# Hope and Charity

An Illustrated History of the Roman Catholic
Diocese of Thunder Bay

Roy H. Piovesana

The Roman Catholic Bishop of Thunder Bay
2002

Published 2002 by The Roman Catholic Bishop of Thunder Bay
P. O. Box 10400
Thunder Bay, Ontario.
P7B 6T8

copyright © Roy H. Piovesana

All rights reserved. No part of this publication may be reproduced, stored in a retrieval system, or transmitted in any form or by any means, electronic, mechanical, photocopying, recording or otherwise (except brief passages for purposes of review) without prior written permission of the publisher.

Cover and Prepress Services
Corporate Graphics Northwest Inc., Thunder Bay, Ontario

Printed in Canada by Friesens Corporation, Altona, Manitoba.

Unless otherwise stated, all photographs are by the author.

National Library of Canada Cataloguing in Publication Data

Piovesana, R. H. (Roy Henry)
Hope and charity:
an illustrated history of the Roman Catholic Diocese of Thunder Bay

Includes bibliographical references and index
ISBN 0-9686836-0-6 (bound)
ISBN 0-9686836-1-4 (pbk.)
1. Catholic Church. Diocese of Thunder Bay – History.
I. Catholic Church. Diocese of Thunder Bay. II. Title
BX1423.T48P55 2002    282'.71312    C2002-900894-8

*To the Memory of my parents*

*Enrico and Christina Piovesana*

# CONTENTS

| | | |
|---|---|---|
| | *Foreword* | ix |
| | *Preface* | xi |
| | **I Formation** | |
| 1 | First Parishes, 1892 – 1952 | 3 |
| 2 | Parishes and Cultural Loyalties, 1892 – 1952 | 65 |
| | **II Diocese** | |
| 3 | Bishop E. Q. Jennings, 1952 – 1969 | 105 |
| 4 | Bishop Norman J. Gallagher, 1970 – 1975 | 181 |
| 5 | Bishop John A. O'Mara, 1976 – 1994 | 215 |
| | **III Towards Jubilee Year 2000** | |
| 6 | Bishop Frederick B. Henry, 1995 – 1998 | 267 |
| 7 | Bishop Frederick J. Colli, 1999 – | 277 |
| | *Necrology, 1952 – 2002* | 289 |
| | *Chronology, 1892 – 2002* | 293 |
| | *Index* | 307 |

### Father Baxter General Assembly
### Fourth Degree
### Knights of Columbus

The Father Baxter General Assembly Fourth Degree Knights of Columbus' association with the publication of a diocesan history goes back to 1960. In 1959, Bishop E.Q. Jennings arranged with Father Francis J. Nelligan, s.j., official historian for the Jesuits, Upper Canada Province, to write a history of the Thunder Bay Diocese. At Bishop Jennings' request, the Father Baxter Assembly agreed to cover all expenses related to Father Nelligan's research and writing. Before his death in May 1970, Father Nelligan completed a lengthy manuscript which was largely a history of Jesuit missionary activity in northwestern Ontario from the seventeenth to the early twentieth century. Bishop Jennings, Bishop Gallagher, and Bishop O'Mara were unsuccessful in engaging the services of another historian to complete the work begun by Father Nelligan. The Father Baxter Assembly, however, remained steadfast in their financial support for the writing and publication of a history of the Roman Catholic Diocese of Thunder Bay. The Most Reverend Frederick J. Colli, D.D., acknowledges with gratitude the significant financial contribution made by the Father Baxter General Assembly Fourth Degree Knights of Columbus to the publication of this work.

# GLOSSARY OF ABBREVIATIONS

| | |
|---|---|
| ACG | Archives of the Chaplain General, National Defence Headquarters, Ottawa |
| ASG | Archives Des Soeurs Grises, Saint-Boniface, Manitoba. |
| ASJUC | Archives of the Society of Jesus, Upper Canada Province, Toronto. |
| CCHA | Canadian Catholic Historical Association |
| CJ | Thunder Bay *Chronicle-Journal* |
| CHR | *Canadian Historical Review* |
| DA | Archives Deschâtelets, Ottawa. (Oblates of Mary Immaculate) |
| DBOMI | *Dictionnaire biographique des Oblats de Marie-Immaculée au Canada* |
| DCB | *Dictionary of Canadian Biography* |
| DJB | *Dictionary of Jesuit Biography* |
| DPA | Archives of the Roman Catholic Diocese of Peterborough |
| DSSMA | Archives of the Roman Catholic Diocese of Sault Ste Marie, North Bay. |
| DTBA | Archives of the Roman Catholic Diocese of Thunder Bay. |
| DTJ | Fort William *Daily Times-Journal* |
| FWJ | *Fort William Journal* |
| FWMH | *Fort William Mining Herald* |
| HAC | *Historical Atlas of Canada* |
| NA | National Archives of Canada |
| PADN | Port Arthur *Daily-News* |
| PANC | Port Arthur *News-Chronicle* |
| SHSB | Archives de la Société de Saint-Boniface, St. Boniface, Manitoba |
| SSJAP | Sisters of St Joseph Archives, Peterborough, Ontario. |
| TBA | City of Thunder Bay Archives. |
| TBHMS | Thunder Bay Historical Museum Society Archives. |

The Most Reverend Frederick J. Colli, D.D.
Fifth Bishop of Thunder Bay, 25 March 1999 –
(John Nistico photo, Thunder Bay)

# FOREWORD

My dear friends,

The publication of a diocesan history is truly an important event in the life of a faith family. This publication for the Diocese of Thunder Bay is the fulfillment of a long awaited desire beginning with Bishop E.Q. Jennings. As our history unfolded, each bishop expressed a desire for a publication of the life of the church in northwestern Ontario and how our faith was spread in the region beginning with the missionaries and continuing with the service of the diocesan clergy and many religious communities.

   I am very pleased that this dream is now a reality and that each of us, through this book, can give thanks for the courage, generosity, and determination of those who have gone before us. In particular, I wish to note the dedication and strong leadership that was shown by Bishop E.Q. Jennings, the first bishop of our diocese. In his wisdom and insight, he was able to carve out and organize our diocesan church as we know it today. Building on his intiatives, Bishop Gallagher and Bishop O'Mara also added to our history in significant ways.

   As we look to our past and give thanks for the work and goodness shown, we cannot but also sense an obligation in each of us to continue to build the kingdom of God in our area. It is not an easy task. As our leaders in the past struggled to do what was best for the Church, we too take up the challenge to continue this building in our own way, by the generous sharing of our gifts and talents for the good of the Church and society.

Along with the establishment of many parishes and missions to serve the spiritual needs of all the people of our area, there were many significant developments in the areas of Catholic education, health care, and social services. The prompting of the Gospel and it's message from the Lord, were the inspiration for many of these developments. Let us together continue this noteworthy tradition and build on these strong foundations.

I would like to thank all who contributed to the publication of this volume, and I am especially grateful to the author, Roy Piovesana, our diocesan archivist/historian. May our history inspire us to seek God's help and grace as together we continue the journey of faith in northwestern Ontario.

Sincerely in Christ,

Bishop of Thunder Bay

# PREFACE

In the first fifty years of its history the Diocese of Thunder Bay evolved from a loose amalgam of parishes and missions with disparate orientations to a unified diocesan church. The Roman Catholic Diocese of Thunder Bay is one of sixty-three in Canada. It was created by Pope Pius XII on 29 April 1952 comprising that part of the Diocese of Sault Ste Marie west of 86 degrees longitude and all territory in Ontario that once came under the ecclesiastical authority of the Archdiocese of St Boniface. This book attempts to describe and analyse the apostolates of bishops, parish priests, and missionaries as they ministered to the spiritual needs of Roman Catholics living within the present confines of the Diocese of Thunder Bay from 1893 to the present. Moreover, it explores how and at what pace Vatican II reforms were implemented in one Canadian diocese and how its bishops attempted to fashion a unified pastoral ministry based on the values and ideals of the Second Vatican Council (1962–1965). Vatican II was like a dividing line ruled on the page of twentieth century Roman Catholic church history: a momentous event which fundamentally altered church architecture, the role of the parish, the Sacred Liturgy, the involvement of the laity in that liturgy, and the relationship of Roman Catholics to members of other Christian denominations.

In December 1998, I was asked to research and write a history of the

Thunder Bay Diocese. Bishop Frederick Colli's hope was that it would be ready for publication in 2002 to mark its fiftieth anniversary. The result is a narrative based primarily on the papers and correspondence of its bishops. The periods dealing with Bishop Frederick Henry and Bishop Frederick Colli, being so close to the present, are dealt with in a cursory manner.

If there is one characteristic which distinguishes the Diocese of Thunder Bay from others in Canada it is the architecture of its churches. The photographs which accompany the text illustrate the transformation of parish and mission churches from rustic structures to modern edifices designed in the spirit of Vatican II where the parish church was meant to accommodate a variety of functions and activities of its faith community.

*Hope and Charity* is an introduction to the history of the Thunder Bay Diocese. The development and changes in the ministry to its Native people, the work of the Catholic Women's League and the Knights of Columbus in the diocese, and in-depth histories of its parishes and missions are some of the topics that merit future consideration by students of history. History is often a reminder of humanity's capacity for charitableness and a source of hope that as we reflect on the past experiences of our parish communities future generations will be reminded of the expression: "See how these Christians love one another."

In the course of the research and writing of this study I have received the generous assistance and cooperation of many. It was indeed an honour for me to be considered for this task in 1998 by Monsignor Roger Bazin, Apostolic Administrator of the diocese , Mr. Larry Grace, and Sr. Bernadette Kinsella, g.s.i.c. Moreover, I must thank Bishop Colli for his support of this publication and for his trust and confidence in my judgements. I owe a special debt of gratitude to the Sisters of St Joseph. Sister Jean Rooney, c.s.j of Mount St. Joseph, Peterborough and Sister Regina Rousseau, c.s.j. in North Bay graciously offered my wife Diane and me accommodations in the mother houses of their congregations in the fall of 1999 while I conducted research in their respective dioceses. Similarly, during my visit to the Archdiocese of Saint-Boniface, we received the generous hospitality of Sister Rolande Lagassé, g.s.i.c. at the Grey Nuns Provincial House. Sister Teresa Sabatini, c.s.j., former archivist with the Roman Catholic Diocese of Thunder Bay, not only organized the parish and bishop's files so valuable to this study but also responded to my research requests from 1999-2001 positively and immediately. Sister Shirley Grexton, c.s.j., J.C.L., Chancellor of the Diocese, enthusiastically responded to a myriad of questions relating to canon law and church organization.

My debt to the Jesuit community, Upper Canada Province, is considerable. Father Michael Murray, s.j., who occupied an office next to mine at the Catholic Pastoral Centre in Thunder Bay, was always a constant source of encouragement, patiently listened to my ramblings on diocesan history, and drew my attention to important works on Catholic church history. Father Jack Lynch's, s.j. translation of several French texts including the early memoirs of Father François Maynard,s.j. filled important gaps in the narrative. Father William Maurice, s.j. placed tables and lists compiled on virtually all of the Jesuits who served in the parishes and missions in the diocese at my disposal. Dr. Jacques Monet, s.j., Director of the Canadian Institute of Jesuit Studies, read several chapters of the manuscript and provided me with the benefit of his wisdom and comments.

The suggestions of others who read all or parts of the manuscript improved the accuracy of the narrative. In this regard I must thank the Most Rev. John A. O'Mara, D.D., the Most Rev. Fred J. Colli, D.D., Monsignor George Bourguignon, Father Michael Murray, s.j., Sister Bernadette Kinsella, g.s.i.c., Guy O'Brien, and Rev. Mr. Charles Johnston.

When I first began my research in 1999, Mr. Brent Scollie of Ottawa graciously provided me with a multitude of references found in the early newspapers of Fort William and Port Arthur relating to parishes in the diocese. In addition, archivists throughout Canada gave me access to a variety of collections all of which enriched the narrative. In this regard, I must express my appreciation to Gilles Lesage, Archives de la Société de Saint-Boniface, St. Boniface, Manitoba; Father Patrick Boyle, s.j., Archives of the Society of Jesus, Upper Canada Province, Toronto; Carole Boily, Archives Des Soeurs Grises, Saint-Boniface, Manitoba; Alex Ross and Tracey Zurick, Thunder Bay Archives; Annette Hamel, Archives Deschâtelets, Ottawa; and Major (Rev) Jean Bourgeois, CD, Archives of the Chaplain General, National Defence Headquarters, Ottawa.

Words cannot express the debt I owe to my wife Diane. In addition to being my companion and research assistant at each of the archives mentioned above, she is my most valued critic. As always, I am deeply grateful for her honesty, diligence, and forebearance.


Roy Piovesana
Thunder Bay, Ontario.
21 July 2002

Geographic limits of the Diocese of Thunder Bay in Northwestern Ontario

# MAP

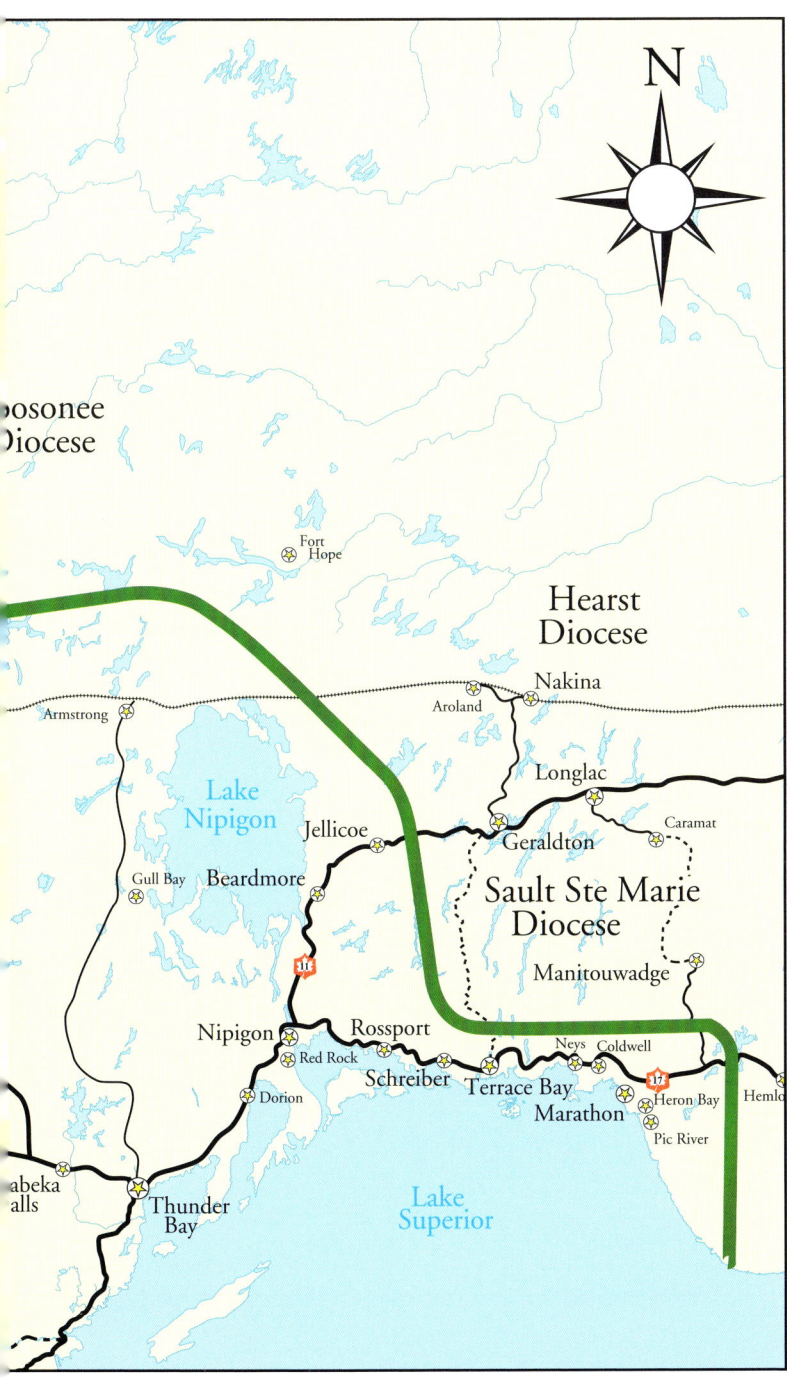

Map illustrated by Kevin Element, 2002

The Fort William Mission showing the Church of the Immaculate Conception, c. 1898
(Thunder Bay Historical Society, 973.28.45B)

St Andrew's Church and Jesuit Residence, Port Arthur, c. 1887.
(Thunder Bay Historical Society, 979.73.10)

# FORMATION
## I

CHAPTER ONE

# FIRST PARISHES

Parishes are the cornerstones of a diocese. Collectively they define its uniqueness and are a measure of its spiritual and temporal strength. The notion of the parish has a distinguished pedigree. Etymologically it is derived from the Greek *paroikia* which in the early Christian church meant "a pilgrim people whose real country and citizenry is in heaven."[1] From the early Middle Ages the structure of the parish has taken a form which essentially remains unchanged to the present. It was understood to be an organization or institution intended to serve the spiritual needs of the faithful under the leadership of a priest in a territorial section of a diocese. The parish's visible symbol was the church itself. Western Europe and England from the twelfth to the eighteenth century had become a land of parishes.[2] The parish had assumed secular as well as religious functions. For example, when the manorial system collapsed in England during the Middle Ages it was the parish that provided help for the aged, sick, and the poor. English parishes continued to fulfill this role until the eighteenth century. So important was the parish in seventeenth and eighteenth France that the inhabitants often referred to their parishes "as if they were separate and individual *pays*."[3] While the secular role of the parish declined during the nineteenth and twentieth centuries, its pastoral role within the Roman Catholic Church was more clearly defined. The Second Vatican

**Catholic Canada, 1893.** (National Archives of Canada, 44439)
The above map entitled "Le Canada Catholique, 1893" (36" x 24") is divided in two sections: the upper section illustrates the ecclesiatical boundaries of the twenty-five Roman Catholic dioceses in Canada while the lower section presents a statistical table giving the number of Roman Catholics being served in each diocese. Almost half of what is now northwestern Ontario came under the ecclesiatical authority of the Archdiocese of Saint-Boniface which extended west of Atikokan, Ontario to Swift Current, Saskatchewan and included approximately 27,000 Roman Catholics.

In 1893, the band of territory north and northwest of Lake Superior came under the ecclesiastical authority of the Peterborough Diocese which included 36,500 Roman Catholics. It stretched from Port Hope, Ontario to an area just west of Thunder Bay. The first bisop of this vast diocese was the Most Reverend Jean-Francois Jamot (1828–1886). When the C.P.R. construction was completed around the north shore of Lake Superior, the Diocese of Peterborough was subdivided and all its territory west of the French River and Lake Nippissing became the Diocese of Sault Ste Marie in 1904.

Council (1962-1965) shifted the emphasis away from the institutional or organizational concept of the parish to "a determined community of Christ's faithful stably established within a particular church (or diocese) and, whose pastoral care, under the authority of the diocesan bishop, is entrusted to a parish priest as its proper pastor."[4]

The first parishes to emerge within the present confines of the Diocese of Thunder Bay did so in response to population growth in northwestern Ontario brought about by the construction of the Canadian Pacific Railway and by the emergence of resource based industries in the region. Immaculate Conception (Fort William Mission), St Patrick (Fort William), St Andrew (Port Arthur), St Agnes (Westfort William), Notre Dame Du Portage (Kenora), and St Mary (Fort Frances) were frontier parishes initially designed to serve Roman Catholics living in and around the small towns of northwestern Ontario. Gradually, Jesuit and Oblate missionaries used these parishes as bases from which to evangelize the Indian and European immigrant populations within an unspecified radius of the parish church. In the course of their travels mission churches were built, some of which later formed the nucleus of parishes established by bishops.

### *The Fort William Mission*

For over fifty years the *Mission de L'Immaculée Conception* on the Fort William Indian Reserve[5] was the cradle of Roman Catholicism in the region north of Lake Superior. It was established in July 1849 by two French Jesuit missionaries, Father Pierre Choné (1808–1879) and Father Nicolas Frémiot (1818–1854) on the left bank of the Mission River at its junction with the Kaministiquia River. A year earlier they had settled temporarily at a spot on the Pigeon River (which formed part of the international boundary between British North America and the United States) with the intent of establishing a mission there. They were drawn to the Kaministiquia River site because the land was more arable and there were greater opportunities to convert Indians to Roman Catholicism.[6] Until its demise in 1906, it was the base and headquarters[7] for Jesuit missionary activity extending over an immense area from Grand Portage and Grand Marais on the northwestern shore of Lake Superior in the United States to White River, 320 km east of Fort William. Equally important, the Church of the Immaculate Conception on the Fort William Mission[8] served the spiritual needs of Indian and European Roman Catholics on the Fort William Indian Reserve and in Fort William.

**Bird's eye view of the Fort William Mission, c. 1898**
This photograph shows the Fort William Mission around 1898 after the fire of 10 April 1895 which destroyed the Church of the Immaculate Conception (centre) and the Sisters of St Joseph residence/orphanage (left). To the right of the church is the Jesuit residence which was headquarters to missionaries who travelled to missions along the north shore of Lake Superior as far east as White River. Between the orphanage and church is the mission cemetery where four Jesuits were buried including Father Joseph Hébert (1834-1893), Father John Blettner (1806-1882), Brother Louis Jérôme (1840-1904) and Father H. Timmon (1828-1893). Immediately behind the orphanage and school is the mission farm which was cultivated each year under the expert supervision of Brother Jérôme – cook and gardener for the Fort William Mission from 1868 until his death in 1904. Fruits and vegetables from the farm were provided for those living on the mission and often for the poor in Fort William. Until a bridge was built across the Kaministiquia River, access to the mission was by boat. ( Thunder Bay Historical Society, 972.2.494)

The *Mission de L'Immaculée Conception* was modelled on the Jesuit Holy Cross Mission at Wikwemikong, also founded by Father Choné in 1844 for the approximately 800 Catholic Indian people living on Manitoulin Island.[9] At both missions a Jesuit residence, a church, an orphanage or school, a farm, and a cemetery were the basic structures around which religious and social life turned. Moreover, there was an on-going exchange of personnel between the two missions depending on the needs of each and the health of the missionaries involved. In the summer of 1892 for example, the Jesuit provincial informed the Most Rev. Richard O'Connor (1838–1913), Bishop of Peterborough, of a personnel change affecting both missions. "Fr. Baudin is strong and would desire more work than he has at Fort William", wrote the Jesuit provincial. "On the other side Fr. Hébert's health is not good and Fort William would be a better place for him because there is little to do."[10]

Since its inception and notwithstanding the lighter workload at the Fort William Mission, at least three Jesuits had been assigned to the *Mission de L'Immaculée Conception* thus providing the canonical requisite for a religious community.[11] A careful examination of the biographical details of the Jesuits who had served at the Fort William Mission during the 1870s and 1880s prompted historian Elizabeth Arthur to comment on their "extraordinary experience and talent".[12] In varying degrees, each had established an exemplary record as a missionary in northern Ontario prior to their arrival at the Fort William Mission. Several not only mastered the Ojibway language but were recognized as Ojibwa scholars throughout North America. Father Alphonse Baudin (1833-1909) for example, Jesuit Superior at the Fort William Mission (1891-1892; 1897-1901) was a gifted linguist. He translated into Ojibway the Gospels and Acts of the Apostles, the Baltimore Catechism and the French-Ojibway Dialogues.[13] Father William Gagnieur (1857–1937),[14] succeeded Baudin as Superior (1893-1895). By the time he had arrived at the Fort William Mission, his list of publications on the language, culture and history of the North American aboriginal people was so impressive that the University of Michigan conferred on him an honorary LL.D. While Joseph Hébert, Alphonse Baudin, and William Gagnieur, as Superiors, tended to the religious and administrative affairs of the Fort William Mission proper, it was usually their assistants who traversed the vast frontier of the Canadian Shield north of Lake Superior to establish new missions and to minister to the Ojibwa people. Whether it was the seventeenth century in their contacts with the Huron or the nineteenth century in their associations with the Ojibwa, the relationship between language

**Father Joseph Hébert, s.j. (1834–1893), c. 1882**
Father Hébert was Superior of the Fort William Mission from 1880 to 1890 and then again in 1893. During those years he played a singular role in the creation of the mission church on the Lake Helen Reserve and the Mountain Chapel as a pilgrimage site on Mount McKay on the Fort William Indian Reserve.
(Thunder Bay Historical Society, 973.105.147i)

**Mountain Chapel on Mount McKay, Fort William First Nation Reserve, June 2000.**
This photograph shows the reconstruction of the original Mountain Chapel built by the Indians of the Fort William Mission in 1888 under the supervision of Father Joseph Hébert, s.j. Father Hébert selected this "enchanting spot" as a place where Mission residents could visit as part of their annual pilgrimage. Here, mass was celebrated followed by a meal and fellowship. When the Fort William Mission property was sold to the Grand Trunk Pacific Railway in 1905, these pilgrimages stopped and the Mountain Chapel fell into a state of disrepair. Later, the chapel's reconstruction was made possible by the thoughtfulness and generosity of a Thunder Bay grain merchant, Senator Norman Paterson. From a photograph of the original structure, he arranged to have local tradesmen build a replica as a historic memorial. On 10 September 1939, fifty-one years to the day after the original chapel was dedicated, Senator Paterson presented Father Alexander Rolland, s.j. with the keys to the new chapel which was large enough to accommodate a priest and an altar server.

and culture and the Jesuit "way of proceeding" among aboriginal peoples remained the same: mastery of their language and a knowledge of their culture was essential in persuading them to become Christians.[15]

The Most Rev. Richard A. O'Connor noted in his journal how "deeply grateful" he was for the "great zeal and unwearied energy of the Jesuit Fathers" who laboured in the western portion of his diocese.[16] In addition to the Fort William Mission, they had been engaged as pastors at St Andrew's in Port Arthur since 1874 and later at St Patrick's in Fort William when it became a parish in 1893. Fathers Joseph Specht, s.j. (1853–1915) and Louis-Napoleon Dugas, s.j. (1862–1928) were just two of the energetic and zealous Jesuit missionaries with whom Bishop O'Connor had frequent contact. Both were fluent in French, English and Ojibway. Both acted as "advance- men" for Bishop O'Connor on his pastoral visits and, at different times, both accompanied him to the missions he chose to visit. The parish records of the Church of the Immaculate Conception, Bishop O'Connor's Journal, and the correspondence Specht and Dugas had with their bishop give us a glimpse of the nature of their ministry and travels in a frontier society.

Joseph Specht was born in the northern French province of Alsace in the town of Haguenau. In his late teens he had decided to become a Jesuit missionary. A more fertile ground than Canada could not have been found for the realization of this calling. Beginning in 1878, a significant phase of his formation as a Jesuit took place at the Fort William Mission. It was there as a scholastic that he studied theology and mastered Ojibway under the guidance of Father John Blettner, s.j. (1806–1882), and it was there that he was ordained by the Most Rev. Bishop Jamot (1828–1886), vicar apostolic of the vicariate of Northern Canada, on 22 May 1880.[17] Following his ordination, Specht, 37, spent nineteen consecutive years at the Fort William Mission and from there embarked on "les grands voyages" which took him around the north shore of Lake Superior from Grand Marais, Beaver Bay, and Grand Portage in Minnesota, USA to First Nation Reserves like Lake Helen, Pays Plat, Pic River, and White River administering the sacraments of baptism, the Eucharist, and marriage. Specht had fifteen different missions to visit – eleven in Canada and four in the United States. Within these missions there were some 1400 Roman Catholics, mostly Indian and Métis.[18] Since they were situated in three dioceses, Specht had three Bishops to deal with– the Bishop of Peterborough, the Bishop of Duluth, Minnesota, and the Bishop of Marquette, Michigan.

As Father Specht surveyed his territory in the spring of 1890 he concluded that in the space of five years "the moral and social condition" of the Indian people in his charge had improved.[19] That the Indians of the Pic Reserve had started the process of farming and building permanent homes around the mission church facilitated his work as a missionary. Moreover, a school had been in operation there for four years. The availability of schools on these reserves was not a given. Although elementary school buildings had been in existence in the Nipigon and Michipicoton River areas during the 1880s, both were closed for seven years for lack of qualified teachers. To Specht's delight, the school at Michipicoton was to be reopened in 1890. For Specht, the absence of a school around the Hudson's Bay Company Nipigon House was particularly lamentable. According to his estimates, five hundred Natives occupied the area and of these, not more than a third were Roman Catholic. More worrisome to Specht was the energetic manner in which the Protestant clergy were directing their efforts in the Nipigon area. During the 1880s, Jesuits could count on the support and sympathy of Junior Chief Trader Henry de Laronde at Nipigon House for their missionary work. They would have delighted in this entry made in his journal: "It being the Conception of the B.V.M., a fête d'obligation, the men did not work."[20] Henry de Laronde carried on a regular correspondence with Father Specht informing him of the health of the elderly native people living in and around Nipigon House. Occasionally, he would raise funds for Specht from the white population in the area so that the missionary could build mission chapels and schools.[21] So devout a Roman Catholic was Henry de Laronde that mass was often celebrated in his home (with many of the Indian people in the area attending)[22] when Jesuit missionaries came through Nipigon or when they were escorting the Bishop through the region on one of his pastoral visits. De Laronde however, had announced his intention to retire from his position at Nipigon House in 1888 and the thought of a Protestant replacing him made Specht anxious. Missionaries like Specht were Bishop O'Connor's pipeline to the remote areas of his Peterborough Diocese. The Jesuit zeal and energy to which O'Connor referred earlier is reflected in the following letter he received from Specht: "This time, I shall go for some 3 or 4 days canoe journey north of Nipigon Lake, to visit some pagan Indians that wish to embrace our holy religion. I am told that there are six hundred of them; but their number is, no doubt exaggerated. At any rate, they must be numerous. I will take with me two good catechists to facilitate my work. On my return home, I hope to be able to give Your Lordship some good news from that far away portion of your

Diocese..."[23] Specht, an indefatigable letter writer, took obvious pride in signing his name "Jos. Specht, s.j. Missionary".

Father Louis Napoleon Dugas shared Specht's unwavering commitment to missionary work in the land north of Lake Superior. He came to the Fort William Mission in the summer of 1899, shortly after Specht had left for Wikwemikong. He covered the same territory as Specht and, like his predecessor, possessed the physical stamina to travel, in the company of native guides, on foot and by dog sled in winter and by canoe when the waterways were passable.[24] Some years, he spent as little as two weeks at the Fort William Mission. In an interview given to a Toronto *Globe* reporter he expressed admiration for the lifestyle of the Indian people. "I prefer to live outside" stated Dugas, "...I am content to sleep in a tepee, as the Indians are nearly always neat and clean. As for their table, they are naturally good cooks, and I enjoy eating with them." The *Globe* interview highlighted the adventurous and heroic side of a Jesuit missionary's travels in northwestern Ontario at the beginning of the twentieth century. Both Specht and Dugas however, used rail transportation as soon as the CPR made its presence felt along the north shore of Lake Superior. Both were provided, for example, with "half-fare permits" which allowed them free travel on freight trains.[25] Jesuits north of Superior served as missionaries and pastors. These roles were never rigidly defined or adhered to. When a Jesuit CPR chaplain was engaged in pastoral work in the eastern extremity of his territory and illness and death necessitated the presence of a priest along the western region of the CPR line, missionaries like Specht and Dugas responded to the call using the convenience of rail travel.

A careful examination of the Fort William Mission registers reveals the comings and goings of Specht and Dugas. They took the registers with them on their travels and recorded the details of baptisms, marriages, and burials in such places as Murillo, Fort William West, Nipigon, Rossport, Pays Plat, Schreiber, Savanne, Heron Bay and the Pic Reserve. Entries were made as the sacraments were administered. For the genealogist or historian, these documents of record have obvious value. If births or marriages were not registered with the Province of Ontario at the time, then these parish registers become the only extant record of where and when some individuals were born, baptised or married.

Bishop O'Connor made regular pastoral visits to the western most reaches of his diocese from 1889 to 1904 usually at two-year intervals in late spring or summer.[26] Over a fifteen year period a well-established travel pattern had emerged. In the company of a young theology student, O'Connor would leave Peterborough by train for Owen Sound on Georgian Bay via Toronto. At Owen Sound he boarded a Canadian Pacific Steamer, (*the Alberta, Athabasca* or *Manitoba*), for a rough two-day journey on Lake Superior to Port Arthur via Sault Ste. Marie.[27] At the Port Arthur wharf he was usually greeted by a large crowd of Roman Catholics including the Jesuit communities from St Andrew's Church and the Fort William Mission. St Andrew's Church, St Joseph's Hospital, St Patrick's Church, The Church of the Immaculate Conception, and St Joseph's convent/orphanage on the Fort William Mission were constants on his visitation schedule. In each of the churches the Bishop celebrated high masses, delivered sermons, and administered the sacrament of confirmation. After several days spent in Fort William and Port Arthur, O'Connor, accompanied by one or two missionaries from the Immaculate Conception Mission (most frequently Fathers Joseph Specht and Louis-Napoléon Dugas), the Bishop's party departed by train for Nipigon station, 116 km east of Port Arthur.[28] St Sylvester Church, founded by Fathers Dominique du Ranquet, s.j. (1813–1900) and Joseph Hébert s.j. (1834–1893), overlooking Lake Helen on the Lake Helen Reserve, was also a constant on O'Connor's itinerary. Here several masses were celebrated after which Indians were confirmed. The Lake Helen reserve was the point of departure for a canoe trip ( including several portages) up the scenic Nipigon River and into Lake Nipigon. Although Specht wanted to spare his Bishop such adventures as treacherous currents and frequent portages associated with canoeing in early spring, their travels in the land north of Lake Superior were no less memorable in battling the elements as the following extract suggests:

> Wednesday July 13. The Bishop's party remained all day on the bank of Lake Nipigon awaiting the arrival of a sailboat, which was expected to come from the Hudson Bay post at the Northwest corner of the lake. The weather was very sultry and about 11 p.m. a heavy downpour of rain, accompanied by vivid flashes of lightning and steady peals of thunder began. In a short time the Bishop and priests were obliged to vacate their balsam beds, as torrents of water flowed through them and wet blankets and coverings. The rain continued until about 2 A.M. and during its continuance the Bishop and priests were obliged to remain standing in the tent, half clad and holding a portion of their clothing in their hands, the water in the meantime coursing through the tent and bathing their feet. After the storm had ceased the whole party ventured outside the tents and the Indians started a fire to dry and warm all water soaked sufferers. Thursday morning, after breakfast, another thunder storm came on lasting for about an hour and after it passed away, blankets and clothing were hung out to dry under the warm

**St Sylvester Mission Church, Lake Helen, 29 May 2000**

In 1880, Jesuit missionary Father Duranquet, s.j. directed parishioners on the Lake Helen Reserve in the construction of this church. The original bell was brought to Lake Helen by Henry de Laronde and was blessed by Father Joseph Specht, s.j. on 7 October 1880. St Sylvester Mission Church underwent extensive renovations during the early 1980s. It is situated on Highway 11 north of Nipigon and until 2001 Sunday Mass was celebrated in the church during the summer months.

sun.[29]... During the trip to Lake Nipigon and return the mosquitoes, black flies and sand flies were very annoying and caused our party to suffer much from their bites and stings. These flies paid special attention to the Bishop and left him many tokens of remembrance to carry away with him."[30]

The religious services associated with the Bishop's pastoral visits were held wherever and whenever Roman Catholics in the region were prepared to gather. All thrived on the ceremony associated with the presence of a bishop in their midst. Knowledge of his party's arrival at places like the Lake Helen Reserve, Rossport, Pays Plat, and the Jackfish Island Reserve provided larger assemblies of people than would otherwise have attended mass. Bishop O'Connor punctiliously recorded in his journal the number attending Mass and the number confirmed. Of those confirmed he made special mention of "converts from paganism." In all of this, the role of Specht and Dugas from the Fort William Mission was to interpret and translate the bishop's sermons to the Indians and to act as catechists in the preparation of candidates for confirmation.[31]

Although Fathers Specht and Dugas were first and foremost missionaries labouring among the native people of northwestern Ontario, they also had pastoral responsibilities. The pastoral ministry of the Jesuit community at the Fort William Mission centred around the Church of the Immaculate Conception where mass was celebrated daily. The Jesuit Superior at the Mission was pastor of a parish that consisted of approximately 250 Indian parishioners.[32] It was the bishop's expectation that the Indian population on the Mission would contribute "according to their means towards the support of their pastor."[33] Interestingly, on any given Sunday the modest church was crowded and "more white people than Indians" were in attendance.[34] Announcements, often made in English and Ojibway, alerted the congregation to special feast days to be celebrated during a particular week. Matrimonial banns were read before the congregation regularly.[35] The cultural duality of the parish was further reflected in its parish registers where the number of baptisms, marriages and burials under the categories of "whites" and "sauvages" were periodically tabulated.[36] Most, if not all, of the "whites" who attended the Church of the Immaculate Conception came from Westfort (Fort William West). Although they had a mission church available to them at the corner of Brown and Frederica Streets Mass was celebrated there on Sundays and then only when a priest from the Fort William Mission was available.[37] The logistics of attending services at the Fort William Mission across the Kaministiquia River from Westfort attested to the devout character of Roman

Catholics living in the area. A bridge had not yet been built to span the Kam River to connect the Fort William Indian Reserve with Westfort. In all seasons but winter therefore, some form of water transport was needed to move people across the river.

The absence of a bridge across the Kaministiquia River created a geographical separation between the Mission and the rapidly expanding town of Fort William. The forces of geography, however, were more than offset by the religious, social and, as will be seen later, the economic links which bound Mission residents to Fort William. In addition to the Church of the Immaculate Conception, the presence of St Joseph's Orphanage further strengthened these links. The Daughters of the Immaculate Heart of Mary (Miss Nardines), whose mother house was situated in Paris France, were the first to assume responsibility for the direction of the orphanage/school in 1870.[38] Because of diminished numbers in their order, they withdrew from missionary work in Fort William. They were replaced in 1885 by the Sisters of St Joseph of Toronto and then Peterborough.[39] Their convent, St Joseph's House, was comprised of two separate structures on the Mission property, one 45' x 60' and the other 40' x 44'.[40] The latter which had two rooms housed the boys; the former housed the Sisters, girls, a chapel, music room and kitchen. A two-room school house was a separate structure accommodating anywhere from 23 to 72 students.[41] On one of his pastoral visits to the Mission, Bishop O'Connor was treated to an "evening of musical and literary entertainment" in the convent "by the Indian children who displayed considerable talent and showed the careful training given to them by the Sisters of St Joseph."[42] Interestingly, this convent/school was an amalgam of white and native orphans and white boarders.

In the early morning of 10 April 1895 (Wednesday of Holy Week) a fire, originating in the convent bake oven, spread and destroyed the convent/orphanage, the Church of the Immaculate Conception and threatened the Jesuit residence.[43] The Fort William Fire Brigade promptly responded to a call for help from the Mission and moved their equipment across the precarious ice surface that still covered the Kam River. "Nearly everything in the church was saved", wrote Father Gagnieur to Bishop O'Connor, "but the good sisters lost a good deal of chattels; about $1,000 they think. Had our roof been shingled the presbytery would have gone." No lives were lost. In the aftermath of the fire, the Sisters of St Joseph used one room in the schoolhouse as a convent and the First Nations Council House as a temporary chapel and schoolhouse. Bishop O'Connor visited the Fort William Mission in May and remained at the Lakehead to initiate the rebuilding of the convent/orphanage and church. By November 1895 both had been rebuilt.[44]

The construction of a new facility gave the Sisters of St Joseph an opportunity to reassess the purpose of their Mission orphanage and school. Would it continue to house white borders and orphans? More important, how would the Sisters of St Joseph continue to finance a cause to which they were deeply committed but for which they had been receiving a meagre annual grant of $500 from the Government of Canada? Perhaps in order to reduce the number of children in their charge and to increase their government appropriations Mother Superior Sister M. Incarnation suggested a new focus for the Mission orphanage. "I take the liberty of submitting to your Lordship's consideration" she wrote, "the idea of having a boarding school or industrial school for Indian children exclusively, taking them from the different reserves where there are no schools established…This would dispense us from the disagreeable task of soliciting alms."[45] For a decade after the fire, the Sisters of St Joseph, the Jesuit community, Bishop O'Connor of Peterborough, and later Bishop D.J. Scollard (1862–1934) of the Sault Ste Marie Diocese, petitioned federal Indian Affairs officials and federal politicians for an increased grant.[46] They argued that the Indian boarding school/orphanage on the Mission was the only one in Canada that received a "fixed contribution" from the federal government to feed, clothe, shelter, and look after the health of a group of children whose numbers ranged from 25 to 75.[47] All others received a per capita grant based on the number of Indian children in residence. The Rat Portage (Kenora) Boarding School for example, which housed some thirty children, received an annual grant of $2155.[48] What possible explanation could be given for this inequitable treatment of St Joseph's Home on the Fort William Mission? Perhaps the presence of white boarders and orphans made the home ineligible for a per capita grant. Or, although St Joseph's Home was a boarding school, it was not classified as an industrial school because no "industrial" programme of instruction was followed.[49] Whatever the reason, the petitions of Bishops, Jesuits, and Sisters of St Joseph went unanswered. When the Mother Superior examined the Annual Report of the Department of Indian Affairs in 1902 the grant for the Mission orphanage "was by far the least of all the grants" even though they did not have the least number of children.

That the Sisters of St Joseph continued their work with the limited financial and human resources at their disposal beggars belief. They accepted all in the spirit of their order. "We tried to storm our dear Patron, St Joseph with prayers," wrote Sister M. Sacred Heart to Bishop O'Connor, "that he might send us more means but as yet he has sent us only poor children."[50] The "poor Indian children", not all Roman Catholics, continued to be placed in the Mission boarding school from several Indian bands including Fort William, Savanne, Nipigon, Pays Plat, Pic River, White River, Chapleau, and Long Lake.[51] Father Prosper Lamarche, s.j., (1855–1928) missionary at the Fort William Mission since 1902, saw little justice in their circumstances and was their most passionate and persistent advocate. Without reasonable financial support from the federal government, he felt the Sisters could not maintain the new convent built after the fire. They could not hire the help necessary to do the heavy work of keeping the furnaces operative and in good repair. Domestic help was not available to do the cleaning and cooking leaving the Sisters free to channel all of their energies into teaching and caring for those in their charge. Lamarche was convinced that Mother Francis (Honora Burke), resident at the Mission since 1885 and later Superior in charge of the convent's direction, who contracted pneumonia due to a typhoid fever epidemic resulting from the contamination of the Kam River water supply in early 1904, died as a result of having no heat in her convent room.[52] "I was told afterwards", wrote Lamarche, "that the room in which she slept was so cold that the water would freeze in the basin and even the quilt of her bed would stick to the wall by frost."

The Sisters of St Joseph on the Fort William Mission trusted that the Government of Canada would eventually recognize the value of their work and increase the appropriations to the orphanage/boarding school. Meanwhile, they had to improvise as they were wont to do and seek financial assistance from those in the immediate area. The people of Fort William had always been generous in support of their efforts.[53] The Sisters questioned whether this support would continue even though the Roman Catholic families of Fort William had their own newly constructed Roman Catholic School to support (St Stanislaus) and a new hospital to pay for.[54] To be sure, the Jesuit community at the Mission had been their bedrock of support. Brother Louis Jérôme, cook and expert gardener at the Mission since 1868, had been providing fruits and vegetables to the orphanage annually. In addition, when Father Lamarche toured his missions he sometimes collected funds on behalf of the Mission orphanage from the camps he visited.[55] Because the Sisters of St Joseph used so much of their flour, the Ogilvie Co. in Westfort would periodically make a financial donation. And at times, they received unexpected donations from individuals. By 1903, the organization of the orphanage/boarding school had not changed from what it had been before the 1895 fire. It continued as an Indian Boarding School and Indian Day School (for which they continued to receive the standard $500 annually which included the teacher's salary), and a Boarding School for white children for which they received a $150 charity grant from the Ontario Government and $5 per month for each child.

What changed the fortunes of the Mission Boarding school/orphanage (and the entire Immaculate Conception Mission for that matter) was the grandiose expansion programme of the Grand Trunk Pacific Railway which had selected Fort William as its western terminus.[56] Negotiations for the transfer of 1600 acres (which included all structures on the Fort William Mission) from the Fort William Indian Reserve to the Grand Trunk Pacific Railway began in early January 1905. The price to be paid for this land by the Grand Trunk to the Fort William First Nation, the Jesuit Community, and the Sisters of St Joseph was negotiable; its acquisition was not. By an act of the Canadian Parliament a national railway company had the power to expropriate lands for its growth and development.[57] The principal players in these negotiations were Mr. S. Bray, Surveyor General of the Department of Indian Affairs, Chief J. B. Pennassi of the Fort William First Nation, the Jesuit Community (Fathers Roger Arpin, pastor, St Patrick Parish and Prosper Lamarche, Superior, Fort William Mission), and the City of Fort William.[58] Bray's recommendation was that the Government of Canada pay up to $250,000 for the property. Understandably, the Jesuits sought an independent assessment of the property's value.[59] The private assessment firm of Mitchell & Ruttan located in Port Arthur placed the property's value at $609,000 with the stipulation that if, in the space of twenty-five years, there was the likelihood that the Grand Trunk Pacific Railway would develop the entire 1600 acres then the value "should be greatly augmented." By March 1905 the City of Fort William and the Grand Trunk Pacific had concluded a final agreement whereby the railway's terminals would be located on the 1600 acres on the Mission which would now be incorporated into the town of Fort William.[60] A year, later financial arrangements were concluded between the Indian Affairs Department and the Fort William First Nations, the Jesuit Community, and the Sisters of St Joseph.[61] Throughout the negotiations for the sale of the land to the Grand Trunk Pacific they contemplated a new location. To replicate what some have termed a "novel religious and educational development"[62], established fifty-eight years earlier, would require a unity of mood and purpose that was found wanting in 1906.

Father Prosper Lamarche implored the Fort William First Nations people to stick together in the move to another location.[63] If their church and school meant anything to them then ideally all families would settle in one place. He left the decision in their hands. Wherever they decided to go as a group the Jesuit community would follow. Lamarche realized, however, that consensus on this issue would be difficult. He was enough of a realist to recognize that when material and spiritual interests came into conflict the former invariably superseded the latter. He also realized that an increasing number of the Fort William Indian Band were no longer hunters and fishers. Their livelihood increasingly became dependent on Fort William's burgeoning economy.[64] Since the early 1890s, members of the Fort William Indian Band cut and sold cordwood on their reserve to Fort William families for domestic use. Moreover, extensive cutting operations were carried out on the reserve by timber and pulp and paper companies. In this instance, the band chief often served as the contractor for the companies seeking wood in close proximity to their operations. Because Band members lived so close to Fort William they took permanent or casual employment with the elevators and CPR sheds along the Kam River to supplement a more traditional livelihood based on subsistence agriculture, trapping, and fishing.

Faced with these economic realities, the Fort William Indian Band had two choices before them once the Grand Trunk Pacific purchase of the Fort William Mission was final: to move to Squaw Bay (Mission Bay)[65] on Lake Superior 10 miles south of the original mission site or to remain close to the Grand Trunk Pacific Railway operations on Mountain Road, approximately 2 miles west of the former mission site. Indian Band Chief Jean Baptiste Penassie, speaking for a significant group on the reserve, was unequivocally opposed to moving to Mission Bay.[66] The land was rocky and unsuitable for farming. Above all, Mission Bay was remote from the town of Fort William where many women on the reserve took employment as domestic servants.[67] Band members also valued the many acts of charity that continually came from the people of Fort William. Would this be jeopardized if they moved to Mission Bay? A strong argument for relocating to Mission Bay however, was put forth by the fishers of the Band. Commercial fisherman of Fort William and Port Arthur passed by on a regular basis and the money made would more than compensate for that lost by the women giving up their work in town. By the spring of 1906, the Fort William Indian Band was hopelessly divided. Twenty-three families opted for Mountain Road while thirty-seven favoured

Mission Bay.[68] Although the Jesuits were inclined to follow the majority, they needed direction from the Most Rev. D.J. Scollard, Bishop of Sault Ste Marie. The Department of Indian Affairs and the Grand Trunk Pacific expected the Fort William Indian Band to be off the Mission site and settled at their new location by early 1906. Bishop Scollard was impressed with the largesse shown by the Jesuit community in offering to follow the majority of the Fort William Indian Band members wherever they might go. He therefore believed that the Chief of the Indian Band and the minority who wished to locate at the base of Mount McKay should acquiesce to the will of the majority and reestablish their community at Mission Bay.[69]

Parenthetically, the move to Mission Bay also entailed the relocation of the historic Mission cemetery. Father Prosper Lamarche estimated that over 500 bodies would have to be exhumed and interred at a new location.[70] In fact, 745 bodies were involved - 381 Indian and 364 non-Indian. The Jesuits flatly rejected a proposal by the Department of Indian Affairs to carry out this difficult task on a tender basis.[71] They argued that cemeteries were Church properties and accepted $4,000 from the Government to do the job themselves. "The bodies have been entrusted to the care of the Church not of the Department", wrote Lamarche. "For over 56 years, we have taken care of some of them who have no relations left, and we shall continue to take care of them without the supervision of the Department." Whether the Jesuits were able to clear and fence the new location, supply new coffins, exhume and reinter, remove crosses and monuments and transport all for $4,000 is uncertain. Their intent was to have the task completed before the onset of frost in 1907.[72]

The move to Mission Bay during 1906 and 1907 spelt the death knell of the Fort William Mission as a unified Roman Catholic community. In the spring of 1907, Chief Penassie lamented the existence of two missions - one at Mission Bay and the other at Mountain Road.[73] He pleaded with Bishop Scollard to provide a church, a priest and a separate cemetery for the people at Mountain Road. The Bishop demonstrated little sympathy for the supplications of the Fort William Indian Band Chief. "He must be a strange character" remarked Bishop Scollard "to expect two priests for a few Indians when there is not sufficient work for one among the whole Band."[74] As for the cemetery, he did not see its creation as a necessity for such a small number of people.[75] By the fall of 1907, a Jesuit residence and church had been rebuilt overlooking Mission Bay on Lake Superior.[76] Missing from this cluster of buildings was the Sisters of St Joseph orphanage/school.

To make the orphanage financially viable, the Sisters of St Joseph had no choice but to leave the Mission and move to Fort William. There, the local citizenry would notice and continue to support it.[77] With the financial support and encouragement of Bishop Scollard[78] and the Jesuits, 3.5 acres of land were purchased at the corner of Arthur and Franklin Streets from Mr. James Murphy for $3,500. On this site a new "Boarding and Industrial School" primarily for Indian children was built in the spring and summer of 1908 for a total cost of $30,500. Given the past financial history of the Mission orphanage, how did the Sisters of St Joseph hope to finance such an ambitious undertaking? Seventeen thousand dollars came from the sale of their Mission property.[79] In addition, they were convinced that prayers to their patron were answered when the family of one of the Sisters made a sizable donation to the new building. And, as they had done so many times before, they visited the various camps along the CPR line soliciting donations.[80] At long last there was also the prospect that St Joseph's Boarding School, once off the Fort William Mission, would receive the same per capita grant from the Government of Canada as other institutions like it across the country.[81] When the new St Joseph's boarding school and orphanage opened its doors on 14 February 1909 a new chapter had begun in its growth and development.

Why is the Fort William Mission important to the history of the Diocese of Thunder Bay? Its establishment in the mid-nineteenth century gave Roman Catholicism a firm presence in northwestern Ontario that preceded the Protestant churches by almost a quarter of century.[82] By the first two decades of the twentieth century Roman Catholics comprised 25-49.9% of the population in established communities along the north shore of Lake Superior.[83] Their closest rival was the Presbyterians with 10-24.9% of the population. In the city of Fort William for example, with a population of 19,858 in 1910 approximately 6,421 or 32.3% were listed as Roman Catholic.[84] To be sure, the predominance of Roman Catholicism along Lake Superior's north shore during the first two decades of the twentieth century must also be attributed to the large number of Roman Catholic European immigrants who settled there. But the Jesuit evangelization of the Indian People and CPR workers from Chapleau to Fort William during the late nineteenth century established fertile ground from which a thriving Roman Catholic community could grow.

From the Fort William Mission the Jesuits and the Sisters of St Joseph filled an important void in a frontier society with the creation of social institutions such as a school, church, and orphanage. At the Church of the Immaculate

Conception a poor and transient population on the Fort William Reserve and in the town of Fort William were baptized, confirmed, married, and buried. On a regular basis, this parish church brought Indians and Europeans together.

The interaction of the two cultures was reflected in the Sisters of St Joseph orphanage/school. When Indian or white children were orphaned or could not be cared for by their parents, the orphanage/boarding school on the Fort William Mission was their refuge. During the 1890s and early 1900s, the educational function of this school was often overshadowed by the compelling need to provide children with the basic necessities of life. The utter frustration of this work was expressed on behalf of the Sisters of St Joseph by Father Prosper Lamarche on the eve of the typhoid epidemic which broke out on the Mission in 1904. "If these children do not receive their education in this school," wrote Lamarche to Bishop O'Connor, "most probably they shall never receive any. But is it right that the Sisters should sacrifice not only their time, since they receive no salary for themselves, but as you can see by Yourself, My Lord, they sacrifice their very life, overworking themselves, in order to feed, clothe and keep these poor Indian children, who are brought more manners every year..."[85] The Sisters of St Joseph and the Jesuits provided a social safety net on the Fort William Mission for the down and out, a safety net not otherwise available in northwestern Ontario at the beginning of the twentieth century.

### *St Agnes Parish, Westfort William.*

Although the purchase of the Fort William Mission property by the Grand Trunk Pacific Railway contributed to the demise of a cohesive Roman Catholic community, the operations of both the Grand Trunk Pacific and the Canadian Northern railways in Westfort proved to be a boon to the fledgling St Agnes mission church situated at the corner of Frederica and Brown Streets.[86] "The Church of the Nativity and St Agnes" was reputedly founded by the Jesuit missionary Father Richard Baxter, s.j. (1821–1904) in the mid-1880s. In the fall of 1887 much publicity surrounded a brief visit to Westfort by the Most Reverend Thomas Dowling, (1840–1924) Bishop of Peterborough, for the blessing of the church and the church bell which had originally been part of the St Rose of Lima Catholic Church at Silver Islet.[87] Although the sacramental records of St Agnes Parish indicate that baptism, marriage and funeral services were periodically celebrated at the original church during the 1890s and early 1900s, the handful of Roman Catholics remaining in Westfort after the Canadian Pacific Railway had moved their headquarters to Eastfort William were unable to prevent the gradual dilapidation of the church.[88] It was not until 1906 when the operations of the Grand Trunk Pacific and Canadian Northern Railways operations were established in Westfort that employment opportunities were sufficient to attract people back to the area and to Sunday Mass. Ward IV of Fort William of which Westfort was a part had grown by 1,133 people from 1907 to 1909 representing a 50.3 per cent increase.[89] "How people are coming fast to Westfort", wrote Father A.A. Ragaru, s.j. to Bishop Scollard. "The immense work rushed on both by the G.T.P. and C.N.R., all around St Agnes' Church brings more people daily. As a consequence the church is much too small for accommodating the people coming to it, and we must give them accommodation and thus to increase the income of the church."[90] A basement was added and a new presbytery was constructed at the back of the church for visiting priests. So confident was the Fort William Separate School Board in the stability and continued growth of Westfort's population that they initiated construction of a Roman Catholic elementary school on the northeast corner of Brown and Mary Streets which opened in September 1910.

Bishop Scollard was equally confident in Westfort's future. On behalf of the Sault Ste Marie Diocese Father H.M. Descoteaux, s.j. purchased a lot on the corner of Brown and Mary Streets directly across from the school and took out a building permit on 24 May 1914 for the construction of a new all brick St Agnes Roman Catholic Church.[91] On the evening of Sunday, 26 July 1914 and on the eve of the outbreak of World War I, Bishop Scollard, assisted by Father Descoteaux and Father Macdonald of St Patrick's Church, officiated at the cornerstone laying ceremony before a crowd of almost 1000.[92] The completed church was solemnly dedicated under the patronage of St Agnes on 15 January 1915.[93] A month later, the Jesuits returned the parish back to the Sault Ste Marie Diocese and Father N.F. McCullough became its first diocesan priest.[94]

Father McCullough provided spiritual leadership to a culturally diverse parish. An examination of the parish's sacramental records from 1913-1920 reveals that those baptised and married at St Agnes listed their nationality as Galician-Austrian, Irish, Italian, Bulgarian, Persian, Swedish and Russian. With the exception of a few whose residence was in Rosslyn Village, South Gillies or Sioux Lookout, most listed their address as some street in Westfort William. Father McCullough's immediate successor, Father William T.

St Agnes Roman Catholic Church, Brown and Mary Streets, Westfort William c. 1926
(Courtesy St Agnes Parish Archives)

St Agnes Church Interior, Easter Sunday, 1936
(Courtesy St Dominic Parish Archives)

Batterton, had this to say about the challenges of ministering to the Italian and Ruthenian (Ukrainian) people of Westfort:

> I have in Westfort about 249 Italians including children…Any who go to church come to St Agnes' Church. I have all the children in the school. [St Martin] The duty rests with me to see that they go to mass on Sunday. I have to prepare them for the Sacraments. In fact I take care of them. Father Tomaselli will tell you that I can do more with them than their own priest. In fact he advises strongly that they be left in my hands. Last week I commenced a new "stunt". To all the Italians who bring their father and mother to church on Sunday I give a little holy picture. Twelve induced their parents to come to church in order to get the picture. Every child in the school who attends mass gets a picture and the boy or girl who obtains the most pictures gets a prize. With regard to the Ruthenians; I have over sixty Ruthenian children attending mass and receiving communion in this church, and many of them bring their parents…[95]

Once the new St Agnes church was constructed in 1914, pastors and parishioners were preoccupied with meeting its day-to-day expenses. More of a burden, however, was the debt (approximately $40,000) incurred in its construction. Bishop Scollard attributed Father McCullough's premature death in 1919 to the stress of dealing with the financial problems facing St Agnes' Parish during the Great War. "Rev. N.F. McCullough" wrote Bishop Scollard, "was an eloquent preacher and a most capable administrator. His struggle to make ends meet and cope with an overwhelming debt during the stressful years of the Great War was a factor in undermining his strength, and left him too weak to battle against the attack of a serious disease…"[96] Bishop Scollard made vague references to "war conditions" and to the "scattering of many of the families" in Westfort as obstacles to dealing with the church debt. In fact, Fort William's population diminished by 6,322 by the end of 1915 of which almost 1,000 were from Westfort.[97] The loss was due mainly to the enlistment of young men in the Canadian Expeditionary Force and to a severe depression in Fort William which caused the exodus of a large proportion of the city's transient population.

From 1918 to the end of the 1930s, St Agnes' Altar Society organized "20th Century Raffles" and bazaars in conjunction with "St Agnes' At Home" socials held in the church hall to raise funds which were applied to the church debt.[98] When Father A.J. Hogan (1891–1966) became pastor in 1935 he solicited promissary notes from each family in the parish in amounts ranging from $10 to $25 and applied the monies raised from this campaign to the church debt. By 1952, St Agnes was free of debt and was recognized both spiritually and financially as being one of the strongest parishes in the new Diocese of Fort William.

### St Patrick Parish, Fort William, Ontario.

The construction of a Roman Catholic Church in Fort William coincided with the incorporation of the town in 1892. The initiative originated with the people. Given the crowded conditions at the Church of the Immaculate Conception on Sundays, Father Alphonse Baudin, s.j., Superior at the Fort William Mission, believed a church in "Fort William East" could be built without much difficulty.[99] A notice appeared in the *Fort William Journal* inviting all persons interested in creating a Roman Catholic Church to meet at McDougall's hall on Sunday, 8 September 1891 at 2:30 P.M.[100] Out of this meeting, attended by twenty-five individuals, a church committee was formed headed by a prominent businessman, James Murphy. In addition to collecting pledges totalling $560 the committee identified the city lot upon which a church, school and convent would be built.[101] Within ten days of the organizational meeting the committee called for tenders to lay the foundations and to construct the church based on plans and specifications drawn up by a prominent local architect and businessman W. R. Graham.[102] By June 1892, construction had begun at the corner of Donald and Archibald streets under the direction of a Mr. H. Rochon.[103] "When the church is completed" reported the *Fort William Journal* "it will be one of the most handsome edifices in town…" In the yet unfinished 40' x 80' frame church, with a sacristy built on the side, the first mass was celebrated on 21 August 1892 before a large congregation by Father Remi Chartier, s.j., (1839–1906) Superior of the Jesuits in the Thunder Bay District and pastor at St Andrew's in Port Arthur.[104] There was a saying among St Patrick parishioners at the time concerning their first church: "The French built it, and the Irish named it." A year later, during his pastoral visit to Fort William, Bishop O'Connor formally established a parish under the patronage of St Patrick and announced to an expectant crowd that a stained glass portrait of St Patrick would be positioned over the main altar and that a resident priest would remain in their midst.[105]

That priest was Father Ludger (Roger) Arpin, s.j. (1841–1918). Father Arpin was born in La Presentation in the Diocese of Saint-Hyacinthe, Que. on 10 April 1841.[106] At the age of 22 he entered the Society of Jesus at Recollect Falls. His formation as a Jesuit included studies in Quebec City, Fordham University, New York, and at Woodstock, Maryland, USA. He was

**Father Ludger Arpin, s.j. c. 1896**
First Pastor of St Patrick Parish
(Courtesy St Dominic Parish Archives)

ordained on 9 September 1877 and took his solemn vows at St Mary's College, Montreal on 15 August 1882. His initiation to fund-raising and building institutions began in 1885 when he became involved in the founding of the College of the Immaculate Conception in Montreal. Shortly thereafter, he spent a brief period (1890-1893) as Superior of the Jesuit community in Sault Ste Marie and then moved further north as the first pastor of St Patrick's parish in Fort William. For the next thirteen years he provided leadership and a vision for a Roman Catholic community in what was still a frontier town in northwestern Ontario.

One of Father Arpin's first priorities as pastor was to have a Roman Catholic elementary school built in the city. The parishioners at St Patrick's, however, were reluctant to follow his lead.[107] To build the school meant increasing their property taxes. For some, the financial commitment to their church was already stretched to the limit as they contributed to the completion of the church and rectory in 1893. Others felt that the creation of a Catholic elementary school in Fort William would create tensions between Roman Catholics and Protestants in the community. The more affluent parishioners were concerned that a separate Roman Catholic school would not provide the quality of education found in the public system. A divided parish on this issue left the "school fund" dormant and postponed action on property acquisition and construction.[108] Father Arpin was understandably frustrated. "…If God sends me good luck, I may have the means to build a first class school." he wrote. " My people are very proud; they want everything fine, but they cannot, they say, pay for it."[109]

But Father Arpin was persistent. In the spring of 1901 he became involved in the formation of a Separate School Board for the town of Fort William. Notice was given of a public meeting of Roman Catholics families to be held in the basement hall of St Patrick's church on 10 April. After a motion that the Roman Catholics assembled wished to form a Separate School Board for Fort William was passed, two trustees from each of the four wards in the city were nominated and elected. Father Arpin was elected a trustee for Ward IV.[110] At a subsequent meeting he was elected Secretary-Treasurer of the newly constituted school board.[111] In this position he reported on the progress of fund-raising for a new Roman Catholic "school house". In the spring of 1901 he was able to convince his parishioners, with Bishop O'Connor's encouragement, to launch a subscription campaign for the Catholic elementary school project. Bishop O'Connor honoured his commitment to be the one of the first to make a personal donation to the cause.[112] At a special meeting of the board on 22 May 1901 Arpin informed trustees that $1,500 had been subscribed. On the basis of this commitment the board struck a committee comprised of Joseph C. McDonald and Father Arpin to consult with local architects and contractors with a view to constructing a school house not to exceed $10,000 when completed. By the fall of that year the property had been acquired on Myles Street and construction had begun. "It is going to be a fine looking building..." wrote Father Arpin as construction progressed. "Protestants cannot believe their eyes to look at such a school; they are literally wild, feel bad and blame the priest to have put such a scheme into the catholic heads, whilst our Catholics seem to have more courage than ever."[113]

St Stanislaus Roman Catholic School in Fort William situated at 241 Myles Street officially opened its doors on Wednesday, 8 January 1902 to 101 Catholic children who had previously attended the public school. In the space of four weeks that number had risen to 130.[114] Father Arpin took great satisfaction in knowing that few Roman Catholic children remained within the Fort William public school. As a four room, two-storey all brick structure it had already been filled to capacity. At the request of Bishop O'Connor five Sisters of St Joseph (Mother St Edward, Sisters Magdalen, Fidelis, St Catherine, and St Philip) agreed to staff the school.[115] That the Sisters of St Joseph would bring the highest standards of instruction to the school was an assurance Bishop O'Connor confidently gave to Father Arpin and his parishioners. "Wherever the Sisters of St Joseph have charge of schools", he wrote "we find that their pupils are taught the secular branches in as satisfactory a manner as the pupils in public schools, and besides the children are well rounded in the knowledge and practise of their religion, a matter that is of the greatest importance..."[116] For their part, the Sisters of St Joseph, operating from their temporary living quarters on the second floor of the school, candidly informed the Bishop of Peterborough of their impressions of the new school and the pupils in their charge. Bright classrooms, hardwood floors throughout, running water, electricity, and hot air furnaces were more than they ever expected. Although their students were not "unruly" as they were led to believe they would be, they found them wanting in basic academic skills.[117] Accordingly, preparation for high school entrance examinations would not take place in 1902. Nevertheless, Roman Catholic elementary education had begun in Fort William. Father Arpin and St Patrick's parish were the prime movers in this development.

St Patrick Roman Catholic Church, Archibald and Donald Streets, Fort William, (Thunder Bay), c. 1945.
(Thunder Bay Historical Society, 984.53.191)

Two years after the opening of St Stanislaus School and a little over a decade since the completion of their church, Father Arpin and the parishioners of St Patrick's had to face the prospect of its renovation and expansion. In 1893 it was designed to serve a small Fort William Roman Catholic population of approximately 811.[118] By 1902 that population had doubled. A lot at the back of the church had been purchased from the McKellar family in the event that expansion was necessary.[119] In the spring of 1904 pastor and parishioners were confident that a major expansion could be undertaken without incurring a burdensome debt. Rather than demolish the existing church the parishioners decided to renovate the interior and exterior to comfortably serve their rapidly expanding congregation.[120]

The magnitude of St Patrick's 1904 renovation prompted the Fort William *Daily Times-Journal* to conclude that it established a landmark in the development of Fort William's Roman Catholic community and represented a symbol in the town's maturity and progress. When renovations were completed the all red brick, thick stone basement structure had its seating capacity increased from 500 to 600. In the interior, a monotonous flat ceiling was transformed into a vaulted structure on which frescos were painted depicting scenes from the life of Christ. The original sacristy on the south side of the church was demolished and replaced with a larger one behind the altar where

View of main altar and interior of St Patrick Church, c. 1908
(Courtesy St Dominic Parish Archives)

daily mass was often celebrated in winter. The triple nave design of the interior gave it a spacious appearance that accented the new oak pews and the stained glass windows gifted to the church by individual parishioners. The names of individuals and societies who contributed to the $14,000 renovation were inscribed in gold lettering on the interior pillars of the church. These renovations gave St Patrick's an elegance that was absent in the original structure and suggested that a core of the parishioners possessed the wherewithal to transform Fort William's only Roman Catholic church into a place of worship that would compare favourably to several existing Protestant churches at the Lakehead. Just as the Christmas season was about to begin in 1904, Bishop O'Connor, assisted by Fathers O. Neault, s.j. (1850–1921) (St Andrew's) Prosper Lamarche, s.j. (Fort William Mission) and pastor Father Arpin, officially blessed the newly renovated chuch.[121]

St Patrick's parish, under the leadership of their pastor Father Arpin, provided the catalyst for the development of Roman Catholic institutions in Fort William at the beginning of the twentieth century. The Fort William Separate School Board, St Stanislaus school, St Patrick's Cemetery, and the Sisters of St Joseph Convent on Myles Street all found their origins with this parish. Little would have been accomplished, however, without the vision and risk-taking of Father Arpin. St Patrick's became the parish around which first and second generation Polish, Slovak, and Italian immigrants rallied. Father Arpin was a source of encouragement to each cultural group to practise their faith within the context of an Anglo-Saxon and French-Canadian dominated parish. For example, he assisted the Slovaks in bringing in a priest from Pennsylvania who spoke their language to give a six-day mission during the Lenten season of 1900. He delighted in the satisfaction and joy they took in hearing sermons in their own language and in socializing among themselves.[122] He also purchased several lots in Fort William's East End knowing that the Slovaks eventually would want to build a church of their own in that part of the city.[123] The Sisters of St Joseph Convent which opened in 1905 across the street from St Stanislaus School on Myles Street also owed its existence to Arpin's initiatives.[124] He purchased five lots on which it was built for $2,000 and the construction cost of $13,000 was borrowed by St Patrick's parish on the security of Diocese of Sault Ste Marie.[125] As long as the Sisters of St Joseph staffed St Stanislaus School they resided at the convent rent free and its maintenance became the responsibility of St Patrick's Parish.[126]

As a tribute to Father Arpin, St Patrick Parish under the leadership of

Father Patrick J. Monahan (later to become the Bishop of Calgary), financed the construction of the only private Roman Catholic high school in northwestern Ontario which was officially opened on 21 November 1928 at 205 Franklin Street South, Thunder Bay. Since some of the funds for its construction came from the estate of Father Arpin the school was appropriately named St Patrick Arpin Memorial High School. From 1928 until the mid-1960s, St Patrick Parish shouldered the entire cost of its operation and administration. With these institutions in place, Fort William's Roman Catholic community was able to grow and flourish.

### *St Andrew Parish, Port Arthur, Ontario.*

St Andrew's parish in Port Arthur predated St Patrick's by almost two decades. The similarities between the two are worth noting. In 1900, both were the only Roman Catholic parishes in their respective towns. With Jesuit pastors, both were inclusive and "territorial" parishes catering to the spiritual needs of a wide spectrum of social groups and classes including a lower class immigrant population. In time, both witnessed segments of their immigrant population branch off to create parishes of their own. Both were in dire need of expansion to accommodate the ever increasing number of Roman Catholics moving into Thunder Bay.

Rebuilding and renewal–necessitated by the tragedy of fire, the increasing size of the parish and later, by changes ushered in by Vatican II of the 1960s –were dominant themes in the history of St Andrew's parish. Only a photographic essay could adequately chronicle the impressive transformations that were made to the interior and exterior of the church over time. Here, it is only possible to sketch out some of the early changes.[127] The first church, situated at the corner of Algoma and Red River Road, was dedicated under the patronage of St Andrew in 1875 to recognize a financial contribution of $100 that had been made to its construction by Scottish Catholic labourers. Its first pastor was Father Richard Baxter, s.j.[128] In 1881 a new church was built to replace the original which had been destroyed by fire. Within a year fire again struck and not only destroyed the vestry where it had originated but also the altar and some of the pews and windows.[129] By Christmas of 1892, the fire damage had been repaired and the church refurnished.[130] A decade later, the generosity of a single parishioner made possible a further renovation to the interior, a renovation that many viewed as being the most impressive thus far in St Andrew's history.[131] This change was completed in the full realization that the St Andrew's of 1903 was too small for the parish it was serving and totally inadequate for the increasing Port Arthur Roman Catholic population it was intended to serve.

Port Arthur's population during the first decade of the twentieth century grew faster than at any other period in its history. From 2,779 in 1900 it increased to 13,214 in 1910.[132] Approximately 20 percent was considered Roman Catholic. Perhaps a more accurate measure of the town's increasing Roman Catholic population was the number of baptisms recorded in St Andrew's parish registers and the enrolment in the separate school. Baptisms had increased dramatically from an average of 32 per year during the period 1891 to 1900 to 52 in 1905, 74 in 1906 and 126 in 1910.[133] From 1906 to 1909 St Andrew's School saw its student population increase by 30%.[134] Father Joseph Grenier, s.j., (1859–1976) pastor of St Andrew's (1906-1913; 1916-1922) estimated that the church had the potential of serving 1,000 - 1,200 Roman Catholics in Port Arthur. In 1906, however, it could seat 275 people comfortably. Three masses were celebrated each Sunday and at each service the church was filled to capacity. Gratifying as this was to Father Grenier he wanted to broaden the circle of those attending mass. Because of the overcrowding many who might have come to church did not. "Despite ourselves", commented Grenier, "we have to conclude that many of these families whose faith is not strong enough to move mountains, do not come to church." By 1906 a new church had become an absolute necessity.

The modern St Andrew's church was the product of prolonged and arduous effort. Pastors and parishioners lacked neither the will nor the vision to build an architecturally distinctive church on the eastern edge of Port Arthur's Waverley Park. Instead, from 1907 to 1924 they struggled with Bishop Scollard's vision of a new church that was significantly at odds with their own. He wanted to scale down what he believed to be extravagant expectations on the part of St Andrew's parishioners. More important perhaps, there was a struggle as to whom would direct and supervise its design and construction - St Andrew's building committee or the bishop. Some have referred to Bishop Scollard "as a pastoral man with a builder's sense."[135] He was not one to delegate decision-making on building projects within his diocese. On the contrary, he made decisions on all details relating to the construction of churches, rectories, schools, and orphanages. His was a benevolent authoritarian leadership style. Not surprisingly, this created tension between bishop, pastors, and parishioners.

The tension became evident as St Andrew's building committee placed before him their vision of a new church based on several architectural designs - one in 1907 and another in 1909. During Bishop Scollard's first pastoral visit to Port Arthur in May 1905 St Andrew's parishioners announced their intentions to get on with the task of building a new church. Two years later, the building committee submitted a general conceptual design (architect unknown) for the Bishop's perusal which had as its most distinguishing characteristic an impressive two tower facade.[136] Scollard's immediate reaction was that the committee was trying to create "an architectural monument for Port Arthur". In his view the construction costs for such an edifice were in the $150,000 - $200,000 range. Scollard argued that a small parish like St Andrew's with approximately 400 families should consider building a church in the $60,000 - $65,000 range. He was not prepared to guarantee a loan larger than $35,000 on the credit of the Diocese of Sault Ste Marie particularly since the parishioners, as of 1907, had only subscribed $6,000 towards their new church. Understandably, he had a multitude of issues in the diocese which demanded his undivided attention before he could give the plans for the Port Arthur church his "minute scrutiny and supervision." Meanwhile, he gave them permission to have the old church moved to the extreme eastern end of the property. If construction were to begin in the fall of 1908, the old church would be out of the way.[137] In addition, he urged that parishioners show their commitment to a new church by contributing generously to the building fund.

Had the old St Andrew's church been comfortable and large enough to allow reasonable numbers of Port Arthur's Roman Catholic population to attend mass and to participate in social events organized by the parish, parishioners would have tolerated Bishop Scollard's conservative approach. His need, however, to examine the minutest details in architectural plans postponed construction and forced a frustrated parish to organize their religious and social affairs around a church building that no longer met their needs and a school where space was at a premium with each passing year as enrolment increased. The building committee therefore pressed Bishop Scollard for decisions and action.[138] The committee was an impressive group. It included several of Port Arthur's leading businessmen and contractors. James Whalen, for example, was the Lakehead's most prominent industrialist. He was born and bred in Port Arthur and established two successful companies - the Western Dry Dock and Ship Building Co. and the Great Lakes Dredging Company. Frank Hamer and J. L. McRae were well-known building contractors. James

M. McGovern, William McBrady and James McTeigue had served on Port Arthur's town council. As the following extract makes clear, Bishop Scollard did not welcome the independent initiatives of this group:[139]

> The trouble out there seems to be that they do not know where their authority ends and where the Bishop's and Priest's authority begins and ends, in reference to the building of churches. It is my duty to consult with the people about the seating capacity of the church required, about the cost which they would be prepared to assume, about the material of construction which they would wish, about the appearance of the building in a general way, and when I get all these ideas it is my duty to sift them carefully, adopt what may be considered for the best and reject what may not be advisable to adopt...I knew I could make my authority prevail in this church matter, but I prefer not to quarrel with the people of Port Arthur. If they want that crude, unarchitectural pile, lacking many conveniences necessary in a Catholic Church, suffering as it surely will all the adverse criticism which any artist who sees it and every priest who uses it for years to come will heap upon it, they are welcome to it as far as I am concerned."

Bishop Scollard vacillated between outright rejection of the building committee's proposals and giving them carte blanche to do as they pleased providing construction costs did not exceed $60,000. By the end of 1907, however, he did not allow the parish to proceed. Instead, he instructed Father Grenier to inform his congregation that construction on the new church would be delayed for "another year or two" because of the high interest rates.

Two years later the building committee commissioned another design by Quebec architect G.E. Tanguay who, interestingly enough, was recommended to the group by Bishop Scollard.[140] So confident were they of the bishop's approval that they went public in November 1909 announcing that Port Arthur was to have a "new cathedral" built on the corner of Arthur (now Red River Road) and Algoma Streets. The design was to be Gothic in style "with two slender spires at the west end of the building towering upwards, each 180 feet high." To be constructed of Bedford stone and lined with brick, it would have a seating capacity of 1250. The estimated cost was $85,000. Mr. Alexander J. McComber, 69, a well-known and respected Port Arthur lawyer, was selected by the committee to travel to North Bay to sell this plan to Bishop Scollard. "It is understood that no difficulty will be met with in the approval of the plans," reported the Port Arthur *Daily-News,* "as the Bishop has signified his willingness of approving any plans that the congregation may choose to submit." They understood wrong. The Bishop did not want to meet with McComber.[141] Instead, he wanted to pore over the architectural drawings. Not surprisingly, he concluded that St Andrew's could not afford the Tanguay design as submitted. Significant changes would have to be made to bring down costs.

As they had done several times before, the building committee, respectfully but firmly, advanced reasons why the Tanguay plan was worth considering.[142] Savings could be made by finishing and furnishing the church in stages, by having the stone hauled to Port Arthur in scows and tugs owned by members of the congregation, and by using stone veneer instead of solid stone in construction. The bishop was assured that the congregation had been made aware of the costs and the financial responsibilities to be borne in the future. "We feel that we can more easily raise the larger amount if the people are enthusiastic in the matter" argued the building committee, "than a smaller amount if the people do not like the plans adopted." To reject the Tanguay plan or to seriously alter it meant further delays. Finally, St Andrew's parishioners wanted to build a church that would stand the test of time practically and aesthetically. Trinity United Church, constructed in 1904-1905 and First Baptist Church set a high architectural standard on the perimeter of Waverly Park. St Andrew's parish had a genuine desire to at least meet this standard in the building of their new church.

Bishop Scollard might not have consistently appreciated the needs and aspirations of St Andrew's parishioners situated as they were at the western extremity of his diocese 1105 km away from the episcopal seat in North Bay. Father Grenier put it succinctly when he said: "At this distance what one does not know one does not love." He did acknowledge publicly on one of his pastoral visits to St Andrew's, the absolute necessity of a new church for Port Arthur. Moreover, he compromised on the total amount to be spent on the new church - from $65,000 to $85,000. There was no compromise, however, on who would direct the planning and construction. "When it comes to the erection of a temple of God," he wrote, "I am the judge of what it should be, and shall continue to exercise that judgement. Criticisms, unkind remarks, and even insults may be levelled at me, but I must do my duty..."[143] To a later generation, Scollard's exercise of his authority might seem unreasonable and even bewildering. But he took his job seriously and wanted to do it well. When it came to assessing construction costs based on architectural designs, his judgement was sound. The tendered price for a "scaled down" version of the Tanguay design came in at $150,000.[144] To have proceeded on this basis would have left the parish with an enormous debt.[145] If the diocese was to guarantee any debt incurred by St Andrew's then it was reasonable that Bishop

Scollard should have the final say as to when the new church would be built. Hence he continued to temporize on approving plans until the architect could scale down costs within the manageable range of $80,000 - $85,000 and until the parish had the necessary cash on hand. Construction began in the summer of 1924. As expected, Bishop Scollard was involved in every facet of the building process.

Prior to and during the erection of their new church, St Andrew's parish explored every avenue to provide religious services to the Roman Catholics of Port Arthur such as having four masses on Sundays instead of three and holding missions at frequent intervals for the men, women and youth of the parish.[146] And the failure to build a new church did not dampen the enthusiasm of parishioners who belonged to organizations such as the Altar Society, choir, the Apostleship of Prayer, the Children of Mary, and the Youth League. At times, some were more active than others but these organizations were in place for those who wanted to participate in the spiritual life of the parish. By the early 1920s, St Andrew's was a vibrant parish and its members had to exercise forbearance as their bishop led them toward the realization of a new church .

With or without a new church the parish continued to serve as the headquarters and home base for Jesuit missionaries who served as chaplains to C.P.R. workers and their families along the north shore of Lake Superior. Father

Laying the Corner Stone, St. Andrew's New R. C. Church, Port Arthur, Ont., July 13, 1924.

**Bishop David Scollard officiates at the laying of the corner stone, St Andrew Parish, 13 July, 1924.**
Altar boys, parishioners and the local citizenry look on intently.
On 3 May 1925 the completed church was dedicated by Bishop Scollard.
(Thunder Bay Historical Society, 981.8.67a)

**St Andrew's Church Interior, c. 1950**
(Thunder Bay Historical Society, 984.53.341)

**St Andrew Roman Catholic Church, 23 July 2001**
292 Red River Road, Thunder Bay.

**St Andrew Parish Dew Drop Inn, 13 August 2002
Red River Road, Thunder Bay.**

Prior to becoming the Dew Drop Inn in 1981, this was the St Andrew's Church that served the Roman Catholics of Port Arthur during the first two decades of the twentieth century. In anticipation of the construction of a new church, this building was moved to its present site in 1907. When the new church was constructed in 1924-1925, the former church served a variety of parish functions.

Richard Baxter, s.j. had established the parameters and standards for this physically demanding work during his years as a railway missionary from 1875-1893.[147] At 72, he retired.[148] Two of his successors - Fathers Edward J. Devine, s.j. and Louis Lafortune, s.j. made singular contributions to this unique apostolate. By the time Devine had been appointed to succeed Baxter in 1893, he had established a reputation among his confreres as an editor, printer, writer, and distinguished orator. His new parish "was five hundred and eighty miles long by four feet ten inches wide." To reach his parishioners, he usually rode in the caboose with the railway crews. During these long hours, his creative mind led him to invent an electrical device that would allow the engine crew to communicate with the caboose. Once patented in 1895 it became known among CPR railway workers as "the Devine Signal." As the following extract from his memoir suggests, the life of a railway missionary was not for the faint of heart:

> I was continually on the road, travelling by freight or passenger trains and sometimes making my tiring journeys along the shores of Lake Superior. I managed to get over the whole area of 586 miles every three months...So frequent were the calls up and down the railway that during the first two years of my ministry on Lake Superior, I made sixty thousand miles, not figures of my imagination, but a mileage record well kept, a tiring task, but my health was good and I did not feel the fatigue. Having four churches to serve, White River, Schreiber, West Fort William and Murillo, I gave one Sunday a month to each church. The rest of the week was given to stations between these points...It was pleasant enough exercising railway ministry in the summer, but winters along Lake Superior, especially in the neighbourhood of White River, were extremely severe, and the stations and section-men's shacks were flimsily built, there was much misery to put up with. Many nights I did not know how to keep warm. I suffered more from cold on Lake Superior than I did years later in Alaska. It was an ordeal, for instance, to go into church at White River when the mercury was thirty degrees below zero, and start a fire to get some heat...[149]

Father Louis Lafortune followed in the footsteps of Devine three years later. He combined the talents of being an exemplary missionary with the administrative ability to organize a parish in a frontier setting like northwestern Ontario. Under his leadership and supervision the Roman Catholics of the railway town of Schreiber, 150 km east of Thunder Bay, built their first mission church in 1896. Sixteen years later it seemed appropriate that he would be reunited with this community to serve as their first resident priest. Through the experiences of Jesuit missionaries passing through St Andrew's rectory, the parish was, and would continue to be, exposed to a regional perspective on the development of Roman Catholicism in northwestern Ontario. Only one other parish in the diocese - Notre Dame du Portage in Kenora - could identify with this experience.

### *Notre Dame du Portage Parish, Kenora, Ontario.*

Notre Dame du Portage parish, Kenora, grew out of a need seen by Archbishop Alexander Taché (1823-1894) of St Bonificace to provide C.P.R. construction workers along the transcontinental line between Kenora (then Rat Portage) and Winnipeg with a permanent chaplain. He was deeply disturbed over reports of excessive drinking and rowdiness among railroad construction workers, one-third of whom were French Canadian Roman Catholics from Manitoba.[150] For this task he selected Father Albert Lacombe, o.m.i., (1827–1916) one of the best known Roman Catholic Oblate missionaries in western Canada.[151] At the request of his bishop Father Lacombe reluctantly left his work among the Cree and Blackfoot and used Rat Portage as a base to minister to railway workers in thirty different C.P.R. camps. Here he was scandalized by the blasphemy, drunkenness and immorality. Hoping to raise the moral consciousness of these people he celebrated mass and delivered sermons wherever he went. At Rat Portage itself he was responsible for the construction in 1881 of a modest log chapel on what is now Main Street. Father Lacombe's presence in Rat Portage ended in the Spring of 1882. He was succeeded by Father Jean-Baptiste Baudin, o.m.i. (1833–1909) who became the first pastor of Notre Dame du Portage parish canonically erected by Archbishop Adélard Langevin on 11 October 1903.[152]

From its inception to 1914 the parish grew at a steady pace. In the early 1880s its congregation consisted of 127 families (324 members) with a little less than half being francophone.[153] By 1890, it had grown sufficiently to warrant the construction of an imposing and majestic church at 222 First Street North of red and grey granite overlooking the Town of Kenora and beautiful Lake of the Woods. In the early 1900s, the congregation was almost equally divided between anglophones and francophones but as the pulp and paper, logging, and mining industries developed around the Lake of the Woods region the English speaking families in the parish began to outnumber the French.[154] At times the issue of language was a source of frustration for the anglophones of the parish as this petition to Archbishop Adélard Langevin suggests:[155]

> We, the undersigned, your Grace's loving and filial children of the parish of Notre Dame du Portage, Ontario, do individually and collectively wish to call your Grace's attention to the fact that while we English speaking people are largely in the majority of this place we seldom hear a good instructive sermon in our mother tongue, and to request your Grace, if it in any way lies in your Grace's power, to let us have a parish priest whose mother tongue is the English language. We would also respectfully mention to your Grace that a large number of our Irish co-religionists abstain from assisting at the services of the church and are in danger of losing the faith of their fathers...

On Christmas eve of 1914 a fire which had originated in the furnace room spread and destroyed the entire church leaving only the massive granite walls intact.[156] The fire represented a $35,000 loss to the parish of which $17,500 was recovered through insurance claims. The process of reconstruction began almost immediately after the fire.[157] Archbishop Langevin granted the parish permission to organize raffles and draws as fund-raising ventures for the new church.[158] During construction, the enlarged structure was built around the remnants of the old. A twenty-five foot transit was added to the rear of the church, four feet was added to the original walls extending the ceiling height to 39.5 feet, and a full basement, hewn out of the granite bedrock on which the church stood, was built under the entire 105 foot length of the church. All stone used in the reconstruction was secured from the church site and more stone was used in the expansion than in the original structure. In the space of eleven months, the church had been rebuilt with an attractive and artistic ceiling, a new auditorium, and an enlarged choir and organ loft above the interior front entrance. That the reconstruction was completed during the economic difficulties associated with the First World War at a cost of $25,000 was a tribute to the sacrifice, resourcefulness and commitment of Notre Dame du Portage parishioners. The first Mass celebrated in the reconstructed church took place on Sunday, 19 December 1915.[159]

The physical renewal of the church necessitated by the tragedy of fire coincided with significant changes to its social make-up. Out of the approximately 98,000 Roman Catholics in the St Boniface diocese in 1910, less than a third were of French origin and the number of Poles almost equalled those whose first language was English.[160] Parish reports submitted to the Archdiocese of St Boniface reflected these changes. Statistics carefully prepared by pastors from 1919 to 1945 reveal an ethnically diverse parish led by English-speaking parishioners (42.5) followed by francophones (39.6), Ukrainian (12.7) and Polish

(4.2). The Polish percentages increased at the expense of the French. Pastors expressed concerns that a significant segment of the parish population was transient ("population flottante") and attributed this phenomenon to the presence of a Backus/Brooks paper mill in Kenora.[161] Since most men in the parish were employed by either the paper mill or the C.P.R. many were obliged to work on Sundays and hence their attendance at Mass was irregular as was their children's catechetical instruction. Mixed marriages had become commonplace and the Oblates took some comfort in knowing that two-thirds of these marriages were from the English segment of the parish. Whatever the social make-up of the parish, sermons and announcements were given in both French and English at Sunday masses. Notre Dame Du Portage was unique during this period in that the Latin and Eastern rite (Ukrainian) Catholics coexisted in the same parish. There is no evidence to suggest that any special accommodations were made for Polish and Ukrainian parishioners.

Like most first parishes in the Diocese of Thunder Bay, a separate school was invariably in close proximity to the parish church. In the case of Notre Dame du Portage, Ecole Mount Carmel was situated immediately beside the church. From its inception the school was staffed by francophone women religious trained in Quebec or Manitoba: from 1914 to 1927 the Reverend Soeurs de la Presentation de Marie de St Hyacinthe staffed the school and were followed by the Sisters of the Holy Names of Jesus and Mary until 1952.[162] Unfortunately, none of the Sisters were licenced to teach in Ontario.[163] They were granted temporary teaching certificates on the understanding that qualified teachers would be hired in subsequent years. From 1914 to 1945 the Kenora Separate School Board paid a high price for having unqualified francophone teachers. Without qualified teachers, the school board could not float debentures to finance the school debt or receive grants from the Ontario Department of Education.[164] The funds the school board received from the Town of Kenora from taxes were insufficient to cover all expenses. The following pronouncement made by Archbishop Langevin in 1914 gives some insight into the economic importance of having parents send their children to the separate school in Kenora:[165]

> FOR THE GREATER GLORY OF GOD AND FAMILY PEACE. We believe in the necessity of publishing the following regulations for the catholic separate school of Kenora, Norman and Keewatin.

1) In the first place, this is a fundamental principle and a solemn obligation for Catholics to pay their taxes to maintain the separate Roman Catholic School.

2) If, in a particular case and for exceptional reasons which the Archbishop shall be the judge, permission may be granted to parents to send their children to the public school...

3) The parish priest will withhold absolution to fathers who refuse to honour this regulation, that is to say, to pay what is required to support the catholic separate school, and to send children to a public school without permission from the parish priest. If the mother encourages the father in this "mauvaise voie", she is as guilty as he is and she desires to be treated in a similar manner.

Bishop Adélard Langevin, o.m.i.
Archbishop of St Boniface.

One can only imagine the conflicts which arose between parishioners and pastors of Notre Dame Parish over this regulation. Beginning in 1926, the parish contributed generously to the operation of the school without adding to the church debt which was liquidated in 1945.[166]

Kenora and Notre Dame Du Portage Parish became the centre from which the "Lake of the Woods Missions" were served by the Oblates of Mary Immaculate. There were two categories of missions: those that served bushmen, hydro workers, and tourists and those that served the Indian population within a 100 km radius of Kenora. In the latter category there were missions at McIntosh, Grassy Narrows, Lac Seul, Wabaskan, and White Dog. At McIntosh was established an Indian Residential School which also served as a residence for the Oblate missionaries. The total Indian population was estimated to be approximately 1,855 individuals of whom 1000 were "pagans", 200 Catholic and the balance nominally Anglican.[167] Grassy Narrows was the main mission situated approximately 66 km north of Kenora with 80 Catholics out of a total population of 125. By 1952 small rustic mission chapels had been built at Sioux Narrows, Willard Lake, Melick and Redditt to serve tourists and workers in the Lake of the Woods region. Oblate missionaries such as Father William Moss, o.m.i. travelled to these missions on a regular basis throughout the year from the Notre Dame Du Portage rectory.[168]

The first parishes described above became the anchors of Roman Catholicism in northwestern Ontario. During the first fifty years of the twentieth century the Jesuits and Oblates that served these parishes attempted to

**Sacred Heart Chapel, Sioux Narrows, 22 May 2002.**
This chapel was blessed and dedicated by Bishop E.Q. Jennings on 29 July 1957. Sacred Heart Chapel was meant to serve Americans and Canadians who moved to their cottages on Lake of the Woods during the summer months. The first chapel was much smaller and situated closer to Highway 71. After considerable protest from Roman Catholics who regularly attended mass at the chapel during the 1940s, it had to be replaced with this larger and more durable building. Since 1938, Sacred Heart Chapel has been served by priests at Notre Dame du Portage Parish, Kenora.

**Commemorative Historical Marker for Father William Moss, o.m.i., Sioux Narrows.**
As a missionary in northwestern Ontario during the 1930s and 1940s, Father William Moss, o.m.i. brooked few comparisons. This simple marker was erected in his honour. The inscription reads: "He built this rustic church in 1938 [Sacred Heart Chapel], and many others on the Lake of the Woods. After 18 years as a missionary he died on October 9, 1952. He loved them all, and his friends of all faith[s] erected this monument to help you to remember a friend."

St Mary Roman Catholic Church, 23 May 2002.
206 Victoria Avenue, Fort Frances.

On 21 September 1893 Father Adélard Langevin, o.m.i., together with two other Oblate missionaries, established the Fort Frances Mission which was primarily intended to serve approximately 100 Indian and Metis on the Couchiching Reserve on Rainy Lake. In the Town of Fort Frances itself, situated on the shores of Rainy River and two miles from Rainy Lake, there was but a handful of Roman Catholics. To serve them, the first mass was celebrated in the home of Mr. Louis Hamel on 9 September 1894. A year later, a small "chapel house" was built and open for worship. Although Father J. B. Baudin, o.m.i. was sent to the Fort Frances mission ("Our Lady of Perpetual Help") to take up permanent residence, the number of Roman Catholics did not warrant a full-time pastor and by 1896 Mass was celebrated in the town every fourth Sunday. It was not until a pulp and paper mill and the C.N.R. established a presence in Fort Frances that the Roman Catholic population began to grow. In 1918, it had fifty-nine Roman Catholic families who attended a small church capable of seating 165 people. Twenty years later, in order to accommodate all parishioners, four masses were celebrated each Sunday. The church shown in this photograph was built in 1950 and dedicated by the Archbishop of St. Boniface on 26 May 1951 under the patronage of Our Lady of Perpetual Help. In 1952, it was named St Mary Church. From 1893 to June 2002 it was served continuously by the Oblates of Mary Immaculate.

Our Lady of Lourdes Parish Church, 23 May 2002.
Couchiching Reserve, Fort Frances.

Our Lady of Lourdes Church Santuary, 23 May 2002

**Our Lady of the Way Church, Pinewood. 23 May 2002.**
This parish church is one of the most attractive in the diocese. It began as a mission church in 1897 served by the Oblate priests from Notre Dame du Portage in Kenora. On 21 September 1898, it was dedicated by Archbishop Adélard Langevin of St Boniface under the patronage of Notre Dame du Chemin ("Our Lady of the Wayside") because voyageurs and explorers visited the church en route to trading posts in the Rainy River District. It was elevated to parish status on 31 October 1900.

Our Lady of Good Counsel Parish Church, 23 May 2002
Rainy River, Ontario.

St Patrick Parish Church, Emo. 23 May 2002
This church was built in 1972 after the original structure had been totally destroyed by fire on 3 September 1971. Today, it is served by the pastor at Our Lady of the Way parish in Pinewood.

cope with ethnically diverse congregations as best they could. In the Kenora and Rainy Lake regions Polish, Ukrainian and Italian Roman Catholics had little choice but to attend services where French and English were the dominant languages. In Thunder Bay, where there were larger concentrations of ethnic groups, national parishes emerged. The establishment and growth of these parishes is the subject of the next chapter.

## Notes

[1] James A. Coriden, et. al., eds., *The Code of Canon Law: A Text and Commentary* (New York: Paulist Press, 1985), p. 415-416.

[2] N.J.G. Pounds, *A History of the English Parish: The Culture of Religion from Augustine to Victoria* (Cambridge: Cambridge University Press, 2000), pp. 3-6.

[3] See John McManners, *Church and Society in Eighteenth-Century France, Volume 1: The Clerical Establishment and Its Social Ramifications* (Oxford: Oxford University Press, 1998), p. 297.

[4] J. Coriden, ed., *The Code of Canon Law,* see canon 515. *Archives of the Roman Catholic Diocese of Thunder Bay* (*DTBA*), 5.10, Box 3, Rev. Francis G. Morrisey, O.M.I., "Statement Regarding the Canonical Requirements relating to the re-establishment of Saint Anthony's Parish, Diocese of Thunder Bay, Ontario," 8 October 1990.

[5] For the geographic extent of the Fort William Indian Reserve see M. Elizabeth Arthur, ed., *Thunder Bay District, 1821-1992* (Toronto: University of Toronto Press, 1973), p. 19.

[6] Archives of the Society of Jesus, Upper Canada. (ASJUC) "Diary of the Mission of the Immaculate Conception of the Jesuit Fathers on Lake Superior in the Year of Our Lord 1848", pp. 30-31.

[7] *DTBA. Church of the Immaculate Conception,Parish Registers, 1848-1914, Vol. I, 1872.* Father Richard Baxter, s.j. (1821-1904) establishes the location of the Fort William Mission in a note inscribed in this first volume: "Head Quarters at the Church of the Immaculate Conception near Fort William, on Kaministiquia River, off Thunder Bay, Prov. Ontario."

[8] For a brief history of the Church of the Immaculate Conception see Arvis Neuert, *The Church That Follows the People* (Thunder Bay, 1991). For the origins and development of the Mission de L'Immaculée Conception see Roch L. Letourneau, "Continuity and Change: Religious and Secular at the Lakehead, 1849-1906" (Honours diss., Lakehead University, 1993).

[9] Patrick Boyle, S.J., *Saint Stanislaus Parish, Copper Cliff, The Early Years 1886-1914* (Toronto, 1998), p. 2. Father Choné was the first Jesuit Superior at Wikwemikong (1844-1848).

[10] Diocese of Peterborough Archives *(DPA)*, The Most Rev. Bishop R.A. O'Connor Papers. Fr. Renaud, s.j. to +R.A. O'Connor, 24 August 1892.

[11] *DTBA*. Father William Maurice, s.j., comp., "Personnel at the Fort William Mission, 1848-1999" (Thunder Bay : St Anne Parish, 1999). See also Patrick Boyle, s.j., *Saint Stanislaus Parish,* p. 6.

[12] Elizabeth Arthur, ed., *Thunder Bay District, 1821-1892,* p. lxxxvii.

[13] Angus J. Macdougall, et. al. eds., *Dictionary of Jesuit Biography: Ministry to English Canada, 1842-1987* (Toronto: Canadian Institute of Jesuit Studies, 1991), pp. 10-11.

[14] *Ibid.*, pp. 120-121.

[15] Bruce G. Trigger, *The Children of Aataentsic: A History of the Huron People to 1660* (Montreal: McGill-Queen's University Press, 1987), p. 468.

[16] *DPA. Journal of Most Rev. Bishop R.A. O'Connor*, 31 December 1893, p. 90.

[17] Angus J. Macdougall, ed., *DJB,* pp. 326-327. Specht, together with Thomas Gagnon, s.j. (1851-1883) were the first to be ordained within the present limits of the Dioceses of Sault

Ste. Marie and Thunder Bay. See Greg Humbert, ed., *Bishop R. H. Dignan, The Minute Book*, p. 420.

[18]*ASJUC*, Joseph Specht, s.j. Papers, Box A-206, "The Indian Missions of Lake Superior, A Letter from Father Specht, 10 September 1897.

[19]*DPA*. O'Connor Papers. Specht to + O'Connor, 23 April 1890.

[20]See Elizabeth Arthur, "The de Larondes of Lake Nipigon", in The Thunder Bay Historical Museum Society, *Papers and Records*, IX (1981), p. 44.

[21]*ASJUC*, Specht Papers, A-206, Henry de Laronde to Father Specht, 10 November 1890.

[22]*DPA*. O'Connor Journal, 6 September 1893, p. 82.

[23]*Ibid.*,O'Connor Papers. Specht to +O'Connor, 23 July 1890.

[24]Toronto *Globe*, 11 August 1900.

[25]*Ibid.*, O'Connor Papers. Prosper Lamarche, s.j. to +O'Connor, 7 January 1901.

[26]*Ibid.*, Specht to +O'Connor, 18 April 1896.

[27]*Ibid.*, *O'Connor Journal*, 23 August 1893, p. 79; 8 July 1897, p. 127; 5 July 1898, p. 142; 2 July 1901, p. 184; 24 October 1902, p. 209.

[28]*Ibid.*, 28 August 1893, p. 80.

[29]*Ibid.*, 13-14 July 1898, pp. 143-144.

[30]*Ibid.*, 20 July 1898, p. 145.

[31]*Ibid.*, 11 September 1893; 8 July 1901, p. 184; 16 July 1901, p. 185.

[32]*DSSMA*. Report of the Mission of the Immaculate Conception, Fort William for the year 1905. Rev. P.E. Lamarche, s.j., Pastor to Bishop D.J. Scollard, Bishop of Sault Ste Marie. The Church of the Immaculate Conception and the Jesuit residence were owned by the Society of Jesus.

[33]*ASJUC*, Alphonse Baudin Papers, Box A-105, +O'Connor to Baudin, 20 January 1899. Bishop O'Connor suggested that all parishioners contribute fifty cents on the oaccasion of baptisms and two dollars for marriages in addition to the usual fees for the dispensation of banns.

[34]*DPA*. O'Connor Papers, Fr. A. Baudin to +O'Connor, 29 August 1891.

[35]*ASJUC*, Box C-409, "Book of Announcements in the Church of the Immaculate Conception, Fort William Mission, 1889-1897.

[36]*DTBA*, Church of the Immaculate Conception, Parish Register, 1892, v. 2. (p. 109, p. 119).

[37]*DSSMA*. Report of the Mission of the Immaculate Conception, 1905. The Westfort Church was registered in the name of the Diocese of Sault Ste Marie and by 1905 still carried a debt of $1100. It was variously referred to by Father Baxter, s.j. in the Mission parish registers "Church of the Nativity of Our Lord and St Agnes", "Church of the Nativity and Saint Agnes", or "Nativity at Fort William."

[38]Sisters of St Joseph Archives, Peterborough. *(SSJAP)*, Sister Evarista's Annals, 1 March 1881. See also Sisters of St Joseph, Peterborough, *As The Tree Grows: Sisters of St Joseph of Peterborough, 1890-1990 (*Peterborough, 1993*)*, pp. 134-135.

[39]*Ibid.*, Sister Annunciation (Mahoney), Sister Francis (Honora Burke), Sister Hilda (McCormick), and Sister Geraldine (Chidwick) arrived at the Fort William Mission in August, 1885.

[40]*DPA*, Sister M. Incarnation to +O'Connor, 23 April 1895.

⁴¹*Ibid.*, O'Connor Journal, 26 August 1893, p. 79.

⁴²*Ibid.*, O'Connor Journal, 25 August 1893, p. 79.

⁴³*Ibid.*, Bishop 0'Connor Papers, W.F. Gagnieur, s.j. to +R.A. O'Connor, 10 April 1895; O'Connor Journal, 10 April 1895, p. 100; For a detailed description of the fire see *Fort William Daily Journal*, 10 April 1895. For Chief Frank Pelletier's personal testimony of the fire see Arvis Neuert, *The Church That Follows The People*, (Thunder Bay, 1991), pp. 7-8. Pelletier was a resident of the orphanage when the fire occurred.

⁴⁴*Ibid.*, O'Connor Journal, 12 July 1897, p. 127. New convent/orphanage, rebuilt at a cost of $7000, was a large two story frame building with a stone foundation. For a detailed description of its interior and exterior physical appearance see the *Fort William Daily Journal*, 30 September 1895. The new Immaculate Conception Church was a wooden structure, painted white, measuring 25' x 30'; sanctuary and vestry alone measured 24' x 27'. Total cost of new construction was $2600.

⁴⁵DPA, O'Connor Papers, Sister M. Incarnation to + O'Connor, 23 April 1895.

⁴⁶DSSMA., Bishop D.J. Scollard Papers, +Scollard to C.A. McCool, 27 June 1905. Scollard restated the arguments of the Jesuits, Sisters of St Joseph and Bishop O'Connor to James Conmee, Roman Catholic Member of Parliament for Thunder–Bay Rainy River (1904-1911) and to the Hon. Frank Oliver, Minister of the Interior in the Laurier government (1905-1911).

⁴⁷DPA, O'Connor Papers, Fr. P. E. Lamarche,s.j. to +O'Connor, 20 June 1902.

⁴⁸*Ibid.*, Sister M. Sacred Heart to +O'Connor, 3 November 1902.

⁴⁹*Ibid.*, J. Paquin, s.j. to Secretary, Dept. of Indian Affairs, 31 March 1898. (copy)

⁵⁰*Ibid.*, O'Connor Papers, Sister M. Sacred Heart to +O'Connor, 7 April 1903.

⁵¹*Ibid.*, Fr. Prosper Lamarche, s.j. to +O'Connor, 4 March 1904.

⁵²*Ibid.*,Fr. Lamarche,s.j. to +O'Connor, 18 February 1904. The contamination of the Kam water supply resulted from a sewer discharging into the river one-half mile above the City of Fort William water intake. See W. L. C. Greer, "The Fort William Water Supply, 1905-1909 in The Thunder Bay Historical Museum Society, *Papers and Records,*II (1974), pp. 1-3.

⁵³*Fort William Journal,* 10 October 1891.On a regular basis the Sisters of St Joseph would publicly thank the people of Fort William for their financial support. In the Town and District column of the *Fort William Journal,* the Sisters of St Joseph placed the following notice: "The Sisters of St Joseph's Convent, Fort William, return most sincere thanks to the people of Fort William East and West, for their generous contributions towards the maintenance of the orphans."

⁵⁴DPA.,O'Connor Papers. Sister M. Sacred Heart to +O'Connor, 3 November 1902.

⁵⁵*Ibid.*, Sr. Sacred Heart to +O'Connor, 7 April 1903.

⁵⁶See Thorold J. Tronrud, *Guardians of Progress: Boosters & Boosterism in Thunder Bay, 1870-1914* (Thunder Bay: Thunder Bay Historical Museum Society, 1993), p. 40, 45. See also, Bruce Muirhead, "The Evolution of the Lakehead's Commercial and Transportation Infrastructure", in Thorold J. Tronud and A. Ernest Epp, eds., *Thunder Bay: From Rivalry to Unity* (Thunder Bay: Thunder Bay Historical Museum Society, 1995), pp. 81-82.

⁵⁷Fort William *Daily Times-Journal*, 18 January 1905.

⁵⁸*Ibid.*, 14 January 1905. See also Thorold J. Tronrud, *Guardians of Progress,* pp. 40, 45. Over $350,000 was given to the Grand Trunk Pacific Railway in municipal aid by the City of Fort William to ensure that the railway would locate there and not Port Arthur.
⁵⁹ASJUC, C-407, file #15, Robert E. Mitchell to Fr. Lamarche, s.j., 13 April 1905. Confidential (copy)
⁶⁰*DTJ*, 30 March 1905.
⁶¹*Ibid.*, 3 April 1906. DSSMA., Bishop D.J. Scollard Papers, Fr. P. E. Lamarche to +Scollard, 26 May 1906. The Fort William Indian Band received approximately $245,000 from the GTP out of which was taken the costs for building the homes near the mountain. Canadian Government officials estimated that the Indian Band would realize a cash settlement of approximately $144,000. The Jesuit community received $53,953 for the church property and an additional $4,000 to re-inter the bodies from the cemetery on the original site to another. In addition, they sold ten acres of land situated at the mouth of the Kaministiquia and Mission Rivers to a Mr. T. P. Kelly for $20,000. For their part, the Sisters of St Joseph received $23,000 for their convent/boarding school.
⁶²See A. Ernest Epp, "The Achievement of Community", in Thorold J. Tronrud and A. Ernest Epp, eds., *Thunder Bay: From Rivalry to Unity,* p. 180.
⁶³*DSSMA.*, Scollard Papers, Fr. P. Lamarche to +Scollard, 11 April 1906.
⁶⁴See Steven High, "Responding to White Encroachment: The Robinson-Superior Ojibwa and the Capitalist Labour Economy, 1880-1914", The Thunder Bay Historical Museum Society, *Papers and Records, XXII, 1994,* pp. 22-39.
⁶⁵For a brief period this was officially referred to by the Indian Affairs Department as "Mission Village, Fort William Indian Reserve, Ontario."
⁶⁶*DSSMA*, Scollard Papers, Jean Baptiste Penaissie to +Scollard, 29 June 1906.
⁶⁷*DTJ*, 11 April 1906.
⁶⁸Fr. Julien Paquin, s.j., missionary and historian, in his history of the Immaculate Conception Mission, gives a different version of the vote: 30 families elected to remain at Mountain Road while 28 families followed the Jesuits to the Mission Bay site.
⁶⁹*ASJUC,* Box C-407, File #16, +Scollard to Fr. Lamarche, 16 April 1905.
⁷⁰*DSSMA.* Scollard Papers, Lamarche to +Scollard, 25 September 1906. See Father William Maurice, s.j., "Burials..."
⁷¹*Ibid.,* Lamarche to +Scollard, 26 May 1906; 25 September 1906.
⁷²Fort William *Mining Herald*, 3 October 1907.
⁷³*DSSMA.* Scollard Papers, J.B. Penassie to +Scollard, 3 April 1907.
⁷⁴*ASJUC,* Box C-407, File #16, +Scollard to Fr. Lamarche, 8 April 1907.
⁷⁵*DSSMA.* Scollard Papers. +Scollard to Lamarche, 21 September 1907.
⁷⁶*Ibid., Scollard Chronicle,* p. 14. "These buildings were erected at the expense of the Society of Jesus from a portion of money received from the Grand Trunk Pacific for the sale of their property at the old Mission."
⁷⁷*Ibid.,* p. 17. SSJAP, Sister Evarista's Annals, 1 March 1907.
⁷⁸*Ibid.,* +Scollard to Father Grenier, 21 May 1908. The Sault Ste. Marie Diocese assumed the financing of the Boarding School and made it a Diocesan institution for the western

portion of the Diocese and encouraged the Catholics of Port Arthur to support it.

[79] *Ibid.* Of this amount $2,000 was paid to the Daughters of the Immaculate Heart of Mary, who preceded them at the Fort William Mission beginning in 1870 and built the first orphanage/school.

[80] Sisters of St Joseph, Peterborough. *As The Tree Grows*, p. 139.

[81] *DSSMA*. Scollard Papers. C.A. McCool to +Scollard, 9 January 1908.

[82] A. Ernest Epp, "The Achievement of Community" in Thorold J. Tronrud and A. Ernest Epp, eds. *Thunder Bay: From Rivalry to Unity*, p. 180.

[83] See Donald Kerr, et. al., *Historical Atlas of Canada, III, Addressing the Twentieth Century, 1891-1961,* (Toronto: University of Toronto Press, 1990), 34.

[84] Thunder Bay Archives (TBA). Series 16, City of Thunder Bay Annual Reports. Annual Report of the Assessment Commissioner, 1910.

[85] *DPA*. O'Connor Papers. P.E. Lamarche to +O'Connor, 4 March 1903.

[86] Fort William *Daily Times-Journal*, 13 July 1918.

[87] *Fort William Journal*, 8 September 1887.

[88] *DTJ*, 26 March 1907.

[89] *TBA*, Series 16, Box 207, file 1-24-25, Assessment Commissioner's Report, 23 November 1909.

[90] *DSSMA*, Rev. A.A. Ragaru, s.j. to +Scollard, 13 July 1910.

[91] *Ibid., Scollard Chronicle,* 11 July 1914, p. 39; See also Fort William *Morning Herald*, 25 May 1914. The estimated cost of construction for the new church was $34,000.

[92] For a detailed description of the ceremony see the *DTJ*, 27 July 1914.

[93] Scollard Chronicle, 17 January 1915, p. 42; See also *DTJ*, 13 July 1918.

[94] *Ibid.,* 11 February 1915, pp. 42-43.

[95] *DTBA*, 5.17, Rev. W.T. Batterton to +Scollard, 2 March 1922.

[96] Scollard Chronicle, p. 60; Father McCullough died on 26 November 1919.

[97] *TBA*, series 16, box 207, file 2-71, Assessment Commissioner's Report, 7 January 1916.

[98] See *DTJ*, 20 August 1918, 11 August 1919, 14 March 1921.

[99] *DPA*. O'Connor Papers. Baudin to +O'Connor, 29 August 1891.

[100] *Fort William Journal*, 5 September 1891.

[101] *DPA*, O'Connor Papers. Baudin to +O'Connor, 8 September 1891. The land was owned by the Sisters of St Joseph; land bequeathed to them by a Mr. Sills. Document does not state where the land was situated or its specific dimensions.

[102] *FWJ*, 19 September 1891.

[103] *Ibid.,* 8 and 29 June 1892.

[104] *Ibid.,* 17 August 1892.

[105] *Ibid.,* 2 September 1893. Bishop O'Connor canonically erected a parish at St Patrick's on Sunday, 26 August 1893. The total cost of the unfinished church was approximately $5,000 of which $3,000 was raised by the people and $2,000 borrowed from the Diocese of Peterborough.

[106] Biographical details taken from eulogy given at Father Arpin's funeral. Latin text translat-

ed by Fr. Rino Zilotto, c.s., St Dominic Parish.

[107] *DPA.* O'Connor Papers. Arpin to +O'Connor, 27 September 1893; 13 December 1893.

[108] *Ibid.,* Arpin to +O'Connor, 24 February 1897.

[109] *Ibid.,* Arpin to +O'Connor, 13 June 1899.

[110] Thunder Bay Catholic District School Board Archives. Minutes of the Separate School Board of Fort William, Ont., 1901, p. 3.

[111] *Ibid.,* 30 April 1901, p. 3.

[112] *DPA.,* Arpin to +O'Connor, 16 April 1901.

[113] *Ibid.,* Arpin to +O'Connor, 25 September 1901. The total cost of the school was approximately $13,000; See O'Connor Journal, 15 January 1902, p. 202.

[114] *Ibid.,* O'Connor Papers. Sister St Edwards to +O'Connor, 19 February 1902.

[115] The remuneration for the Sisters of St Joseph was set at $300 per year per teacher. Minutes of the Separate School Board of Fort William, 1901, p. 4.

[116] *DPA.,* +O'Connor to Arpin, 1 January 1902.

[117] *Ibid.,* Sr. St Vincent to +O'Connor, 13 January 1902.

[118] Canada. Census, 1901.

[119] *DPA.* O'Connor Papers. Arpin to +O'Connor, 1 September 1893; 27 September 1893; 13 December 1893.

[120] For a detailed description of the renovations see The Fort William *Daily Times-Journal,* 6 May 1904, 28 May 1904 and 19 November 1904. See also *DTBA*, Box 801, Harry Mireault, "Old St Patrick's Church" .

[121] *DPA*, O'Connor Journal, 20 November 1904, p. 239.

[122] *Ibid.,* Arpin to +O'Connor, 2 March 1899; 23 January 1900; 20 March 1900.

[123] *Ibid.,* Arpin to +O'Connor, 28 November 1903.

[124] *Ibid.,* Arpin to +O'Connor, 23 October 1903.

[125] *DSSMA.* Scollard Chronicle, 8 December 1905, p. 9.

[126] *DTBA*, 5.17/30, "Memo of an agreement between the Rev. St Joseph's Sisters and St Patrick Parish, Fort William, Ont. sanctioned by his Lordship D.J. Scollard", 1 February 1906.

[127] For an early history of St Andrew's Parish see Rev. Francis J. Nelligan, s.j., "The Early History of St Andrew's Parish", in *St Andrew's Catholic Church Centennial, 1875-1975* (Thunder Bay, 1975).

[128] See Elinor Barr, "Richard Baxter" in *DCB, XIII,* 44-45.

[129] *DPA*, O'Connor Journal, 21 September 1892, p. 69. The damage, estimated at $1791, was covered by insurance.

[130] *Ibid.,* 31 December 1892, p. 73; 27 August 1893, p. 80. Bishop O'Connor noted in his Journal that the cost of repairs and new furnishings totalled $3,625. "Of this amount $1462 were given by subscriptions; $814 were realized from a Bazaar and the balance obtained from some church lots that were sold and from the church revenues..."

[131] *Ibid.,* Father Oliver Neault, s.j. to +O'Connor, 8 June 1903.

[132] *TBA*, file 2559.

133 St. Andrew's Parish Registers, Port Arthur, Ontario. Baptisms, 1878-1907, Vol. 1-B; Baptisms, 1908-1935, Vol. 1-C.

134 *ASJCF*, B-16-D, 9, Annual Letters, 1906-1909. In 1906 the school had 230 students. By 1909 that had increased to 330 necessitating the addition of four classes and an equal number of teachers.

135 *Bishop David Joseph Scollard: A Chronicle*. Edited with an introduction by Gregory J. Humbert (North Bay: The Diocese of Sault Ste. Marie, n.d.), xxvi.

136 *ASJUC*, C-410, file #4, +D.J. Scollard to Fr. Joseph Grenier, s.j., 18 May 1907.

137 The church was moved in July 1907 on to a concrete sub-basement which was subsequently used as a church hall. After the move repairs had to be made to the cracked walls.

138 Port Arthur *Daily-News*, 8 November 1909. The following made up the building committee: Father J.A. Grenier, s.j., chairman; Messrs. D. Dwyer, W.F. Fortune, M.J. Kenny, George Horrigan, J. McTeigue, A.J. McComber, Alphonse Guerard, William McBrady, Dr. J.M. McGrady, Albert Guerard, Thomas Redden, James Whalen, John Redden, John Hourigan, F. Hamer, E. Bonin, J.M. McGovern, J.L. McRae, H. Chausse, C.E. Duffy and Joseph Redden.

139 *Ibid.*, +Scollard to Grenier, 15 June 1907.

140 Port Arthur *Daily-News*, 8 November 1909.

141 *ASJUC*, C-410, file #4, +Scollard to Grenier, 28 December 1909.

142 *Ibid.*, Building Committee to +Scollard, 14 January 1910.

143 *Ibid.*, +Scollard to Grenier, 20 April 1910.

144 *Ibid.*, +Scollard to Grenier, 1 June 1910.

145 *Ibid.*, +Scollard to Grenier, 15 December 1910. Scollard estimated that the parish could not handle a debt of $65,000-$70,000.

146 *ASJCF*, B-16-D, 11. "Notes from the Annual Letters, 1910-1912, Port Arthur, Ont., 12 February 1913.

147 See Elinor Barr, "Richard Baxter", in *DCB, XIII*, (Toronto: University of Toronto Press, 1994), 44-45. See also A.J. Macdougall, ed., *Dictionary of Jesuit Biography*, pp. 11-12.

148 *DPA*, Journal of the Most Rev. R.A. O'Connor, 30 June 1893, p. 76. Baxter's retirement and Devine's appointment is given some notice. "Among the Jesuit Fathers who attend the mission in the western portion of the Diocese, some changes were made by the Superior during the months of May and June. Rev. R. Baxter, a venerable and aged missionary of 72 years, who had labored faithfully and zealously for many years throughout Algoma was superannuated and Rev. E. Devine was sent in his place to attend Fort William and the stations along that portion of the C.P. Railroad."

149 *ASJUC*, Box A-217.a, Fr. E.J. Devine, s.j. Memoirs, 1879-1921.

150 Kenora *Daily Miner and News*, 9 May 1956.

151 For details on Father Lacombe's activities in northwestern Ontario see Raymond Huel, "Albert Lacombe", in *DCB*, XIV, 1911-1920, pp. 573-574; Gaston Carrière, o.m.i., ed., *Dictionnaire biographique des Oblats de Marie- Immaculée au Canada, II,* (Ottawa: Éditions de L'Université d'Ottawa, 1977), 219-222; Pierre Berton, *The National Dream, 1871-1881* (Toronto: McClelland & Stewart, 1970), pp. 298-299.

[152] See George C. Salamon, o.m.i., and J.N. Davidson, *A History of the Catholic Church in the Kenora (Rat Portrage) Region*, 1982. pp. 9-10; See also references in *Kenora Miner and News*, 26 December 1914 for establishment of Notre Dame du Portage Parish.

[153] Notre Dame du Portage Parish Records. Parish Register of Baptisms, Marriages and Burials, Vol. I, 28 January 1881 - 17 August 1886. Census of Parish taken on 3 January 1884, pp. 76-85.

[154] Archives de la Société Historique de Saint-Boniface *(SHSB)*. Box 11, file 212, 4 February 1914.

[155] *Ibid.*, Parishioners to His Grace Louis Philippe Adélard Langevin, o.m.i., Archbishop of St Boniface, [1 January 1903], Box 11, file 211.

[156] For a detailed description of the fire see the *Kenora Miner and News*, Saturday, 26 December 1914. The newspaper was published twice weekly.

[157] *SHSB*, box 11, file 211, Rev. F.A. Dugas to Archbishop of St Boniface, 28 July 1917. At the time of the fire Kenora had 139 families - 70 English and 69 French forming a population of 712 (365 French and 347 English).

[158] *Ibid.*, box 11, file 211, Chancellor to Rev. J.W. Vezina, o.m.i., 17 April 1915.

[159] *Ibid.*, 22 December 1915.

[160] R. Perrin, "Adélard Langevin", *DCB, XIV*, 597.

[161] *Ibid.*, Parish report, 24 February 1928.

[162] *Ibid.*, box 11, file 212, reports from 1914-1945; See also *Catholic Yearbook 1940*, pp. 58-59.

[163] *Ibid.*, — to +Langevin, 22 January 1908.

[164] *Ibid.*, box 18, file 368, R. Baribeau to +Yelle, 28 June 1937.

[165] *Ibid.*, 6 April 1914.

[166] *Ibid.*, Rev. P.H. Gonneville, o.m.i. to +Cabana, 18 October 1944; Gonneville to +Cabana, 24 October 1944.

[167] *DA*, L 501, "Profile of missions attached to Kenora", 1 January 1949.

[168] *DTBA*, 8.32, Fr. G. LeBleu, o.m.i to +EQJ, 28 December 1954.

CHAPTER TWO

## PARISHES AND CULTURAL LOYALTIES

The thousands of European immigrants that entered Canada between 1891 and 1911 had a profound impact on the creation and complexion of Roman Catholic parishes within Canadian dioceses. The Archdiocese of St Boniface for example, which, until1951, included all Ontario parishes and missions west of Atikokan, had 24,000 Catholics in 1893. By 1915 that number had increased to 160,000.[1] One third were francophone, another third were Ukrainian, and the remaining third was comprised of Germans, anglophones, and Poles. The Most Reverend Adélard Langevin, o.m.i (1855–1915), Archbishop of St. Boniface, believed that if a "living" Roman Catholic culture was to flourish in North America language was as important as denominational education. He was influenced in his thinking by some American Catholic leaders who advocated that ethnic communities be allowed to evolve where each would preserve its language and culture with the parish church serving as the centre of religious and social life. To translate this vision into reality required the presence of multilingual priests and women religious willing to serve the various cultural groups coming together in Catholic parishes. It was argued that without these communities the faith of individuals and entire families would be lost through assimilation. To many within the British Canadian political establishment cultural homogeneity through assimilation was desirable and welcomed. That this view was held by influential segments of the anglophone Catholic clergy and laity was disturbing to individuals like Archbishop Langevin. Canadian ethnic communities in which Roman Catholicism was the dominant religion, however, found solace in Canon Law which was sensitive to immigrants whose spiritual needs could not be met in a traditional "territorial" parish where the dominant language was English or French. At the discretion of a bishop, parishes could be established based on language and "the nationality of the Christian faithful."[2]

What role then did language and culture (other than English and French) play in the formation of parishes within the present confines of the Thunder Bay Diocese during the first two decades of the twentieth century? The main centre for the emergence of national parishes within northwestern Ontario was Fort William's East End (in Ward I) where significant numbers of Slovaks, Italians, Poles and Ukrainians settled.[3] From the early 1890s European immigrants had been drawn to the area by seasonal employment opportunities as "dock labourers" and "coal heavers"[4] at the Canadian Pacific Railway freight sheds and the James Murphy coal handling facilities along the northern banks of the Kaministiquia River. According to the Fort William Assessment Commissioner Reports, the city's population increased significantly from 20,644 (1911) to 22,884 (1912). Most of the increase showed up in Ward I which had a population of 8,384 in 1912 representing one-third of Fort William's total population.[5]

To the local citizenry the East End was commonly referred to as the "coal docks." The CPR yards formed its dominant western boundary and, in a real sense, cut it off from the rest of the city. To the south and south-east it was bound by the Kaministiquia and Neebing Rivers respectively. Scottish street names like McBain, McDonald, McIntosh, McLaughlin, McLeod, McPherson, and McTavish belied the ethnic character of the area where Slovak, Italian, Ukrainian and Polish families took up residence. Because census officials often had difficulty knowing what languages were spoken by individuals classified as Hungarians, Galicians and Ruthenians and because of the transient nature of the immigrant population, it was difficult to determine what ethnic groups dominated the area. Slovakia, for example, came under the aegis of the Austrian-Hungarian Empire and the Magyars prior to 1918 and therefore Slovak speaking people were often listed as Hungarians. Galicians might have spoken either Ukrainian or Polish and Ruthenians spoke a Ukrainian dialect. More than any others, the Slovaks and Italians had a significant transient population. Many of these young single immigrants would work in the CPR

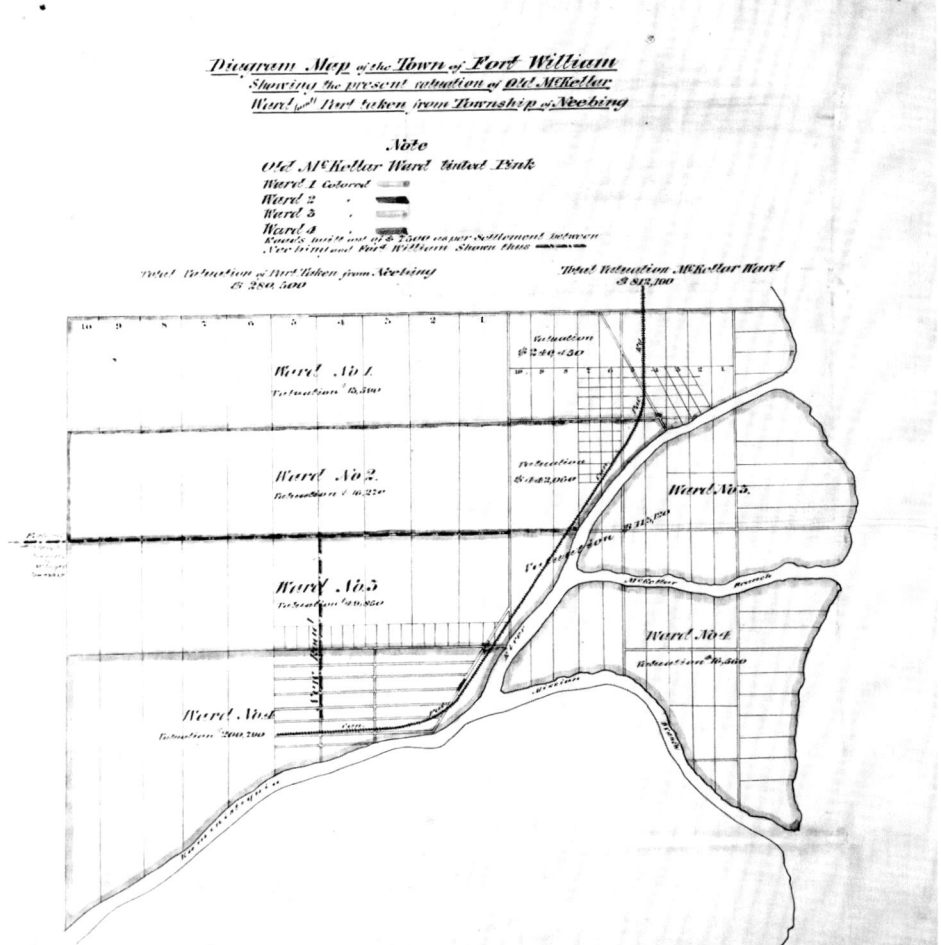

**Diagram Map of the Town of Fort William, c. 1894 (Ontario Archives, D-8)**
Map illustrates the location and extent of the Wards in Fort William used for property assessment and election purposes. Ward I extends across the top of the map with the city's East End or "coal docks" shown in the upper right hand corner. Some politicians referred to the East End as the city's "foreign quarter" where large numbers of Italians, Slovaks, and Ukrainians took up residence. The CPR line which runs along the northern bank of the Kaministiquia River and then extends north tended to separate the East End from the rest of Ward I and the city itself.

freight sheds and coal docks from the opening of navigation in April to the onset of winter and then return to their respective countries. The Slovaks rather than the Italians were more likely to have planted permanent roots in the area by building and owning their own homes.[6] Residences were seriously overcrowded. It was not unusual to have a three-room or six-room dwelling occupied by 10-19 inhabitants the majority of which were immigrant boarders or "sojourners". According to *The Report of a Preliminary and General Social Survey of Fort William*, (1913)[7] directed by the Methodist and Presbyterian Churches of Canada, the vast majority of these men were Roman Catholic. Whether the East End's residents were transient or permanent, Slovak, Italian, or Polish, their common bond was that 98% considered themselves to be Roman Catholic. The construction of three "national" Roman Catholic churches and one Ukrainian Catholic church in this part of Fort William from 1907 to 1921 reflected this reality.

## St Peter Parish, Fort William, Ontario.

A community of Slovaks with a keen desire to have their own church led by a Slovak-speaking pastor had been identified as part of St. Patrick's parish as early as 1893.[8] An important step in the realization of this goal was the founding of the First Catholic Slovak Union, St. Joseph's Lodge No. 402 (Jednota) in Fort William on 18 April 1902. As a fraternal mutual benefit society it provided leadership in fundraising and community formation. Recognizing the urgency of providing a church for the "foreign element" in Fort William, Bishop Scollard approved the purchase of several lots in the "coal docks" in the summer of 1906 from the Hudson's Bay Company which, together with those acquired by Father Arpin, s.j. three years earlier, established the future site of a church on the corner of Connelly and McIntosh streets.[9] Although the Bishop's intent was to have the church serve the entire Catholic immigrant population of Fort William's East End, it was mainly the Slovak population that provided the financial wherewithal for its creation. Knowing that the Slovaks were taking aggressive steps towards the creation of a church, a delegation of Italian married men approached Father Albini Primeau, s.j., (1865–1937) pastor of St. Patrick's Parish, with a proposal to create an Italian church.[10] Although Primeau himself did not think this to be a prudent move, he agreed to present their wishes to the Bishop anticipating a negative response. Failing a church of their own, the Italians expressed a desire to have a separate Mass set aside for themselves in the proposed new church celebrated by an Italian-speaking priest. In the planning stages for St. Peter's, they took a wait and see approach. They would contribute financially to its creation if and when construction began.

To find a suitable pastor for this immigrant and largely Roman Catholic population Bishop Scollard turned to the Society of Jesus. He approached Father Edward Lecompte, s.j., Superior General of the independent mission of the Jesuits in Canada, hoping that a Slovak Jesuit from Hungary might be persuaded to accept an apostolate among an immigrant population in a small frontier community in northwestern Ontario. Although the Hungarian Provincial could not spare a priest for this purpose, Father Lecompte offered the services of Father François Maynard s.j., 38, who had demonstrated a remarkable facility in modern languages and who had already taken up residence at St. Patrick's rectory to serve the missions west of Fort William.[11]

Father François Maynard (1868–1956), like Father Arpin, was born in the small Quebec town of La Présentation. His early education and formation as a Jesuit took place in the Diocese of St. Hyacinthe where he was ordained on 24 August 1901 at the Convent of the Precious Blood. Prior to his arrival in Fort William on 5 July 1905 he had spent fifteen years as Superior of a Jesuit classical college in Montreal - the College Ste Marie. When he began his apostolate among the immigrants of Fort William's East End in May 1907 his first concern was to learn a language or languages that would allow him to communicate with the majority of his future parishioners. He had been through this once before. Father Maynard spoke little English just after he left Montreal. It was only with the help and forebearance of the French-Canadian and Irish families at St Agnes mission church in Westfort that he was able to develop a fluency in English. In a similar fashion, he became familiar with the predominant languages in Fort William's "foreign quarter". He walked the streets of the East End, visited immigrant families and conversed with the people as best he could.[12] If he was to become an effective pastor in this neighbourhood he concluded that fluency in Slovak and Italian would be essential. The Slovak language presented him with the greatest challenge. It was not until he acquired a Slovak grammar and Slovak-Magyar dictionary that he was able to develop a facility in this language which eventually earned him the everlasting confidence and affection of the Slovak people. In the presence of a large crowd of Slovaks, Italians, Urkainians, and other Catholics from Fort William and Port Arthur he gave his first sermon in Slovak and Italian on 28

July 1907 at the laying of the cornerstone of St. Peter's Church.[13]

Construction was well under way when the entire brick-veneered edifice was destroyed by fire on Saturday, 3 November 1907.[14] What caused the fire? Father Maynard offered the "charitable theory" of a tramp who sought shelter in the basement of the church and started a fire for warmth. The fire ignited the construction debris left in the basement which in turn spread to the building proper. One can only imagine the deep sense of anguish and discouragement this tragedy brought to the people. Father Maynard, however, referred to it as a "happy accident."[15] In his opinion, the local contractor Joseph LeBrun had not built a church that would have stood the test of time. Regrettably, the builder's insurance policy did not cover the entire $15,000 construction cost leaving the parishioners to make up the difference which was mainly owed to workers in unpaid wages. In the aftermath of the fire, Father Maynard rented the small Finnish Church on Christie Street between McLaughlin and McIntosh until the basement of the Slovak church (which was originally intended to be used as a schoolroom for Catholic immigrant children) could be renovated and made suitable for services. The parish prudently decided to postpone reconstruction until all debts were paid and additional funds raised.

During this three year interlude significant steps were taken in the spiritual and physical growth of the parish. From 1 January 1908 to 1 August 1910, Father Maynard celebrated 330 baptisms, 90 marriages and 100 funerals (of which 70 were children).[16] In May 1908 he invited a young Italian-speaking Jesuit from Montreal to give a mission. Because the missionary spoke in a northern Italian dialect to a predominantly southern Italian audience, the mission was not well attended. It demonstrated to the Italians of the East End, however, that they too were an integral part of a growing parish community. A year later, the first Corpus Christi outdoor procession in Fort William and Port Arthur was organized at St. Peter's.[17] The feast of Corpus Christi frequently had been celebrated this way at the Church of the Immaculate Conception on the Fort William Mission. The Mission had the advantage of being separated from the town of Fort William and therefore had few concerns about possible interference from non-Catholic groups. In the East End, Father Maynard saw little risk in carrying the Blessed Sacrament outside by restricting the procession to the perimeter of St. Peter's church property. Parishioners also participated in a celebration on 3 August 1910 of the blessing of the church bell by Bishop Scollard.[18] Made in France specifically for St. Peter's Parish with the inscription: "Pius X, Bishop Scollard, F. Maynard, s.j.,

**St Peter (Slovak) Roman Catholic Church and School, c. 1924**
(Courtesy St Peter Parish Archives)
To the left of the church is St Peter Roman Catholic Separate School which opened in September, 1911 with four classrooms. This photograph shows an enlarged school with eight classrooms. Students from the school attended special services at either St Peter or St Dominic Churches depending on whether their parents were Italian or Slovak. Throughout a school year, however, attendance at either church was not rigidly based on nationality. Both churches became an integral part of each student's life while attending St Peter's School.

1910" the bell gave the essentials of the genesis of the parish and as "the voice of the people" was ready to be rung in welcome, rejoicing, and mourning. Those attending the ceremony anxiously awaited the day when the bell would be elevated to its proper position in the belfry of the completed church.

Father Maynard approached this moment with some anxiety. By the spring of 1911 the parish had just paid off a debt of $2,000 resulting from the 1907 church fire leaving $120 in the parish coffers. Accordingly, he was inclined to wait another year or two to augment the building fund and to improve his fluency in Slovak. Notwithstanding the respect parishioners had for their pastor's sage advice, the majority opted to have the church reconstruction begin immediately. The decision was made easier by a fortuitous infusion of $3,000 into the building fund with the sale of 3 lots of church property to the Fort William Separate School Board for the construction of St. Peter's School.[19] Reconstruction began on 19 June and all work was completed by 1 October 1911. A week later, on a bright and crisp Sunday morning, Bishop Scollard blessed and dedicated the new church under the patronage of St. Peter.[20] The church was filled to capacity and, in the presence of a 125 voice choir made up of parishioners, their sons and daughters and children from St. Peter's School, Bishop Scollard delivered his congratulatory remarks in English followed by Father Maynard's homily in Slovak. St. Peter's Roman Catholic Church thus became home to one of the first Slovak parishes in Canada and the first of several to serve the spiritual needs of Fort William's immigrant population.

The formation of St. Peter's parish and the reconstruction of its church was a testament to the power of cultural loyalties, the deep commitment of the Slovak people to their faith, and the talented leadership of a caring, sensitive pastor. Would the Slovak ethos of the parish endure? Bishop Scollard and his successor, Bishop Ralph Dignan had their doubts.[21] Father Maynard had no such doubts. So confident was he of its survival that he had the inscriptions on the Stations of the Cross etched in Slovak. Moreover, the seriousness with which he approached the study of Slovak was a poignant reminder to parishioners of the esteem he had for their language and culture.

It was ironic therefore that Father Maynard's departure from St. Peter's revolved around language and culture. Bishop Scollard it seemed lacked confidence in Father Maynard's fluency in Slovak and therefore wished to provide Fort William's Slovak people with "a priest who knew the Slovak language well."[22] In his notebook written sometime after 1914, Maynard viewed the Bishop's enigmatic judgement in this matter with some bitterness. To be sure, Maynard was sufficiently fluent in Slovak to communicate effectively with his parishioners. According to Maynard, a group of American Slovak priests who were part of an organization that rivalled the established Slovak Society of St. Joseph "cast an envious eye on the Slovak parish in Fort William".[23] They communicated directly with Bishop Scollard with a view to assuming responsibility for its administration. That the Bishop was receptive to these overtures disturbed Father Maynard. Where were these priests in 1906 when they were most needed? Were his labours over the past seven years in establishing a financially sound and efficiently run parish being taken for granted? Consideration of these questions evoked such negative thoughts in his mind that he asked his Jesuit Provincial to be relieved of his responsibilities at St. Peter's. Accordingly, on 4 November 1914 he officially took his leave from the parish and was replaced by Father Ján Novotny, a Slovak-speaking priest residing in the United States.

Bishop Scollard's seemingly good intentions of bringing native born Slovak priests to St. Peter's resulted in a period of instability and discord between pastors and parishioners during the 1920s and early 1930s. Father Novotny remained as pastor until 1921 and then left after a serious misunderstanding with the congregation over financial matters.[24] His successor Rev. Karl Gross, from North Dakota faced similar disagreements with the parish over money matters and realized in the space of one year (1922) that he could not lead the parish since he was perceived as not being of their race. These tensions culminated in 1934 when St. Peter's church committee "forcibly threw out the Rev. Emery Vodicka".[25] The Most Rev. Ralph Hubert Dignan, the second bishop of the Diocese of Sault Ste. Marie (1934-1958), looked back on this unsettled period and welcomed the stability brought to the parish by the Slovak Benedictine Order from St. Andrew's Abbey, Cleveland, Ohio.

Once the Benedictines ended their tenure at St. Peter's[26] on 18 April 1950 a native of the parish,[27] Father Joseph S. Reguly (1918-1988), was called upon to succeed them just as the new Diocese of Fort William was about to be formed. Father Reguly was one of four priests to be ordained from the parish. After completing his studies at St Augustine's Seminary in London he was ordained by Bishop Ralph H. Dignan from the Pro-Cathedral in North Bay on 10 April 1943. Prior to his appointment as pastor of St. Peter's he served as Assistant Pastor at Holy Trinity Parish, Sudbury (1943-1946, 1949), St. Patrick's Parish, Thunder Bay, (1946-1949) and Our Lady of Mount Carmel Parish, Sault Ste. Marie (1950). He was ever mindful of the Slovak ethos which had been sustained by the Benedictine Fathers at St. Peter's and his responsibility in its continuance. To quote Father Reguly:[28]

> The Benedictine Fathers have taken good care of St. Peter's Parish...for a number of years. There have been priests there who were well qualified to run the parish satisfactorily. They were able to preach well in Slovak and minister to the needs of the people in that language. In this matter, I would certainly fall short of what they were able to do. There may even be an objection from the parish on that score. However, I am but a curate, Your Excellency, and I feel that I have no right to make any choice regarding the parish to which I might be sent. Wherever you send me, there I will go.

Interior, St Peter's (Slovak) Roman Catholic Church, 23 July 2002.
Apart from the alterations made to accommodate the Vatican II liturgy, this church interior has changed little over the years. The ornate altar at the front was originally intended for the Pro-Cathedral of the Assumption in North Bay but was the wrong size. St Peter's Parish purchased it from the Sault Ste Marie Diocese in 1931. The altar was fully restored in 1997. The murals on the ceiling by Canadian artist L. Scott Young depicting aspects of the lives of Jesus, Mary, Joseph, and the Saints were mounted in 1949 and today represent the only complete extant works of the artist left in Canada and the United States. Today, St Peter's Parish continues to serve the Roman Catholics of the East End most of whom have Slovak and Italian cultural backgrounds.

**St Peter's Stations of the Cross inscribed in Slovak.**
Father François Maynard, s.j. demonstrated his faith in the survival of the Slovak ethos of St Peter's Parish by having the inscriptions on the Stations of the Cross done in Slovak.

His service to St. Peter's lasted for 38 years, the longest of any pastor in the parish's history.

## Italian Parishes in Fort William and Port Arthur

The origins of the Italian parishes in Thunder Bay may be found in St. Peter's. As mentioned above, Father Maynard occasionally invited an Italian-speaking priest to give a mission for the benefit of his Italian parishioners. A Rev. Francesco Crociata gave one of these missions during the first week of December, 1911.[29] Little was known of his background except that he had spent some time in the Archdiocese of St. Boniface at Prince Albert Saskatchewan.[30] According to Father Maynard, he had succeeded in capturing the affection and confidence of the Italian people. Since Crociata was not attached to any parish or diocese he might have viewed the Diocese of Sault Ste. Marie as a place to establish his niche. On the basis of vague "satisfactory testimonials" Bishop Scollard granted him permission "to labour among the Italians of Port Arthur and Fort William."

Crociata's enthusiasm and energy galvanized the Italian communities of Thunder Bay into action resulting in the construction of two churches - St. Joseph's and St. Anthony's. In early January 1912, a group of Fort William Italians met in St. Peter's church basement to form an organizational committee to direct the fundraising and construction of their own church. Sufficient financial contributions had been made at this meeting to enable the group to purchase two 25 lots at the corner of McLaughlin and Connolly Streets on which to build their church.[31] By June, a modest, all wooden structure was completed from which religious services could be held.

In Port Arthur Father Crociata's dream was to "build a beautiful church in the name of St. Anthony of Padua."[32] To this end he organized a fund-raising drive directed at the Italian, English and French-speaking parishioners who up to this time had attended St. Andrew's parish. Understandably, Father Grenier, s.j., pastor of St. Andrew's, took exception to Father Crociata's solicitations among his parishioners and registered his complaints with Bishop Scollard. Father Grenier himself had been desperately trying to raise funds for a new St Andrew's church in Port Arthur. He viewed Father Crociata's efforts as undermining his own. In his defence Father Crociata argued that the English and French-speaking members of St. Andrew's parish willingly contributed to St. Anthony's building fund because they were disgruntled with the overcrowded conditions there and the

**St Joseph Italian parishioners at the front entrance of their church, c. 1913**
The occasion for this photograph might have been a Corpus Christi procession in Fort William's East End the first of which was organized by Father Maynard, s.j. of St Peter's Parish in 1909. Shown here is a group of St Joseph's parishioners gathered around their church shortly after its construction in 1912. Windows had not yet been installed and the wooden exterior was unpainted. In the centre behind the altar boys stands Father Francis Crociata (with the black beard) and to his right is Father Maynard, Pastor of St Peter's Parish. To his left are two other priests who might be the pastors of Holy Rosary Parish (St Casimir) and the Ukrainian Catholic parish. Gathered around the statue are members of the Italian band. Peter Belluz, a prominent businessman in the East End of Fort William, is standing third from the left. The two altar boys on each side of the cross are
Henry and William Tiboni.
(Courtesy Ron Belluz)

repeated delays in building a new church.³³ He simply viewed his efforts as a means of strengthening the Roman Catholic presence in Port Arthur.

That stronger presence became a reality with the construction of St Anthony's church at the corner of Banning and Dufferin Streets. By August 1912 approximately 100 families (predominantly Italian but also including English and French-speaking members from St. Andrew's) had been identified as forming the core of the parish.³⁴ This was augmented by an unspecified number of Italian men boarding at various residences nearby. The official opening and dedication of the church by Father Crociata at midnight Mass on 24 December 1912 suggests the higher profile it enjoyed over St. Joseph's in Fort William which was not officially dedicated until Sunday, 19 January 1913.³⁵ In fact, St. Joseph's was a mission church of St. Anthony's until 1921. Father Crociata served both parishes until his departure in 1914. He was one of the first diocesan priests to serve in what is now the present Diocese of Thunder Bay. Moreover, he was an example of a priest with the linguistic prerequisites of serving an ethnic community but whose inexplicable movement from one diocese to another called into question the soundness of his training and judgement as an administrator and spiritual leader.

Father Crociata was dismissed from the Diocese of Sault Ste Marie and his administration of St. Joseph's and St. Anthony's parishes because of financial mismanagement and "grave charges against his moral character."³⁶ Father Maynard, through his communications with Bishop Scollard, became aware that, as Father Crociata supervised the "precipitous constructions" of the two Italian churches in Thunder Bay, monies advanced by the Diocese to him were not spent prudently, that building materials were not paid for, that workers wages were left in default and that bad cheques were written. Had Bishop Scollard known of Crociata's brief sojourn in the United States and in the Burlington Diocese and had sought references from those who knew him, all of this might have been avoided. Interestingly, Bishop Scollard was asked by the Bishop of Pembroke whether it was safe to hire a Father Francis Crociata who was seeking a position in his diocese shortly after his departure from Thunder Bay.³⁷ "[It would] take much searching to find a more unworthy man in the ranks of the priesthood than this same Francis Crociata," replied Bishop Scollard. "The further away from Pembroke and every other Diocese he is the better."³⁸

This character assessment of Father Crociata must be balanced with the obvious affection the parishioners of St. Joseph's had for their first parish priest

# PARISHES AND CULTURAL LOYALTIES

**First Communion class with Father Agnelo Sansone in St Joseph Church, c. 1915**
When this photograph was taken, the interior of St Joseph Italian Church was unfinished. There were no pews and the interior walls were yet to be painted or plastered. Young students from St Peter's School posing for this photograph might have participated in a Christmas play or religious service relating to the Christmas season.

as reflected in this extract from Father François Maynard's *Notebook:*[39]

At the moment of the departure of the Bishop from the rectory of St. Peter's Slovak Church [705 McIntosh Street] a great crowd of Italian men and women were crowded together in the street and sidewalk. The Italian women were very close to the entrance. They protested loudly to the Bishop against the sending away of their pastor. The Bishop told them: "He is going to leave."...The Bishop said nothing more and could not move from the entrance of the gate. I signalled to the Italians to allow the Bishop to pass through, that I would lead him to the car which was not far from there. The Italians shook their fists at the Bishop...One could read the indignation on their faces. When the Bishop took his seat in the car with Father Lussier [assistant pastor at St. Patrick's church], I signalled the driver to leave. The Italians continued to shake their fists at the Bishop who produced an uneasy smile...The car turned right on Connolly Street...and left the Italian crowd. Then the small stones began to rain down on the car which was carrying the Bishop and Father Lussier. Then all was calm [in] the Coal Dock[s]. The next day I visited Father Lussier and asked him his impression of the visit. He told me that a stone had fallen at the foot of the Bishop in the car. At five o'clock that day, the Bishop telephoned me asking...if Abbe Crociata had left Fort William. I informed the Bishop that the Abbe

**St Joseph Italian Roman Catholic Church, c. 1924**
By 1924 a rectory had been added to the back of the church and its overall appearance seemed rustic but finished. St Peter's Roman Catholic Church and the Ukrainian Greek Orthodox Church are visible in the background.
(Courtesy St Dominic Parish Archives)

was to leave that very evening...The Bishop left that evening from Port Arthur. To his great surprise he boarded the train and in the sleeping car he found the Italian priest. Later the Bishop told me that he spent the night without sleeping. At every moment he saw and felt in his heart the fist of his travelling companion...

Father Crociata's differences with Bishop Scollard were differences of style rather than substance. He was over-zealous in his desire to create two parish churches for the Italians of Fort William and Port Arthur and paid scant attention to sound financial management that would be important to the Ordinary of any diocese. Following the departure of Father Crociata several priests came to Thunder Bay at the behest of Bishop Scollard to minister to the spiritual needs of its Italian community. Several years were to elapse before both parishes had a pastor of their own who was prepared to remain with the people and lead them through difficult economic times.

The extreme poverty experienced by both parishes during the years 1914-1945 was their main challenge to survival. Neither had the remarkable economic stability of the Slovak parish. The poverty of the Italian parishes manifested itself in the unfinished appearance of their churches and in the struggle of their pastors to rise above the level of abject poverty. St. Joseph's in Fort William for example, was a mere wooden shell, without seating accommodation for the congregation and inadequately heated by an old stove situated in a dugout basement.[40] This was in stark contrast to the concrete and brick-veneered appearance of St. Peter's Slovak Church which was frequently visible in photographs taken of St. Joseph's from the corner of Connolly and McLaughlin Streets. St. Anthony's Church in Port Arthur was of a higher standard structurally than St Joseph Italian Roman Catholic Church. It was built on a concrete foundation and had a priest's residence immediately beside the church. This might explain why several priests - Fathers Vincent Juliano and Domenico Tomaselli - served St. Joseph's from the more comfortable living quarters at St. Anthony's. On 22 December 1914, however, fire destroyed the roof of St Anthony's and after it was extinguished the water and ice damage made the rest of the structure unsalvageable.[41] Lawyers attempting to settle the insurance claims on the church revealed the desperate economic circumstances in which Father Juliano found himself. "I attended on Father Juliano" wrote A. J. McComber, a prominent Port Arthur lawyer and member of St. Andrew's parish "and requested that he hand me the policies, but this he refused to do so stating that he had handed the policies to the Parish Committee and that the money [$4,000] was to be deposited in a bank here, and to be used in the construction of a new building. He further complained that he had no clothing himself, and that as the money belonged to the Italians, it should not be sent to North Bay, but should be used here, and intimated that he would require some of it for his personal use."[42] Juliano's defiance of the Bishop's wishes resulted in his dismissal from the Diocese.[43] Bishop Scollard could not ignore, however, the financial constraints under which the Italian priests in Fort William and Port Arthur laboured. He appealed to Rome on their behalf and received some financial relief as the following letter suggests:[44]

> I am very glad that you have made known to me the serious burdens which weigh so heavily on the Italian Churches of Fort William and Port Arthur, and that you have thus given me the opportunity of relieving just a little of the pecuniary sacrifices which they constantly cost Your Lordship. The enclosed cheque for $400 you will please divide equally between the two parishes. I cannot say how much I appreciate your pastoral zeal on behalf of the poor Italians who have made their homes in your jurisdiction and any-

thing that I can ever do to show that appreciation will be done most readily...

The moral rather than the pecuniary support from the Vatican for the Italian priests recognized the missionary dimension of their apostolate which did not involve conversion as much as it did the provision of the rites of passage celebrated in the ministration of the sacraments to Italian immigrants attempting to find a better life in Canada.

Rev. Domenico A. Tomaselli devoted most of his religious career in long-term service to the Italian immigrants of Fort William and Port Arthur. Born in Guardia Framonte, Italy on 20 April 1876 and ordained twenty-one years later in Ceritti San Nita, Italy he came to Canada at age 39 after a brief sojourn in the United States.[45] Bishop Scollard appointed him pastor of both St. Anthony's and St. Joseph's on 10 May 1915.[46] Since most of Tomaselli's energies were directed towards the reconstruction of St. Anthony's church following the fire which destroyed the original structure a year earlier, he did little more than celebrate Mass every Sunday at St Joseph's during the five years he was pastor there. For both parishes, however, he organized the elaborate religious ceremonies for the installation and blessing of their church bells.[47] This ritual signalled a symbolic watershed in the development of both parishes since the bell would be the instrument alerting all in the neighbourhood to the rites of passage mentioned earlier. Father William McCullough, pastor of St Agnes parish in Westfort and Bishop Scollard's appointee to officiate at both ceremonies, explained it this way:[48]

> The bell...is a product of God's earth, the copper and zinc of which it is composed having been taken out of the earth for the glory and service of God. It is to voice the joys and sorrows of the people in their prayers and praise, and will be the voice of God calling them to meet in His house for worship. At baptisms it will ring to tell the joy and new blessings brought into their lives; for weddings it will peal the story of joy's increase in the home life, ringing a glad paean, and, when death enters the home, its notes will tell that the duties of life have been discharged and that the soul has passed to await judgement at the bar of God and meet Him face to face.

At St. Joseph's for example, an average of five baptismal ceremonies per week were performed during the years Father Tomaselli was pastor.[49] During the war years, marriages were few but after 1919 at least one marriage per month was celebrated.

As the regular tempo of sacramental celebrations continued, pastors and parishioners at both parishes carried out improvements to their churches.[50] Given the poverty of the Italian congregations at the time, the desire to beautify their parish churches reflected how important it was in their lives. In the minds of some, no church could have rivalled those in their native Italy. But in a modest way St. Joseph's and St. Anthony's came to convey an image of beauty, tranquillity, stability, and remoteness from the days of hard work that were the norms in their lives in a northern Canadian frontier environment. Moreover, the liturgy of the Roman Catholic Church and the sermons delivered in Italian were an important link to the life they once knew and left in Italy.

During the interwar years both Italian parishes shouldered significant debt. To remove this debt was constantly in the minds of the pastors whose success in doing so rested mainly on the financial sacrifices of first-generation Italian immigrants. St. Anthony's parish was better able to liquidate their debt than was St. Joseph's. Although the majority of St. Anthony's congregation was comprised of Italian immigrants a significant minority were English and French-speaking whose financial circumstances permitted them to contribute to the church coffers more generously than the Italians.[51] Prominent English-speaking parishioners also tended to lead fund-raising projects like teas and bazaars the profits of which were directed toward "assisting Father Tomaselli to clear his church of debt."[52] Like Father Crociata before him, Father Tomaselli recognized the value of attracting parishioners from St. Andrew's to his parish. At the nadir of the depression, he did this openly by announcing that Port Arthur English and French-speaking Roman Catholics, without running counter to the directives of the Bishop, had the option of attending and financially supporting St. Anthony's parish.[53] Once again, the Jesuits at St. Andrew's were annoyed at Tomaselli's loose interpretation of the Bishop's wishes. Father William Dunn, s.j. (1875–1967), pastor at St. Andrew's, interpreted Bishop Dignan's formal directive to both pastors on this issue to mean that all non-Italian Roman Catholics in Port Arthur were in all conscience bound to support St Andrew's parish. The competition for parishioners between the two Port Arthur parishes continued to be a bone of contention long after the 1930s.  St Joseph's Italian Parish in Fort William relied solely on its first generation Italian immigrant congregation to pay off a $8,000 debt owing to the Diocese of Sault Ste. Marie accumulated during the 1920s and 1930s to run the day-to-day affairs of the parish and to make fundamental renovations to the church. Coping with debt not only distracted St Joseph pastors from the spiritual development of their parish but also took its toll on

Monsignor Domenico Tomaselli, c. 1932
Pastor of St Anthony Parish, 1915 – 1940
(Thunder Bay Historical Society)

St Anthony (Italian) Roman Catholic Church, Port Arthur, 25 April 1940.
The automobiles shown in this photograph parked on Banning Street were part of Monsignor Tomaselli's funeral cortège.
(St Dominic Parish Archives)

Interior of St Anthony (Italian) Roman Catholic Church, Christmas Eve, 1940.
(St Dominic Parish Archives)

their personal well-being. In 1921, Father Don Ferdinando Capresi (c.1863-1933) became St Joseph's first full-time pastor. He was born in Florence, Italy and was ordained in 1888. It is not known when he left his homeland for America but we do know that prior to his arrival in Canada (sometime after World War I) he ministered to an Italian community in Philadelphia.[54] It was said of Father Capresi that he came to Canada as a missionary priest "to devote his life, his time and his talents to the Italian immigrants - that he might give them the many consolations of their religion." Parishioners at the time saw him as "a good man", a "saintly man", and one who lived in abject poverty in Fort William's East End. They vividly recall that often during the winter months of the late 1920s and early 1930s weekday masses[55] were not held in the church proper but in a room in the rectory kept warm by a small wood burning stove because the parish could not afford to purchase coal to fuel the main furnace. That Father Capresi would solicit alms for the poor of the parish and for himself was a poignant act which endeared him to all parishioners. It also underscored the grim reality that the parishioners of St. Dominic's could ill-afford to financially support their pastor and parish church during the early 1930s let alone pay off debts owing to the Diocese of Sault Ste. Marie.

This responsibility was left for Father Capresi's successor, Rev. Arthur Joseph Murray (1897-1968). Father Murray was St. Dominic's sole non-Italian born pastor. He was born in Glanworth, Ireland and took his elementary and secondary education in Galway. Shortly after World War I, he spent two years studying at the Gregorian University in Rome where he developed a remarkable fluency and eloquence in Italian.[56] The precise time of his arrival in Canada is not clear but we do know that he attended the Grand Seminary in Montreal and was ordained there in June 1923. Shortly thereafter, Bishop Scollard invited him to serve in his Diocese first as a curate (assistant pastor) at Sacred Heart Parish, Sault Ste Marie and then to minister to the Italians of North Bay.[57] A decade later when Father Capresi became seriously ill, Bishop Dignan assigned Father Murray to St Joseph's parish in Fort William as pastor.

St. Dominic's Italian congregation was quickly drawn to Father Murray's "good mannered, polite and affable" ways. He was a populist priest who tended to the spiritual and material needs of his parishioners and who, like his predecessor, lived in poverty without outwardly complaining. In order to avoid having two parishes in the Sault Ste Marie Diocese with the same name, Bishop Dignan changed the name of St Joseph in Fort William to St Dominic in 1936.[58] A year later Father Murray initiated a "Silver Jubilee Year Special Debt Reduction Drive."[59] The following appeal emphasizes the transient nature of the Italian immigrant population in Fort William's East End and the difficult economic circumstances in which the parish found itself:

> Twenty-five years ago this Italian Church was built at a great personal sacrifice by the then Italian-born residents of the Fort William Coal Docks. In the intervening years more than fifty per cent of these pioneering families have moved away. The burden of debt has since been carried by those who have remained; but owing to present economic conditions they are powerless to meet even the current expenses of this Parish.
>
> For over five years I have attempted to shoulder this burden. My poor people, during this year, the Silver Jubilee Year of the Parish, [sic] have paid off, from their meagre means, over $2500.00 of this outstanding debt. There still remains over $5000 to be paid.
>
> Will you not, in your charity, lend a helping hand. Any contribution, however small, will be gratefully received; and on Christmas Night, the twenty-fifth anniversary of the official opening of this church, your name will be remembered in the Holy Sacrifice of the Mass.
>
> And may I remain,
>
> Sincerely yours in Christ,
>
> A.J. Murray, P.P.

Eight years after this appeal was made, St. Dominic's Church Men's Club canvassed the 260 families of the parish and raised sufficient funds to eliminate the debt.[60] To celebrate this memorable event, a banquet was organized on 4 April 1945 at the Italian Hall on McLaughlin Street. In the presence of 350 well-wishers, Father Murray paid tribute to the "least of the Brethren as well as those in high position whether they had contributed the only dollar they had in their purse or had given a substantial sum towards the paying off of this long-standing debt."

In March 1946 Father Murray was relieved of his responsibilities as pastor of St Dominic's.[61] His successors were never to experience the difficulties of leading and caring for a parish during an economic depression. Future pastors would have the good fortune of prosperity in which to minister to the spiritual needs of Fort William's Italian community.

## Holy Rosary Roman Catholic (Polish) Parish, Fort William, Ontario.

For Thunder Bay's Polish Roman Catholic community church construction preceded parish formation.[62] In May 1921 about eighty Polish families had made financial contributions towards the purchase of property and the construction of a modest all-wooden church at the corner of Mackenzie and Robertson streets in Fort William's East End approximately six blocks west of the CPR tracks.[63] With church and property free of debt and registered in the names of three "trustees"[64], they hoped to attract a Polish priest to lead them in parish formation. The first notion of forming a Polish parish in Fort William emerged out of a mission offered in December 1921 at St. Peter's by a Polish-born Oblate, Father François-Boniface Kowalski[65] (1878-1954) o.m.i., pastor of the Roman Catholic parish in Beausejour Manitoba. He believed that its creation was an absolute necessity if these people were to remain Roman Catholics. "Some of the Poles refuse to go to St. Peter's Church altogether," wrote Father Kowalski, "and as they do not feel at home in the other churches, they do not go to mass on Sundays at all."[66] He was confident that Thunder Bay's Polish population was able and willing to support a "good Polish- speaking" priest.

To find the right match between a Polish-speaking priest and the Polish community in Thunder Bay would tax the resourcefulness of any Canadian bishop at the time. Priests from the United States actively seeking a position with an ethnic parish in Canada were, according to Father Kowalski, suspect. Had they proven themselves in the United States they would not be seeking a position in Canada. Until a priest could be found, Bishop Scollard accepted the offer of a Father Francis B. Tomanek to be pastor of the Polish parish in Fort William. Born in Slovakia, he spoke Slovak and English and promised to learn Polish. Little is known about his background until he arrived in Fort William in 1921 where he served as administrator of St. Peter's parish for three months. His departure from St. Peter's was accompanied by warm testimonials, a gift of a "substantial purse", and a farewell banquet. Bishop Scollard demonstrated confidence in Tomanek by having him formally install Father Martin Pazurick as the incoming pastor of St. Peter's and by appointing him to be the officiating priest at the dedication of Our Lady of the Holy Rosary Church.

From the outset Father Tomanek's vision of the Polish Parish was flawed and ran counter to the aspirations of the congregation he was appointed to serve. He favoured the development of a "mixed parish"(Polish and English) which, he argued, would assist the Polish people to integrate into the mainstream of Canadian life.[67] Moreover, he stood firmly against the establishment of "purely foreign parishes." This view manifested itself in the church's dedication ceremonies held on Sunday, 1 October 1922. If Holy Rosary Church was intended to serve all Polish-speaking Roman Catholics in Fort William, then it must have seemed odd for those in attendance at the 11:00 a.m. dedication Mass that the first sermons were delivered in English and Slovak. Only one sermon, that delivered by Father Cox, s.j.(1868–1947), pastor of St. Andrew's parish, in the afternoon, was translated into Polish by Father Tomanek. Equally bewildering must have been the singing of the Slovak national hymn and "O Canada" at the end of the dedication ceremonies.

Father Tomanek it seemed was more interested in securing a position for himself within the Sault Ste Marie Diocese than in leading Fort William's Polish community in the formation of their own parish. His inability to speak fluent Polish hampered his efforts in this regard. In fact, he was disdainful of his Polish congregation suggesting to Bishop Scollard that they were ignorant in all matters pertaining to the Roman Catholic faith.[68] Accordingly, he argued that they should be "ruled" like all other English-speaking parishes in the diocese. He flirted with the idea of having an English-speaking group purchase the church from the "trustees" to create a "mixed" parish where the spiritual needs of the Poles would be taken care of but where they would be excluded from having a voice in matters relating to the pastor and to the management of the church. Put simply, he wanted to create another English parish in Fort William.

Had Father Tomanek listened to his parishioners he would have discovered that the Polish people wanted their parish to evolve along similar lines as St. Peter's. Unfortunately, he did not have the tolerance and compassion of a Father Maynard in leading a congregation whose language and culture was different from his own. If the Polish church was to be governed by the same rules as St. Peter's this meant that a language other than English was to dominate its spiritual and temporal affairs.[69] Those who initially contributed funds for its construction were Polish-born. Funds were collected by canvassers on the understanding that a Polish-speaking priest would be secured to conduct services in the Polish language.[70] It was further understood that while English-speaking Roman Catholics were welcomed to Holy Rosary Church they were not to become part of the parish community. The Polish people were insulted to be told that a mixed parish would serve to acculturate them to Canadian life. By 1922 most were Canadian citizens and believed they had become sufficiently familiar with Canadian institutions.[71]

In the weeks immediately following the dedication ceremonies members of the Polish congregation concluded that they could not support a pastor whom they could not understand, whose gratuitous and snide remarks from the pulpit portrayed them as " a bunch of fools", and who favoured "other nationalities" in the administration of parish affairs.[72] Father Tomanek's position within the parish was untenable. In leaving Fort William, he was an orphaned priest unattached to any parish or diocese. While Bishop Scollard unsuccessfully attempted to have him placed in some diocese in the United States he faced an uncertain future in December of 1922. "At the present, I am living from my own money," wrote Tomanek to Bishop Scollard, "having no income whatsoever. Should your Lordship not succeed to find a place for me in the United States, I am ready to take any place in Canada, preferring in the first place your Diocese."[73] Father Tomanek was the first of six pastors who, for a variety of reasons, came into serious conflict with the Polish congregation.[74]

A major source of conflict between pastor and parishioners during the late 1920s was the question of who was the legitimate owner of Fort William's Polish Church. Was it a group of "trustees" who originally led the way in its construction or was it the Episcopal Corporation of the Diocese of Sault Ste. Marie? This was the question that dogged both Father Anthony Gorek and Bishop Scollard from 1929 to 1934. Father Kowalski had alerted Bishop Scollard to the issue of church ownership in 1921 when he noted that the Holy Rosary Church property had been registered in the names of several "trustees" instead of with the Diocese of Sault Ste. Marie.[75] From his experience in Manitoba serious problems arose between trustees in whose names a church was registered and the transfer of the same to a diocese. He suggested that Bishop Scollard solve the problem by agreeing to provide them with a priest in return for the transfer of the property to the diocese. For reasons unknown, the bishop did not do this. Therefore, the perception of some Holy Rosary parishioners that they were the owners of the church and that the priest was a "hired hand" prevailed. Father Gorek's well-intended actions on behalf of Bishop Scollard in attempting to solve the problem of church ownership heightened tensions within the parish. He convened a special meeting of parishioners who then voted to transfer the church property to the Sault Ste. Marie Diocese.[76] This action prompted another group within the parish to form themselves into the Polish National Church with the avowed object of removing Father Gorek from the parish and settling the matter of church ownership in court. Interestingly, "The Polish National Church" was given some official recognition in that twenty-one of their members were counted in the Fort William Assessment Commissioner's Report of 1931.[77] This group began to hold services at a Finnish church at the corner of Rowand and McMurray Streets led by a Rev. Palaszweski, a Roman Catholic priest from Chicago who was a member of the so-called Polish National Catholic Church.

Both sides in this parish dispute sought legal counsel. The lawyers' correspondence with Bishop Scollard gives us a dispassionate perspective on the conflict. Those who referred to themselves as the "National Catholic Polish Church" sought the advise of the Fort William law firm, Dyke & Beeman. John A. Dyke claimed to have known "large numbers of Parishioners on both sides of the controversy" and "the viewpoint of each side very well."[78] When approached by the "dissentient Parishioners" he was inclined to "stand aloof" from the matter and counselled them to settle the matter among themselves. From his conversations with these parishioners he concluded that the essence of the problem lay in the style and personality of Father Anthony Gorek who "has not acted as a Priest should." This polite and diplomatic assessment was corroborated by A. J. McComber, a Port Arthur lawyer and a member of St. Andrew's parish acting on behalf of Bishop Scollard. McComber, in his conversations with Mr. Joseph Clemens (Klenarowicz) – one of the trustees holding the Church property at the time it was conveyed to the Episcopal Corporation and who supported the action – concluded that Father Gorek's problem was his use of "intemperate" language and that he was "given to publicly denouncing people by name in Church."[79] Mr. Clemens' view was that had a priest other than Father Gorek been in charge of the parish the problem of church ownership would have been settled amicably and those who had left the church would have returned to begin rebuilding a strong and unified congregation.

Regrettably, a suit regarding the ownership of the Polish Church in Fort William was brought before the Supreme Court of Ontario in December 1932. The plaintiffs argued that Holy Rosary Church was built as a Polish Independent or National Church; that it rightfully belonged to those who originally donated funds for its construction and that a minority of the congregation had wrongfully deeded the property to the Sault Ste. Marie Diocese without the knowledge or approval of the Bishop. After seven days of hearing testimony the judge in the case ruled that when the plaintiffs formed the National Polish Church they had ceased to be members of Our Lady of the

Holy Rosary Parish and of the Roman Catholic Church and hence forfeited all rights to the church property; that they were therefore not entitled to question the transfer of property to the Diocese and that the property rightfully and legally became that of The Roman Catholic Episcopal Corporation of the Diocese of Sault Ste. Marie.[80]

During the 1920s and 1930s the Holy Rosary parish was a house divided. Strained relations between pastors and parishioners which persisted well after the court case had concluded caused many to leave the parish, to attend other churches in Fort William or to cease going to church altogether. Needless to say, to be quarrelling in court over church matters was an embarrassment to them as Polish Roman Catholics.[81] For those who remained in the parish, supporting their church was a financial burden. During the height of the depression it was questionable whether they were capable of supporting a parish priest. Out of sheer desperation one of their pastors, Father William Demski[82], announced at a Sunday service in 1933 that in order to assist at Mass parishioners were obliged to contribute twenty-five cents towards the church's fuel bill.[83] In 1936, the name of the parish was changed to St Casimir by Bishop Dignan. The name change coincided with the arrival in 1937 of Rev. Dr. John Wojnowski from the Regina Diocese. Under his leadership order, calm, and a sense of unity was brought to the parish.[84] He was a humble, learned and devout priest who "did excellent spiritual work among the scattered Polish parishioners at the Lakehead". As a temporary administrator, Father Wojnowski began the systematic recording of baptisms and marriages in the sacramental registers. His untimely death in 1941 was a tragic loss to the parish as they were beginning to recover from years of internal discord. Fortunately, Father Wojnowski was succeeded by a young American-born Polish-speaking priest - Father Joseph Stankiewicz - who was to continue the process of unifying St. Casimir's congregation.

Father Stankiewicz (1910–2002) arrived at an important juncture in the parish's history. Not only were the various factions within being drawn together but the end of the Second World War brought approximately 250-300 Polish refugees to Thunder Bay.[85] They were escaping from the communist political regime which had assumed political power in their homeland during the late 1940s. Father Stankiewicz was born, raised and educated in the United States but ordained in the Pro-Cathedral, North Bay in the Sault Ste. Marie Diocese by Bishop Ralph Dignan on 28 February 1938. [86] Prior to his appointment as pastor of St. Casimir's on 24 October 1941,[87] he had spent brief periods as assistant pastor of St Agnes and St. Patrick parishes. The simple wooden church built in 1921 was woefully inadequate for the strong and growing Thunder Bay Polish congregation. It is a tribute to Father Stankewicz's leadership and administrative ability that the parish had accumulated over $50,000 in a building fund by 1950.[88] With this demonstration of financial and moral commitment he petitioned the bishop for permission to begin construction on a new church. "I had a meeting with both our building and financial committees", he enthusiastically wrote to Bishop Dignan, "and both sources are anxious to start building a new church. They are willing to start canvassing for more funds provided we start building this year."[89]

By spring 1952 Bishop Dignan was aware of Pope Pius XII's intention of severing the western portion of his diocese to create the new Diocese of Fort William. Not surprisingly, Bishop Dignan was either non-committal or negative as Father Stankewicz requested permission to proceed with the various stages of new church construction. As soon as the new Diocese of Fort William was created with the Most Rev. Edward Quentin Jennings as its first Bishop, events in the creation of the new St. Casimir's church moved swiftly. Father Stankewicz and his church building committee set a precedent in the diocese by being the first parish to create a second generation church on the original site. The old church was demolished using volunteer labour[90]; construction of the new church began in June 1952. For a few months, masses were celebrated in the Ogden Street Public school directly across the street. As construction on the new church progressed, the new church basement was used as a temporary place of worship on Sundays and holy days of obligation.[91] Daily Mass as well as nuptials, funerals and baptisms were held at St Peter's. During construction the parish launched a fund-raising drive to augment the $65,000 already raised. To the credit of the Polish congregation and their pastor the handsome new edifice was completed in early 1953 with a small debt of $20,000.

Some mention must be made of the significant numbers of Ukrainian Catholics who were part of "territorial" parishes like Notre Dame in Kenora or members of ethnic parishes like St Peter's or St Casimir's in Thunder Bay. Ukrainians who came from Galicia were Byzantine or Eastern Rite Catholics, but more generally were referred to in their homeland as "Uniates" or "Greek Catholics". The number of Greek Catholics in Fort William, for example, rose from 481 in 1911 to 2,640 in 1941.[92] Significant numbers of Ukrainian Catholics in a diocese presented bishops with a problem. Since most worshipped

Father Joseph Stankiewicz with First Communion class on steps of original St Casimir Church, McKenzie and Robertson Streets, Fort William. c. 1948
The back row of altar boys are identified in this photograph. (L.-R: Ron Belluz, Stanley Cano, Alex Delvecchio, Robert Zelinski, (holding cross) Stanley Pasko.
(Courtesy Cyril Cano)

**St Casimir (Polish) Roman Catholic Church and Rectory, 10 July 2002**
613 McKenzie Street, Thunder Bay, Ontario.
This was one of the first "second generation" churches in the diocese to be built on the same site as the original structure. Construction began in 1952 and was completed a year later. The rectory to the left of the church was erected in 1958. Since the mid-1990s, St Casimir and Our Lady Queen of Poland parishes in Thunder Bay have been served by the Franciscan Fathers. (o.f.m., conv.)

according to the Eastern rite and since the Holy See had prohibited married priests of this rite from entering North America, they were without religious services. Accordingly, Rome gave Ukrainians in Canada their own bishop. In December 1912 Nykyta Budka, apostolic exarch of Canada, "took possession of his see in Winnipeg."[93] Thereafter, Canadian Ukrainian Catholics were removed from the Latin Hierarchy and came under the ecclessiatical authority of the Ukrainian bishop in Canada. In 1913, the Ukrainians of Fort William came together to form their own parish and built a magnificent church at 500 Connolly Street in 1916 (St. Mary's Ukrainian Catholic Church of the Transfiguration) diagonally across from St Peter's in Fort William's East End .[94]

Soon after Bishop Budka's appointment, the Ukrainians of Westfort also built a church of their own. When St. Agnes Parish built a new church in 1914, they purchased the old church, dismantled it and re-built a new one with little resemblance to the old at 1611 Mountain Avenue in 1915-1916.[95] It was not until 28 September 1919 that the church was dedicated as the Ukrainian Catholic Church of the Ascension of Our Lord. As Ukrainian Catholic Churches began to emerge throughout northwestern Ontario after 1912 census records began to reflect the numbers of individuals who considered themselves "Greek" or "Ukrainian" Catholics. In Fort William for example, the Assessment Commissioner's Reports recorded 2,640 as being "Greek" Catholic in 1941. These reports made no claims to being an accurate religious census. Only through a careful examination of parish sacramental registers and census documents is it possible to ascertain approximately how many Ukrainian Catholics remained in the Latin rite parishes and how many branched off to form separate parishes under the Ukrainian Eparchy of Toronto.[96]

National parishes either grew out of territorial parishes like St Patrick in Fort William or St Andrew in Port Arthur or simply emerged because a cultural group was determined to form one of their own. That these parishes survived the stresses and strains of two world wars and the world-wide economic depression of the 1930s is a testament to their commitment to the Roman Catholic faith and to the power of cultural loyalties in creating and sustaining religious institutions.

Survival also depended on the pastors associated with each parish during the formative years. The early history of St Peter's illustrates for example, the importance of stability provided by religious communities. As Jesuits, both Father Ludger Arpin, s.j. and Father François Maynard, s.j. encouraged the Slovak people of Fort William to form their own parish and empowered them

**Ukrainian Catholic Church of the Transfiguration, 18 December 1980.**
629 McIntosh Street, Thunder Bay.
This church was built during the years 1916–1919. The inscription on the plaque on the exterior wall to the right of the front steps reads: "Ukrainian Catholic Church of Tranfiguration J.C. Blessed by His Lordship The Rt. Rev. Nicetas Budka, Bishop of Canadian Ukrainian." This was one of many Ukrainian Catholic Churches built following the establishment of the Ukrainian Catholic Eparchy in Canada. St Peter, St Dominic and the Church of the Transfiguration formed a trilogy of Catholic churches in Fort William's East End. Every June during the 1940s and 1950s, to commemorate the Feast of Corpus Christi, a procession organized by the three parishes would pass through the streets of the East End and celebrate Benediction in front of each church.

to take charge of its temporal affairs. Perhaps it was because they were members of a Canadian cultural minority themselves that they in turn were able to empathize with a Slovak minority wanting to hear sermons and receive the sacraments in a language they understood.

As the Fort William and Port Arthur national parishes were about to become part of the new Fort William Diocese survival was assured. With the exception of St Casimir, all were debt free. St Peter's had accumulated a sufficient surplus to be able to construct one of the finest rectorys in the diocese. Bishop Ralph Dignan was so impressed with the residence that he recommended it to the Most Rev E.Q. Jennings as being fit for a bishop. The number of families attached to each parish continued to grow and each reported having active sodalities such as a Legion of Mary, Holy Name and Altar Societies. Above all, these national parish churches became centres around which many immigrant families organized their social lives.

## Notes

[1] Roberto Perin, "Adélard Langevin", in *DCB*, XIV, 599.
[2] James A. Coriden, ed., *The Code of Canon Law*, p. 416.
[3] *TBA.*, Series 16, Fort Williamm Assessment Commissioner's Reports, 1904-1951, boxes 207-5255. The Assessment Commissioner for the City of Fort William made this statement in his 1913 Report: "…We feel it is extremely difficult to obtain accurate information in our canvassing especially in the foreign quarter." In 1911 the main ethnic groups in Fort William were: Italian (1265), Polish (968), Slovak (1222), and Ruthenian (495).
[4] Canada. Census, 1901. Microfilm Reel 6458; City of Thunder Bay Archives (TBA), Series 16, 207, *Assessment Commissioner's Report, 1910*.
[5] *TBA*, Fort William *Assessment Commissioner's Report, 1912*, box 207, file 46.
[6] *Ibid.*, 234, City of Fort William Assessment Rolls (Ward 1), 1911. Data collected on 30 September 1910 for the 1911 taxation year. On the basis of surnames listed in the assessment roll for the street names mentioned above 42.3 per cent were Slovak, 21.7 per cent Italian, 12 per cent Ukrainian, 9 per cent Polish and 7.9 per cent English.
[7] *Report of a Preliminary and General Social Survey of Fort William, March, 1913*. Directed by The Department of Temperance and moral Reform of the Methodist Church and The Board of Social Service and Evangelism of the Presbyterian Church, p. 11.
[8] St. Patrick's Cathedral. Parish Registers, Baptisms, 1893-1914; Marriages, 1893-1914.

[9] *DSSMA. Scollard Chronicle*, 1 January 1907, p. 13; 12 August 1906, p. 12.

[10] *Ibid.*, + Scollard Papers, J.A. Primeau , s.j. to +Scollard, 22 April 1907.

[11] Angus J. Macdougall, ed., *et. al, Dictionary of Jesuit Biography*, p. 212. Maynard, *Mes Cahier,* 10 June 1906. Father Maynard visited the missions of St. Agnes, Westfort, Murillo and Baird all of which were within a 30 mile radius of Fort William.

[12] *ASJUC*, François Maynard, *Mes Cahier*, 1 June 1907.

[13] *TBA*, 234, Fort William Assessment Rolls, 1911. St. Peter's Roman Catholic Church, under the name of Father Maynard, occupied lots 1-7 on McIntosh Street (block 38) and McLeod Street (lots 8-12).

[14] For a description of the fire in the local press see Fort William *Daily Times-Journal*, 4 November 1907; Port Arthur *Daily News*, 4 November 1907. These reports indicate that the Fort William Fire Department was alerted at 12:15 A.M. on 3 November. "The building was of brick veneer, the main part being 45' x 80', nave 30' x 20' and sacristy 16' x 24'. The massive tower, which was a splendid feature in the two cities, was completely ruined."

[15] Maynard, *Cahiers,* 10 November 1907.

[16] *Ibid.*, Maynard, *Cahier*, 1 August 1910. St. Peter Parish Baptism, Marriage and Death registers, 1908-1910.

[17] *Ibid.*, François Maynard, *Cahiers*, 21 June 1909.

[18] *Ibid.*, 3 August 1910. The bell weighed 365 pounds and cost $367.

[19] *DSSMA, Scollard Chronicle*, 1 August 1911, p. 28. See also Maynard, *Cahiers*, 1 March 1911. St. Peter's Roman Catholic Separate School officially opened in September 1911. The four-room school accommodated "the beginners" while the "older pupils" from the East End attended St. Stanislaus School on Myles Street.

[20] *Ibid.*, 8 October 1911, p. 28.

[21] *DTBA*, Box 8.17, François Maynard to Andrew Potosky, 21 June 1946. The Diocese is grateful to Mr. Steve Potosky for the donation and translation of a series of letters between Father Maynard and Andrew Potosky.

[22] *DSSMA, Scollard Chronicle*, 1 October 1914, p. 40; 8 April 1921, p. 68.

[23] *ASJUC*, Maynard, *Cahiers*, 1914.

[24] *DSSMA*, Scollard Chronicle, 8 April 1921, p. 68

[25] *Ibid.*, Ralph Hubert Dignan, *Sources: The Journal*, ed. Greg J. Humbert, (North Bay: Diocese of Sault Ste Marie, 1995), pp. 20-21. Bishop Dignan was severely critical of the Rcv. Emery Vodicka referring to him as "an eccentric...old Hungarian priest" who was in his early 70s and resided at St. Joseph's hospital.

[26] *Ibid.*, Dignan, *The Minute Book*, 17 March 1950, p. 285.

[27] St. Peter's History, p. 24. *DTBA*, 4.01. Rev. J.S. Reguly file.

[28] *DSSMA*. + Dignan Papers, Rev. Joseph Reguly to Bishop R.H. Dignan, 4 March 1950. The Abbot of St. Andrew's Abbey, Cleveland, Ohio agreed to surrender St. Peter's Parish on 18 April 1950. Father Joseph S. Reguly was formally appointed pastor on 8 May 1950.

[29] Maynard, *Cahiers*, 3 December 1911; *Scollard Chronicle*, 1911, p. 31.

[30] *DTJ*, 2 January 1912.

[31] Thunder Bay Land Registry Office, title search for Block 37, lots 9 and 10. Date of this

registry was 4 December 1912. The lots were sold for $791.31 by the Pigeon River Lumber Company to a group of trustees representing St. Joseph's Parish, namely, Frank M. Ross, Angelo Descepolo, Louis Belluz, Bruno Mazza, Father Francis Crociata and the Episcopal Corporation of Sault Ste. Marie.

[32] *DTBA*, Box 5.10, Father F. Crociata to +Scollard, 19 October 1912.

[33] *Ibid.*, Crociata claimed that he had raised $2085 from St. Andrew's English-speaking parishioners and provided Bishop Scollard with their names and how much they each had contributed.

[34] Port Arthur *Daily News*, 5 August 1912.

[35] See Port Arthur *Daily News*, 24 December 1912; Fort William *Morning Herald*, 11 January 1913.

[36] *DSSMA, Scollard Chronicle*, p. 32.

[37] *Ibid.*, Bishop D.J. Scollard Papers, +P.F. Ryan to +Scollard, 26 November 1914.

[38] *Ibid.*, +Scollard to +Ryan, 26 November 1914.

[39] Maynard, *Notebook*, 12 May 1914.

[40] See Roy and Diane Piovesana, *St. Dominic Parish: A History, 1912-1987* (Diocese of Thunder Bay, 1987), p. 6.

[41] For a description of the fire see The Port Arthur *Daily News*, 22 December 1914.

[42] *DSSMA*, +Scollard Papers, A.J. McComber to +Scollard, 28 December 1914.

[43] Ibid., *Scollard Chronicle*, p. 43.

[44] *Ibid.*, Scollard Papers, Bishop P.F. Stagui, Delgatio Apostolica, to +Scollard, 27 September 1915.

[45] For biographical details on the life of Father Domenico Tomaselli see the *DTJ,* 22 and 24 April 1940.

[46] *DSSMA, Scollard Chronicle*, 1915, p. 43.

[47] For a detailed description of these ceremonies see Port Arthur *News-Chronicle*, 19 February 1917 (St. Anthony) and *DTJ*, 11 August 1919. (St. Dominic)

[48] *DTJ*, 11 August 1919.

[49] Piovesana, *St. Dominic Parish: A History*, p. 9.

[50] *Ibid.*, p. 10.

[51] *DSSMA*, +Dignan Papers, +Dignan to Judge Kenny, 17 June 1932.

[52] *Ibid.*, +Scollard Papers, Mrs. Muldoon to +Scollard, 12 April 1920.

[53] *Ibid.*, Rev. J.F. Cox, S.J. to + Scollard, 6 June 1930; See also +Dignan Papers, M.J. Kenny, Senior Judge, District of Thunder Bay to +Dignan, 9 January 1933.

[54] Piovesana, *St. Dominic Parish*, p. 6.

[55] As the first full-time pastor of St. Dominic's Parish, Father Capresi began celebrating regular masses on Sundays at 8:00 and 10:30 A.M. and every weekday at 7:30 A.M. All sermons were in Italian. See Piovesana, *St. Dominic Parish*, p. 7.

[56] *DSSMA*, Scollard Papers, Albert Uriguress to +Scollard, 8 April 1923.

[57] *Ibid.*, *Scollard Chronicle*, 1 November 1924, p. 77; 83.

[58] Italian Church in Fort William's East End was changed from St. Joseph's to St. Dominic's

on 3 April 1936 by Bishop Ralph H. Dignan. See *Dignan Journal*, Appendix Four (Titles of Churches), p. 434.

59*DTBA*, Box 8.12, St. Dominic Files.

60Piovesana, *St. Dominic Parish*, pp. 8-9.

61*DSSMA*, Bishop R.H. Dignan Papers, +Dignan to Rev. A.J. Murray, 3 October 1946.

62*TBA*, 210, Assessment Commissioner Reports, Nos. 42, 43, and 80. By 1921 there were approximately 500 Polish people living in Fort William most of whom resided in Ward I.

63*DTBA*, 8.11, "Father F.B. Tomanek Notes, 1 October 1922." The Polish community of Fort William contributed $4100 toward the construction of the church and borrowed another $2350 from several members of the Polish congregation.

64The three trustees were William Kulczicki, Nikolas Kucy, and Joseph Klinarowicz (Joseph Clemens). See *DSSMA*, Bishop D.J. Scollard Papers, The Supreme Court of Ontario. "Examination for Discovery of the Plaintiff Peter Bemben, held at the Court House, Port Arthur, Monday, January 25th, 1932.

65Father François-Boniface Kowalski (1878-1954) was born in Kleszczcwo, Poland. As an Oblate he came to Canada to minister to the Polish and Ukrainian Roman Catholics of Manitoba. He returned to his native Poland in 1922. See Gaston Carrierère, O.M.I., *Dictionaire biographique des Oblats de Marie-Immaculée du Canada, II,* (Ottawa: Éditions De L'Université D'Ottawa, 1977), 204-205.

66*DSSMA*, +Scollard Papers, Rev. F.B. Kowalski, o.m.i. to +Scollard, 30 December 1921. The mission was held in St. Peter's Church from 11-18 December 1921.

67*DTJ*, 20 November 1922.

68*DSSMA*., Rev. F.B. Tomanek to +Scollard, 20 November 1922.

69*Ibid.*, 8.11, "Provisory Rules. The Holy Rosary Church, Fort William, Ont. October 22, 1922. Approved by Bishop D.J. Scollard, North Bay, 17 October 1922.

70*Ibid.*, +Scollard Papers, "Judgement of John McKay on the ownership of Holy Rosary Church, Fort William.", 18 November 1933.

71*DTJ*, 23 November 1922.

72*DSSMA*, Joseph Clemens and J. Walsh to +Scollard, 12 December 1922. See also *DTBA*, 8.11, Holy Rosary Congregation to +Scollard, 8 November 1922.

73*Ibid.*, +Scollard Papers, F. B. Tomanek to +Scollard, 4 December 1922.

74*DTBA*, 8.11. From 1922-1929 Fathers Glinski, Tabourski, Ziemba and Lukasik succeeded Father Tomanek. Little is known about any of these priests.

75*DSSMA*, F.B. Kowalski, o.m.i. to +Scollard, 30 December 1921.

76*Ibid.*, +Scollard Papers, Anthony Gorek to +Scollard, 23 September 1929. According to lawyer John A. Dyke deeding the church and church property to the Diocese of Sault Ste. Marie was without proper authority and without the knowledge and consent of the Bishop. See John A.Dyke to +Scollard, 23 October 1929.

77*TBA*, Series 16, *Fort William Assessment Commissioner's Report*, box 209, file 5-23, 30 January 1932.

78*Ibid.,* John A. Dyke to +Scollard, 23 October 1929.

79*Ibid.,* A.J. McComber, K.C., to +Scollard, 17 September 1932.

[80] *DSSMA*, Legal Judgement, 18 November 1933. [give details of source]

[81] *Ibid.,* A.J. McComber to +Scollard, 17 September 1932,

[82] *Ibid.,* Alfred A. Nicole, Archbishop of Winnipeg to +Scollard, 2 August 1933.

[83] *Ibid.,* R.H. Dignan Papers, Rev. P. J. Mcguire to +Dignan, 23 February 1937.

[84] *Ibid.,* R.H. Dignan, *The Journal,* edited by Greg J. Humbert, (North Bay: Diocese of Sault Ste. Marie, 1995), p. 116. Father Demski had been pastor at St. Casimir's for five years and in 1937 Bishop Dignan revoked his faculties in the Diocese of Sault Ste. Marie because "the Bishop did not want to have him become automatically incardinated as he was most unsuitable."

[85] *TBA*, 212, 213. Assessment Commissioner's Reports. In 1937 the Polish population was listed as 735, in 1940, 844; and in 1944, 1029. By 1949 it had risen to 1321.

[86] *Ibid.,* R.H. Dignan, *The Minute Book,* pp. 166-168. Father Joseph Stankiewcz was born on 21 March 1910 at Exeter, Pennsylvania and educated in the public and secondary schools there. He pursued post-secondary business studies at Wiles-Barr Business College and at the University of Pennsylvania night school program. It is not clear when he decided to enter the priesthood but he took his philosophy and theological studies at St. Mary's College, Orchard Lake, Michigan. It is also not clear when and why he came to Canada. He was ordained to the first and second minor orders (4 February 1938), subdiaconate (6 February 1938), diaconate (13 February 1938) and the Holy Priesthood ( 20 February 1938) by Bishop Ralph Dignan in the Pro-Cathedral, North Bay, Ontario.

[87] *Ibid.,* p. 210.

[88] *Ibid.,* +Dignan Papers, Rev. J.B. Stankiewicz to +Dignan, 1 June 1950

[89] *Ibid.,* J. B. Stankiewicz to +Dignan, 16 April 1951.

[90] *DTBA*, 8.11, Father Stankiewicz to +E.Q. Jennings, 24 May 1952; EQJ to Fr. Stankiewicz, 26 May 1952.

[91] *Ibid.,* 3.02/23, Annual Parish Report, 10 January 1953.

[92] *TBA*, series 16, Assessment Commissioner's Reports, 1911-1941.

[93] For the religious career of Bishop Budka in Canada see Stella Hryniuk, "Pioneer Bishop, Pioneer Times: Nykyta Budka in Canada", in Canadian Catholic Historical Association (CCHA), *Historical Studies*, 55 (1988), 21-41.

[94] *DSSMA*, A. J. Byrnes to +Scollard, 22 November 1911; A.J. McComber to +Scollard, 25 January 1912.

[95] For a brief history of the Westfort Ukrainian Catholic Church of the Ascension see *DTJ*, 22 October 1969.

[96] Notre Dame du Portage in Kenora for example, has a parish register (Volume "R") of baptisms, marriages and deaths of Ukrainian Catholics dated from 1913 to 1937.

# DIOCESE
## II

CHAPTER THREE

# BISHOP EDWARD QUENTIN JENNINGS

As its first Bishop, the Most Rev. E.Q. Jennings guided the clergy and laity in establishing the spiritual and material foundations of the Roman Catholic Diocese of Thunder Bay. This process was made easier during the 1950s and 1960s by the unprecedented prosperity and population growth in Canada and northwestern Ontario. Founding new parishes and missions, organizing a diocesan council of the Catholic Women's League, launching a diocesan fund-raising campaign, attending the Second Vatican Council and beginning the implementation of its reforms, grappling with the problems of catholic secondary education in Thunder Bay, and initiating the design and construction of a new St Patrick's Cathedral were some of the tasks that engaged Bishop Jennings during his seventeen-year tenure at the helm of the Thunder Bay Diocese.

Edward Quentin Jennings, son of Patrick Jennings and Elizabeth Wallace, was born on 4 October 1896 in the hamlet of Little River outside of Saint John, New Brunswick.[1] His family had sufficient means to provide him with a fine Catholic academic education in Saint John where he attended St Malachi Elementary School and then St John High School graduating in 1915.[2] At 19 his formal education was interrupted when he joined the

Canadian Expeditionary Force on 9 May 1916 and became part of the 6th Canadian Siege Battery Regiment as a gunner.[3] He served with this regiment in England, France, Belgium, and Germany. Like thousands of Canadian soldiers who experienced the horrors of trench warfare during World War I, he was in and out of military hospitals suffering from head wounds, shell gas wounds, and the dreadful effects of mustard gas used by German forces against Allied troops. In the fall of 1919, following his discharge from the Canadian army, he enrolled at St Francis Xavier University, Antigonish, Nova Scotia receiving a Bachelor of Arts degree in 1922. Three years of further study at Holy Heart Seminary, Halifax, culminated in his ordination to the priesthood on 27 December 1925 by the Most Reverend Edward Alfred LeBlanc at Saint John, N.B. for the Edmonton Diocese.[4]

The religious career of Father Edward Jennings was to grow and flourish in Western Canada. His superiors in the Edmonton Diocese soon recognized his industriousness and inclination for pastoral work and administrative affairs. From the date of his ordination to the outbreak of World War II he held the positions of Assistant Pastor (1925-1927) and Rector of St Joseph's Cathedral in Edmonton (1937-1941). His administrative responsibilities in the Edmonton Diocese as Secretary to Archbishop Henry Joseph O'Leary (1927-1934) and as Chancellor (1934-1941) prepared him for the Episcopal appointments which were to follow. Within a decade of his appointment as Auxiliary Bishop of Vancouver in 1941, Bishop Jennings accepted the responsibility of organizing two new Canadian dioceses, namely, Kamloops, B.C.(1946) and Fort William, Ontario (1952). Both encompassed vast and sparsely populated areas, both were considered mission dioceses destined to serve significant native populations and both were created out of sections from adjoining dioceses.[5] In the case of Fort William, the new diocese comprised that part of the Diocese of Sault Ste. Marie west of 86th degree longitude and all territory in Ontario that once came under the aegis of the Archdiocese of St Boniface.[6]

The selection of Bishop Jennings as the first shepherd of the Fort William Diocese was based on the exemplary spiritual leadership that he had provided in Kamloops.[7] "I have the honour of informing Your Excellency", wrote The Most Rev. Ildebrando Antoniutti, Apostolic Delegate to Canada, "that the Holy Father has deigned to designate you as Bishop of the newly erected Diocese of Fort William in Ontario. This is a promotion for Your Excellency who has worked with such...great zeal in Kamloops and a recognition of your merits in the development of that Diocese." The newly formed Diocese of

The Most Reverend Edward Quentin Jennings, D.D.
First Bishop of Thunder Bay, 26 August 1952–16 September 1969

Installation ceremony of the Most Rev. E.Q. Jennings in St Patrick's Cathedral, Fort William, 26 August 1952. (Thunder Bay Historical Society, 978-13-111b)

Fort William was considered bilingual with 18 parishes and 72 missions at widely dispersed points. With approximately 32,000 Roman Catholics served by 50 priests and 160 women religious, it covered a vast geographic area of 170,600 square km[8] bound on the west by the Ontario-Manitoba border, on the north by 53 latitude, on the south by the Canada-United States boundary and on the east by a line which coincided with the Pic River. Bishop Jennings was understandably honoured by the trust and confidence placed in him by this appointment. Once it was made official in *L'Osservatore Romano* on 21 May 1952 he began the process of taking possession of the new diocese from Kamloops where he was still Apostolic Administrator until his successor was named. In addition, he tended to organizational matters for his installation which was to take place at St Patrick's Church, now elevated to the status of a cathedral.[9]

The modest size of St Patrick's sanctuary determined the nature of the installation ceremony. His inclination was to keep it modest and simple.[10] On the morning of 26 August 1952 St Patrick's Cathedral was filled to capacity and those present witnessed a milestone in Fort William's history. Papal bulls formally erecting the new Diocese of Fort William and installing the Most Reverend Edward Quentin Jennings as its first bishop were proclaimed by the Apostolic Delegate to Canada.[11] In the presence of His Excellency Archbishop Baudoux, Coadjutor of St Boniface, the clergy and women religious of the diocese and the Roman Catholic laity from Thunder Bay and region, Bishop Jennings celebrated a Pontifical High Mass and read his inaugural address in both of Canada's official languages. To Pope Pius XII he pledged his loyalty. To all in his diocese he pledged his devoted service.

To the first Bishop of Thunder Bay went the responsibility of settling matters of finance and property transfers between the two dioceses from which his was created. In all of this, Bishop Ralph Dignan of Sault Ste. Marie was forthright and accommodating. He claimed that his diocese had lost its best region to the newly created episcopal see of Fort William[12] and that the Thunder Bay area parishes were financially sound.[13] Since 1935 he had encouraged his pastors to deposit their surplus or building funds with the chancery office to finance debtor parishes in the Sault Ste. Marie Diocese. He transferred approximately $200,000 to the Fort William Diocese which represented funds collected from Thunder Bay parishes for three specific purposes, namely, the Priests' Infirm Fund used to care for diocesan priests during periods of illness or old age; the St Patrick's Parish Fund to be used at some future date for the construction of a new church; and the Campaign Fund, begun in 1949, and earmarked to develop catholic higher education in the Thunder Bay area. The transfer of assets between the Archdiocese of St Boniface and the Fort William Diocese was the reverse of what it was with the Sault Ste. Marie Diocese and on a smaller scale. Fort William owed St Boniface approximately $25,000 which was transferred in the fall of 1953.[14] Once these matters of finance were settled, Bishop Jennings was able to give his undivided attention to issues which prompted the creation of his diocese.

Roman Catholic dioceses are erected by the Vatican on the recommendation of Apostolic Delegates and bishops in response "to the needs of the faithful, in accordance with local circumstances."[15] What, then, were the needs of the faithful that gave rise to a new diocese in northwestern Ontario? A centrally located episcopal see that would ensure the extension of pastoral care to the growing Roman Catholic population in the region north of Superior was the rationale given in Bishop Jennings' installation address.[16] The population was not only growing but becoming ethnically diverse. Historically, parishes and missions between Thunder Bay and Lake of the Woods were served by the Missionary Oblates of Mary Immaculate of French expression. Linguistically, they recognized their limitations in administering the sacraments to congregations where the language of the majority was neither French nor English but Polish, German, Italian, and Ukrainian. Father Patrick J. McGuire, the first Rector of St Patrick's Cathedral, recognized this fact and was somewhat bewildered at the Vatican's classification of the Fort William Diocese as bilingual. "I find this idea of a bilingual diocese rather amusing between you and me", wrote Father McGuire to Bishop Jennings. "I think you will find we have more Slovaks and Italians than French."[17] The cosmopolitan Roman Catholic population which had emerged in northwestern Ontario after World War II cried out for more attention than had been given them in the past. Moreover, a centrally located episcopal see was essential if the small parishes and missions along the north shore of Lake Superior and from Thunder Bay to the Manitoba border were to be administered efficiently. Often, the Bishops of Sault Ste. Marie and St Boniface found it difficult to give their undivided attention to important parochial issues in the western or eastern extremities of their dioceses 1000 km away. For example, John A. Dyke, a Fort William lawyer who acted as legal counsel to the "dissentient Parishioners" in the Holy Rosary (Polish) Parish dispute in Fort William from 1929-1932 believed that the conflict might have been averted or settled out of court had Bishop Scollard spent time in Fort William mediating matters between disgruntled parishioners and their pastor.[18] As for the Archbishop of St Boniface, the territory in his diocese beyond Kenora, Fort Frances and Rainy River was *terra incognita*. He was often unaware of the pockets of native and immigrant Roman Catholics that had settled along the C.N.R. line in northwestern Ontario. Jesuit missionary Alexander Rolland, s.j., for example, requesting faculties in the Archdiocese of St Boniface, had to inform Archbishop Georges Cabana that it was the Jesuits and not the Oblates who ministered to the Indians living in Ghost River, 15 km east of Sioux Lookout.[19] Roman Catholics associated with missions such as Atikokan candidly expressed to visiting priests that because of their isolation they felt no attachment to the St Boniface Diocese or its work.[20] Parishes and missions in northwestern Ontario would be difficult to serve given the human and financial resources available to any bishop during the first half of the twentieth century. The experiences of Roman Catholics living in these communities prior to the formation of the Fort William Diocese, however, reveal that their requests for

**Heraldic Crest of the Diocese of Fort William, 1953.**
Shortly after the Fort William Diocese was created in 1952 Bishop Jennings commissioned artist Cyril Cassidy to prepare a coat of arms or heraldic crest for the diocese. Under the Bishop's mitre are three symbols (left to right): the heart, recalling the love for men of Jesus Christ, Saviour, Leader, Teacher; the shamrock, recalling St Patrick, patron saint of the cathedral in Fort William; the crescent moon, a symbol of the Blessed Virgin Mary, principal patroness of the Fort William Diocese, under the title Our Lady of Charity. In the lower section is a fort representing the origins of the City of Fort William.

religious services and spiritual leadership were inadequately met. The creation of the Fort William Diocese would not remove the inconveniences of great distances separating a bishop from his flock but it held out the promise of engendering a deeper sense of belonging among parishes and missions to their diocese.

The founding and development of parishes in the small towns of northwestern Ontario provided the litmus test of Bishop Jennings' administrative and pastoral skills. Atikokan, Sioux Lookout, Ignace, Dryden, Red Lake, and Balmertown, attracted thousands of workers seeking employment with the Canadian Pacific and Canadian National Railways and with the pulp and paper, iron ore and gold mining operations that emerged in the region. To serve their spiritual needs he reached out to various religious orders and con-

**First Priests' Retreat, Diocese of Fort William 1953.**
*(DTBA)*
Front: (L-R). Alexander Greengrass, Joseph B. Stankiewicz, Eugene Hebert, T.J. McCarthy, s.j., Most Rev. E.Q. Jennings, Albert J. Hogan, Emmett Bunyan, John Roenicke, Francis J. Meyer. Insert: James J. Muldoon.
Back: (l-r) Joachim Bortignon, Garret Morris, Joseph McHugh, Lawrence Wittig, Roy Carey, James Cowan, Armand Moreau, Reginald Carroll, Joseph Reguly, Joseph Cano, John Montag, A. Marcel Dugal, F. Regis St James, Daniel China, Edward Gallagher, B. Shumay(Ukrainian), Leo Laliberte.

gregations of priests including The Missionaries of La Salette, Franciscans, Consolata Missionaries, The Congregation of Missionaries of St Charles (Scalabrinians; formerly the Pious Society of St Charles Borromeo) and The Missionary Oblates of Mary Immaculate, St Peter's Province, whose linguistic dexterity and missionary zeal made their apostolates among a largely immigrant population credible and endearing. These missionary priests willingly and enthusiastically accepted Bishop Jennings' invitation to undertake pastoral work in his diocese and, in an unplanned way, the small parishes in the region served as bases from which they came to direct larger parishes in Thunder Bay. For an emergent diocese which produced few "home-grown" priests, these religious orders and congregations made a singular contribution to its development.

*St Patrick Parish, Atikokan*

St Patrick Parish, Atikokan was one of the first in the diocese's western region that demanded the attention of Bishop Jennings. Atikokan, a small community 180 km west of Thunder Bay on Highway 11/17 and 130 km east of Fort Frances, was considered an improvement district during the 1920s with a population of 325 most of whom found employment with the C.N.R. The handful of Roman Catholics in the town were periodically served by Father Arthur Dallaire, o.m.i. from Fort Frances where he was pastor of St Mary's Parish.[21] It was not until 1931 that the construction of a small wooden chapel was made possible by a five hundred dollar donation through The Catholic Church Extension Society. It was the wish of the donor to the Society that the chapel be dedicated to St Patrick.[22] During the depression years the seventy to one hundred Roman Catholics of Atikokan had struggled to maintain the chapel where mass was celebrated once or twice a month.[23] By the early 1940s the development of the Steep Rock Iron Mines 8 km north of Atikokan was a boon to the town's economy and became the site of one of the largest iron ore mining operations in the world. On a pastoral visit to St Patrick chapel in June 1942 Archbishop Georges Cabana observed the significant increase in attendance since his last visit.[24] Several of the 200 who gathered to meet him requested that a priest visit their chapel as frequently as possible to say mass. He responded by assigning Father Édouard Maurice, O.M..I.(1916-1972) as the resident priest for Atikokan. As a young priest who had spent the previous eight years as a professor at the Oblate Collège Mathieu in Gravelbourg,

St Patrick Roman Catholic Church, 23 May 2002
119 Hawthorne Road
Atikokan, Ontario.

Saskatchewan, his first priority was the establishment of a bilingual separate school rather than the construction of a larger church.[25] The St Boniface Archdiocese provided moral support for this initiative and suggested that the school committee work closely with Father Maurice and look to St Joseph's Parish in Dryden as a model which had a separate elementary school staffed by the Sisters of St Joseph from Crookston, Minnesota. The priorities of Atikokan's Roman Catholic community, however, were at odds with those of their pastor. Foremost in their minds was the construction of a new church and rectory. Father Maurice left Atikokan with the issues of a separate school and a new church unresolved.

The development of Atikokan's Roman Catholic community during the 1950s and 1960s depended on the financial circumstances of its parishioners and the zeal of its pastors. In 1952, Bishop Jennings considered it a mission with "practically the status of a parish."[26] Within weeks of his installation the resident priest at St Patrick's chapel, Father Stanislaus Gauvin, requested a transfer out of the diocese for health reasons. What is more, as a francophone, he felt inadequate serving an English and growing cosmopolitan parish.[27] During his brief sojourn in Atikokan he clearly identified the need for a larger church in the centre of town as a means of ameliorating the indifference Roman Catholics had towards their faith and of improving their attendance at Sunday Mass.[28] Prior to his departure in April 1953 he apologetically lamented the dreadful living conditions and financial circumstances his successor would have to face. "The church at Atikokan is too small," he wrote in his annual parish report. "The rectory was improved but it is cold and too small. No stove, no fridge, no housekeeper…I was not able to take a decent salary but I did not come here for the money. The condition is one of a missionary. I paid many things out of my personal money." For Father Gauvin's successor, however, the spiritual development of the parish would prove to be a more daunting challenge than the physical discomforts. "A strong and healthy priest is required in Atikokan", observed a visiting priest. "There is so much to do. The population is growing, there are many Catholics who don't practice their religion any more. There is no separate school and therefore the young generation is ignorant: many children are coming to church but they don't seem to know anything about Mass and the Sacraments. What a pity! Poor people!"[29] Bishop Jennings acceded to Father Gauvin's request for a move and arranged with Paul Emile Cardinal Léger to have him transferred to the Montreal Diocese.[30] In the fall of 1953 he was replaced by Father Lawrence

Wittig (1909–1977).³¹ Under his supervision the former chapel was replaced by a much larger church in the residential subdivision of Dunbar Heights.³² A year after his arrival, he proudly invited Bishop Jennings to visit Atikokan to bless and officially open the new church and the separate elementary school. In the mid-1950s, St Patrick's Parish ideally demanded the attention of two priests. Bishop Jennings' fortuitous contacts with The Congregation of the Missionaries of St Charles (Scalabrinians) provided him with an opportunity to realize this ideal.

The Scalabrinian Congregation was founded in Piacenza, Italy in 1887 by Blessed John Baptist Scalabrini. Their charism was to follow and serve the spiritual needs of Italian immigrants.³³ It was in New York City that they established their first North American mission in 1888. From the United States they branched off to Australia, Chili, Argentina, and Brazil to administer multicultural parishes and ethnic missions. With approximately twenty-five thousand Italians emigrating to Canada each year during the 1950s it is not surprising that they assumed responsibility for their first Canadian parish in Hamilton, Ontario in 1953.³⁴ A year later, the Scalabrinian Provincial Superior (headquartered in Chicago) offered the services of two priests for the Fort William Diocese.³⁵

St Patrick's was not an Italian parish but the Scalabrinians viewed it as falling within the scope of their work as missionaries to immigrants. In the spring of 1958 Fathers Giulio Gragnani, c.s. (1911–1984) and Anthony Carrano, c.s.³⁶ (1921–1993) took up residence in Atikokan and energetically engaged themselves in pastoral work. They visited each Catholic family and blessed their homes. From Christmas Day 1959, mass was celebrated every Sunday in the nearby missions of Coldstream and Sapawe.³⁷ During the summers of 1960 and 1961 they organized a religious summer school attended by 160 students and staffed by two Sisters of St Joseph (Crookston, Minnesota). St Patrick's parishioners organized a committee to eliminate the church debt. Through a house to house subscription campaign spread over five years the debt was reduced from $65,000 in 1960 to $29,000 in 1966.³⁸ In addition, a new home was purchased by the parish close to the church to serve as a rectory. A request from parishioners to establish a mission chapel on Eva Lake on the northeast boundary of Quetico Provincial Park was welcomed by Father Gragnani as the parish's religious contribution to Canada's centennial. The chapel, "Our Lady of the Lake", was intended as a place where "the voyageur" would be able to stop and "refresh his soul."³⁹ It took the parish three years to raise the necessary funds to build this chapel but when it was completed in the spring of 1969 it more than lived up to its original intent as a place where travellers, cottage owners on Eva Lake, and visitors to Quetico Park could attend mass and services on Sundays during spring and summer.[40]

All this was done at a time when the Steep Rock Iron Mines operations were being scaled down resulting in major layoffs and the exodus of families from the parish.[41] The ability of St Patrick's parishioners to support a pastor and maintain a parish church was tied to the fortunes of this one major industry. A comment frequently found in parish reports during the 1960s related to the fluctuating employment levels in the town. The number of new Catholic families coming into the parish never made up for those that left. Father Gragnani served on the Atikokan Industrial and Development Committee which visited Minneapolis, Minnesota to promote the town's potential for industrial development.[42] The Scalabrinians assumed civic responsibilities for diversifying the local economy hoping that their efforts would have a positive impact on the financial well-being of the town and indirectly on their parish. The stability of the Atikokan economy and the future availability of priests serving in the diocese would determine if St Patrick's could fulfill its mandate as a parish.

The Scalabrinian presence at St Patrick's, Atikokan provided them with a base from which to accept responsibilities in other communities in northwestern Ontario and in Thunder Bay. In 1959, for example, they administered St Augustine's Parish in Baird and its associated missions of Hymers, Harstone and Kakabeka Falls.[43] These were small rural communities west of Thunder Bay's city limits with a total of 82 Catholic families among them. In the early 1960s, Father Joseph Favotto, c.s. travelled from Baird to Ignace on a regular basis to visit the Italian families, to bless their homes and to hear their confessions.[44] Although the Scalabrinians welcomed the tranquillity and natural setting of Atikokan and Baird, they soon looked for more demanding responsibilities associated with larger (preferably Italian) parishes. An opportunity presented itself when St Anthony's Parish in Port Arthur desperately needed an assistant pastor who was fluent in both Italian and English.  Accordingly, in 1959 the Scalabrinian Provincial was delighted to oblige Bishop Jennings in providing a full time assistant pastor for Port Arthur's Italian parish.[45]

St Anthony's was the parish around which the Scalabrinian Fathers wanted to concentrate their pastoral efforts in the Thunder Bay Diocese.[46] From the mid-1960s they had made known their desire to assume responsibility for the parish if and when the incumbent pastor were to retire. Father Joachim Bortignon

**St Augustine Roman Catholic Church, 2001.**
R. R. # 11, Townline Road, Thunder Bay.
Bishop Ralph Dignan of Sault Ste Marie canonically erected St Augustine Parish in Baird which also included the missions of Harstone and Hymers with the Rev. Joseph Carmel McHugh as its first resident parish priest, succeeding Rev. V. J. McGivney.
(Courtesy Rev. Henryk Augustynowicz)

St Theresa Parish Church, 28 July 2001.
R. R. 11 Townline Road, Kakabeka Falls.

(1902–1977) had been pastor at St Anthony's since 1955 and led the parish in their desire to build a new church to replace the existing structure on the corner of Banning and Dufferin Streets. Bishop Jennings had always been impressed with Father Bortignon's pastoral and administrative style and left any decision of retirement to him alone. A careful examination of St Anthony's statistical data submitted to the Bishop from 1955 to1968 reveals a parish growing spiritually and financially stronger each year. When Father Bortignon first arrived, it had approximately 425 families and celebrated on average approximately two marriages and eight baptisms a month.[47] Ten years later average monthly marriages had risen by ten per cent and baptisms by 43 per cent. Attendance at Sunday masses was consistently high during this same period. Moreover, St Anthony's building fund had risen from $14,500 in 1955 to $78,000 in 1966. The project in Father Bortignon's "mind and heart" was the new church and he entertained no intention of retiring until that dream became a reality.[48] Regrettably, construction bids received in 1967 for the new church were too high and the project was postponed indefinitely. A year later, Father Bortignon decided to retire and Bishop Jennings formally offered the direction of the parish to the Scalabrinian Fathers.[49] They returned the administration of Baird (1968) and Atikokan (1976) back to the diocese and St Anthony's became the bedrock of their apostolate in Thunder Bay.

### *Sacred Heart Parish, Sioux Lookout*

Sacred Heart Parish, Sioux Lookout, unlike St Patrick's in Atikokan, had the advantage of evolving gradually in a northwestern Ontario town with a stable economy. Sioux Lookout, 550 km northwest of Thunder Bay and 100 km north of Dryden was incorporated as a town in 1912 and, at the time, its principal employer was the Canadian National Railways.[50] The diversification of its economy began with the "Red Lake Gold Rush" of 1926 when Sioux Lookout served as an aviation gateway to Ontario mining communities inaccessible by road north of the 50th parallel. After World War II, its economy was further nurtured by the logging operations of The Great Lakes Paper Company which had established a camp at Valora, 22 km west of the town. Great Lakes Paper purchased the Patricia Lumber Company[51] in 1952 to expand the production of railway ties sold to the C.N.R. and to begin the manufacture of finished lumber. The presence of a radar station 20 km north of the town as an integral part of the Pinetree Line of air defence built along the 49th parallel contributed significantly to its economy. The radar station was manned by 50 members of the 915th Aircraft and Warning Squadron from the Goremier Air Force Base, New Hampshire, U.S.A. The combination of the radar station, the C.N.R., Patricia Lumber Company, air service to northern communities, and the logging operations of the Great Lakes Paper Company provided secure employment in Sioux Lookout with a population of 2300 in the late 1940s . Most were English-speaking with significant concentrations of Italian, Ukrainian and Polish immigrants. The small francophone population was transient and worked mainly in the logging industry. Roman Catholics made up approximately 32.6 per cent of the total population by the time the Diocese of Fort William was established.

The Missionary Oblates of Mary Immaculate intervened at two critical stages in the development of Sacred Heart Parish, namely, its founding in 1912-1913 and, fifty-six years later, in its spiritual renewal and construction of a new parish church. From Notre Dame du Portage Parish in Kenora, missionary Father Cornelius O'Dwyer, o.m.i. (1862-1934) travelled along the Canadian Pacific and Grand Trunk rail lines in northwestern Ontario and ministered to small groups of Roman Catholics in the towns of Sioux Lookout, Dryden and Ignace.[52] From 1909–1912, he visited Sioux Lookout once a month and "gathered the few Catholics off the gumbo streets into a restaurant on Front Street for a brief mass and a few words of encouragement."[53] In 1913, the Catholic community erected a 50' x 34' building that was to serve as the first Sacred Heart Church. The church bell, made in France, arrived and installed in 1913, was decorated with the Oblate emblem and the inscription: "E. Planet, ptre o.m.i., 1913". Father Edouard Planet (1877-1941), although credited with being the first resident priest, simply followed in the footsteps of his predecessor Father O'Dwyer in being a missionary priest in charge of Sioux Lookout.[54] At the beginning of World War I the parishioners were petitioning the Archbishop of St Boniface for a "Resident English speaking priest."[55]

Sacred Heart Parish welcomed its first resident diocesan priest in 1917. For thirty years thereafter it survived the crises of war and depression but the responsibilities of supporting a separate school, church maintenance, and providing services to missions around Sioux Lookout (Hudson, Ignace, Superior Junction, Dinorwic) were often too demanding for one priest. A Roman Catholic complex consisting of Sacred Heart Church, a rectory, a convent, and the Sacred Heart Separate School (established in 1926) were situated together on King Street. Although the parish financially supported the school, the pastor during the 1930s, Father F. Poitras, not only wanted more instruction in the French language but attempted to lessen the financial burden on the parish by suggesting that the Loretto Sisters, who had staffed the school since its inception, accept a lesser remuneration.[56] This they refused to do. Although they had significant support among the Roman Catholics of Sioux Lookout no amount of convincing could keep them in the community under trying conditions. The Superior General of the congregation explained the situation this way:[57]

> We have the impression that the present pastor at Sioux Lookout is not satisfied with the efforts of the nuns who are there. They are doing their best...and following in the footsteps of the members of the community who preceded them in the same school...It was on the very urgent request of one of the former pastors that we undertook the school at Sioux Lookout and until now it has been most encouraging to feel that we were privileged to teach religion in a region where it was so much needed...It would hardly be for God's honour and glory to continue our work there under present conditions.

Under difficult circumstances, Archbishop Emile Yelle of St Boniface was able to obtain the services of the School Sisters of Notre Dame to staff the school after the departure of the Loretto Sisters in 1939. Neither the pastors at Sacred Heart Parish nor the Archbishop of the St Boniface Diocese were able to provide religious services on a frequent and regular basis to the missions attached to Sioux Lookout or the lumber camps that had emerged in the area. To travel to Ignace, 145 km away on a regular basis required an automobile and all the time and expense that came with it. The lumber camps in the vicinity of Sioux Lookout, however, were in a different category. In the late 1940s The Great Lakes Paper Company, headquartered in Fort William, operated lumber camps at Valora. Working in the camps were a significant group of devout Lithuanian Roman Catholics who requested, through Great Lakes Paper personnel, to have mass celebrated at Valora on a regular basis.[58] Great Lakes Paper was prepared to pay for the transportation of the priest to and from Valora and for his upkeep while at the camps. Even under these circumstances, the pastor from Sacred Heart Church in Sioux Lookout could only manage to visit Valora twice during a six month period in 1947. Clearly, the Sioux Lookout parish and surrounding missions and lumber camps demanded the attention of an energetic pastor.

The Archbishop of St Boniface managed to fill this void temporarily by attracting the Consolata Missionaries to Sioux Lookout.[59] The Consolata Missionaries' Institute, founded at Turin, Italy in 1901 by Blessed Joseph Allamano, was dedicated to serving all missions around the world.[60] Sacred Heart Parish was the first they served in Canada when Father Luigi Amadio, (b. 1916) i.m.c. was appointed pastor in 1948.[61] He immediately impressed Archbishop Cabana and later, Bishop Jennings of Fort William, with his hard work and efficiency. In the space of three years, he made significant renovations to the parish church and, at the request of his bishop, helped organize a chapter of the Catholic Women's League in the town.[62] Above all, during his seven years at Sacred Heart Parish he provided regular religious services which were often neglected by his predecessor. The isolation of Father Amadio from other members of his congregation and the isolation of being in Sioux Lookout for seven years prompted his departure and the returning of the parish back to the Fort William Diocese.[63] Father Amadio had occasional assistance from one of his confreres but most of the time he was alone. Travelling to Hudson 25 km away and to Ignace, in addition to providing services for American servicemen stationed at the radar scanning station on the outskirts of Sioux Lookout had become burdensome. In 1955, the Consolata Missionaries had more commitments than their complement of priests in Canada could handle. Few, if any, would be coming from Italy to support their missionary work in North America.[64] Father Amadio remained in Sioux Lookout long enough (September 1955) to give Bishop Jennings an opportunity to find a replacement.

The Bishop of Fort William appealed to the Oblates, St Peter Province, Ottawa to assume responsibility for the 1196 Roman Catholics in Sioux Lookout and associated missions.[65] They agreed and in 1956 assigned two of their most capable and dedicated priests to Sacred Heart Parish.[66] Prior to their arrival Bishop Jennings wanted to formally erect the Sacred Heart Parish in Sioux Lookout and establish its boundaries since this was not done previously by the Archbishop of St Boniface.[67] Sacred Heart Parish, canonically erected on 25 April 1955, covered an area of 3200 sq. km with a widely dispersed population and united physically by the C.N.R., C.P.R. and Trans Canada Highway passing through it on which were situated the various communities to be served by the Oblates. Along the southern boundary of the parish (C.P.R. and Trans Canada Highway) was English River, Ignace, and Dinorwic; along the C.N.R. line was Fowler, Robinson, Superior Junction, Sioux Lookout and Richan. Sacred Heart Parish became the norm for those

Sacred Heart Roman Catholic Church, 20 May 2002
128 King Street
Sioux Lookout, Ontario.

Construction began on this church in May 1968. The first mass was celebrated in the new Sacred Heart Church on Holy Thursday, 3 April 1969. On 21 September 1969 it was dedicated by the Most Reverend E. Q. Jennings. This was the first of several newly constructed churches in the diocese accessible at ground level.

**Interior of Sacred Heart Church, Sioux Lookout, 20 May 2002**
This church was the first "second generation" church in the diocese to reflect the ideals of Vatican II where seating arrangements for the laity surround the sanctuary. The transition between the nave of the church and the sanctuary is virtually seamless.

created in northwestern Ontario during the 1950s. The parish church was situated in the most populated community within its territorial limits. The pastor(s) used the parish church as a base from which to serve smaller communities 20 to 200 km away. It was this kind of parish that was confided to Father Denis Shea, o.m.i. and the Oblates in August, 1955. As pastor, Father Shea assumed an aggressive and enthusiastic style to the liturgy and parish administration. He instituted a weekly Wednesday evening mass to accommodate a significant segment of Sioux Lookout's Roman Catholic population on shiftwork.[68] Two masses were celebrated each Sunday. The regularity of this mass schedule resulted in a significant increase in attendance and in those receiving the sacraments. Frequently, both Sunday masses were so well attended that some people had to stand outside the church doors. While he looked after Sunday masses at Sacred Heart Church, his associate, Father Brennan travelled to Hudson on alternate Sundays and in the afternoons on these Sundays to Wabigoon where mass was celebrated for a handful of Roman Catholics in the community hall. In Ignace, 145 km south of Sioux Lookout, Father Brennan drew on all his human and spiritual resources to bring increasing numbers of the eighty Roman Catholic families to Sunday masses celebrated on the first and third Sundays of each month.

The success of the Oblate priests in Sioux Lookout manifested itself in plans to build a new church in 1963. In that year, property on King Street was acquired, fund-raising began in 1965 and by October 1967 the parish had engaged the services of an architect to design a church that would accommodate 400 people and meet all requirements of the new liturgy that emanated from Vatican II.[69] The promise of a new church energized and united all members of the Sacred Heart Parish in the two years preceding its official opening and dedication by Bishop Jennings on Sunday, 21 September 1969.[70] Interestingly, this was one of Bishop Jennings last official acts during his tenure as Bishop of Thunder Bay. Sacred Heart Parish at Sioux Lookout was to become an anchor for the Roman Catholic Church in the northerly reaches of the Thunder Bay Diocese.

Just as the Oblate Fathers in Sioux Lookout were about to launch a fund-raising campaign for a new church, Bishop Jennings prevailed upon their goodwill yet again to assume responsibility for St Agnes Parish in Fort William, the second largest in the city.[71] "Our manpower is habitually inadequate" wrote Bishop Jennings to the Oblate Provincial. At St Agnes, Monsignor A. J. Hogan retired in July 1965 after thirty years as pastor.[72] The Oblates graciously accepted and sent Father John Davis, o.m.i. as pastor, and Fathers Wilfred Mally, o.m.i. and Edward MacNeil, o.m.i. as assistant pastors. Thus began a thirty year tenure for the Oblates (St Peter's Province) at St Agnes Parish.

Father Davis inherited a near ideal parish. It was comprised of 1100 families residing mainly in the Westfort area of Thunder Bay. He was gratified with the parishioners' devotion to the Eucharist which he attributed to the spiritual leadership given by Monsignor Hogan over the years.[73] In addition, over a five year period beginning in 1965 the parish averaged 112 baptisms and 35 marriages per year. Moreover, the priests were regularly involved with thriving parish organizations such as The Catholic Women's League, senior and junior youth clubs and the Legion of Mary. On a regular basis they visited the three separate schools within the boundaries of the parish - St Martin, St Mark and St Anne. In 1969, the parish was without debt. This permitted funds to be set aside for the construction of a new parish church to replace the existing one built in 1914 which suffered from serious structural weaknesses. The launching of this project came a decade later and it was the Oblates who guided St Agnes parishioners in its realization.

## *St Joseph Parish, Dryden*

St Joseph Parish in Dryden was unique among those emerging in the western portion of the diocese. At no point in its early history was it directed by a religious congregation of priests. Instead, diocesan priests, together with a core of selflessly devoted Roman Catholic families, brought the parish through the trying years of the 1930s and 1940s to a point in 1952 when it was well on its way to taking its place among the major parishes within the Diocese of Thunder Bay. Like Sacred Heart Parish in Sioux Lookout, it had the advantage of developing in a town with a stable economy driven by the pulp and paper industry.[74]

Dryden is situated on the C.P.R. line and on the Trans Canada Highway 360 km west of Thunder Bay and 140 km east of Kenora. With a population of approximately 1190 in 1921 its early religious make-up was predominantly Protestant. By the mid-1920s, the Methodists and Presbyterians had firmly established a presence in the town with churches on the corner of Princess and Van Horne Streets. It was from the Methodist congregation that Father Cornelius O'Dwyer, o.m.i, an Oblate missionary from Notre Dame du Portage Parish in Kenora, purchased a modest wooden structure as a place of worship.[75] When

St Joseph Roman Catholic Church, 21 May 2002
96 Van Horne Avenue
Dryden, Ontario.

Dryden's first resident priest Father Joseph Bellavance (b. 1907) arrived, he stepped into a sparsely decorated church where the Stations of the Cross were conspicuously absent and the only visible religious icon was a large statue of St Joseph positioned beside the alter at the front of the church.[76] He celebrated his first mass in St Joseph's Church on Sunday, 12 July 1925 assisted by a few members of the congregation. Of the thirty-five Catholic families identified in Dryden in 1925, Father Bellavance felt that he could count on fifteen for financial support.[77] He began the well-established practices in Roman Catholic missions and parishes of celebrating mass on Sundays and weekday mornings, of having benediction and reciting the Holy Rosary on Sunday evenings and, from time to time, administering the sacraments of baptism and marriage. He was acutely aware of his isolation in Dryden with Kenora as the closest town 133 km to the west. This feeling of isolation and of existing on the frontier of the Roman Catholic world was further accentuated every fortnight when he, together with a devoted Dryden parishioner, Jack Skillen, travelled to Ignace (100 km by train and 115 km by road east) only to be met with indifference. This indifference perhaps manifested itself in the meagre Sunday collection in Ignace of $7 - $8 which did not cover his travel expenses from Dryden. In August of 1928 he left Dryden to become the founding pastor in Vassar, Manitoba. His successor, Father Donald McDougall (1908-1965), realized in the 1930s that in order for the Roman Catholics of Dryden to support a resident priest and to maintain a modest church and rectory they would have to depend on the Archdiocese of St Boniface and the Catholic Church Extension Society for limited financial support.[78]

The appointment of Father Marcel Dugal as pastor of St Joseph Parish in 1942 marked a watershed in its history.[79] His previous training and experiences in both business and theology prepared him for pastoral work in Dryden.[80] He first turned his attention to the organization of a Roman Catholic Separate School Board and once the trustees had been elected he was appointed its first secretary-treasurer. In the fall of 1943, St Joseph's Separate School was opened on Arthur Street and a year later the Sisters of St Joseph of Crookston, Minnesota arrived to staff the school.[81]

The construction of a new parish church to replace the original structure did not materialize as easily as Dryden's first separate school. The existing St Joseph's Church was large enough to accommodate Dryden's practising Roman Catholics but too small if the majority of Catholics were to attend mass on a regular basis. Father Dugal's youthful enthusiasm and popularity brought more children and adults to Sunday masses. From 1949 to 1951 his approach to constructing a new church was cautious and financially responsible. Construction materials were purchased and paid for and plans for the new church, with precise cost estimates, were submitted to Bishop Cabana for approval.[82] The beginning of construction coincided with the formation of the Fort William Diocese. In December 1952 Father Dugal celebrated the first mass in the basement of the new church. Two years later, Bishop Jennings blessed the completed and furnished St Joseph's Church at 96 Van Horne Street. From that moment, a strong bond of mutual support developed between St Joseph's Parish in Dryden and the Diocese of Thunder Bay. Under Father Dugal's leadership, the parish enthusiastically supported diocesan fund-raising initiatives as a recompense for the support and encouragement given them by their bishop. "In all my years in the Ministry, Your Excellency", wrote Father Dugal, "you are the first bishop to take the time to write comments on the Annual Reports and you are the first Bishop to offer a generous helping hand to St Joseph Parish, although the parish was established in 1925."[83]

### *Immaculate Conception Parish, Ignace*

Immaculate Conception Parish, Ignace may attribute its birth to the determination and persistence of Bishop Jennings in providing the human and financial resources needed for parish formation. He believed that as the diocese grew so too would Ignace evolve from a mission to a parish.[84] This evolution, however, was slow and arduous. As a mission Ignace was a burden to serve; as a parish its future was always uncertain.

The absence of a viable Roman Catholic culture in Ignace was evident as early as the 1920s and 1930s. A modest wooden frame chapel was situated on the corner of Garden and East Streets beside the Catholic cemetery [85] and given the name Immaculate Conception Church by Father Rudolphe Bélanger, pastor of St Joseph Parish in Dryden, who periodically celebrated mass in Ignace.[86] His predecessor, Father Joseph Bellavance, was astonished by the fractured nature of the early Roman Catholic community in the town. "According to what I can see, there exists an implacable hatred between the people of the country and the "foreigners", observed Father Bellavance on one of his visits to Ignace in the summer of 1925. "There are Slovaks, Italians, Poles, Ruthenians, English and French. There is no common interest in the church. They give as little as possible and do as little as they can."[87] At the request of Father Bélanger, two sisters of the Holy Names of Jesus and Mary came to Ignace during the summer of 1935 to provide religious instruction to 30 children of Roman Catholic families.[88] In this group, the sisters observed that one-third had received some "Catholic formation at home" but only one was able to make the Sign of the Cross and recite the "Our Father" and "Hail Mary." Without a Roman Catholic Separate School and the indifference of most Roman Catholic families in Ignace to their faith,[89] the early formation of Roman Catholics in that community was highly unlikely. Financially, Father Bélanger was prophetic in his belief that the Ignace mission would not likely become self-supporting and repay its indebtedness to the dioceses of which it was a part. Although this statement was made in the context of the depression of the 1930s, better times did not alter its reality. The old adage that the Roman Catholic Church was the church of the poor was no better reflected than in Ignace. Roman Catholic priests visiting the mission during the 1940s soon realized that the Anglicans and Presbyterians "were in a better social condition" than Roman Catholics.[90]

The inability of Ignace Roman Catholics to support a pastor or the isolation of Ignace from other established communities did not deter Bishop Jennings from providing religious services to the town. He could not ignore the appeals of the Ladies of St Teresa and the Catholic Women's League to have mass said in their town at least once a month.[91] At times, six or seven months would elapse without a visit from a Catholic priest. It was the fundraising activities of the Catholic women of Ignace, and not the revenues collected from Sunday collections, that provided the financial means for the upkeep of the parish church and for the beginning of a building fund.[92] Prior to Holy Week of 1957 their fund-raising efforts were reflected in the purchase of new pews for the church and the stations of the cross which Bishop Jennings canonically erected on 13 April.[93] On the strength of this spark of hope, Bishop Jennings explored avenues to provide the seventy-one Roman Catholic families in Ignace (thirty-nine of whom were Italian-speaking) with its first resident priest and pastor.

That priest was Father Bernard Campbell (b.1929). Prior to his arrival in Ignace he had been assistant pastor at St Patrick's Cathedral in Fort William. Initially he had planned to reside in Sioux Lookout and serve Ignace from there. As others before him realized, travelling to Ignace from Sioux Lookout was time-consuming and in winter, often treacherous. In December 1960, Father Campbell wisely decided to take up permanent residence in Ignace and temporarily lived in a local motel and had meals at the homes of various parishioners.[94] From Ignace he planned to serve two logging camps operated by the Great Lakes Paper Company - Valora ( 80Km north) and Graham ( 82 km east) - both with a handful of Roman Catholic families.

Father Campbell's early hope for the development of the Ignace parish soon gave way to disappointment. His main goal was to lead the Roman Catholic families of Ignace in the construction of a new rectory and church. After two years he concluded that the struggle would "be long and difficult."[95] Sunday collections were dismal. The majority of parishioners worked for the Canadian Pacific Railway and the uncertainty of their employment due to layoffs or lost jobs made them understandably reticent to contribute even a small portion of their disposable income to the church.[96] During the summer months the Ignace-Upsala region attracted hundreds of American tourists many of whom attended Sunday mass at the Immaculate Conception Church. Although its worn appearance and meagre furnishings might have encouraged them to be generous in their offerings, Father Campbell was disappointed that this was not so.[97] In the long term, however, it was the revenues generated from the

American tourists that contributed to the up-keep of the Ignace church.

During the 1960s the Roman Catholics of Ignace did not have the means to construct a new church or to support a priest. It became painfully clear that funds for a new rectory and church were to come from special fund-raising projects undertaken by a minority of parishioners and from the Diocese of Thunder Bay. To afford the purchase of a lot on which to build a pre-fabricated rectory and to eventually build a new church, the parish accumulated funds through the cutting and sale of pulpwood to the Dryden paper mill, through loans from the Diocese and bank, and through grants given by the Catholic Church Extension Society.[98] All of this permitted the parish to construct a crypt church in November 1966. "We have moved into the new church basement on Sunday and offered our first masses there", wrote Father Campbell enthusiastically to Bishop Jennings, "a joyful day for our little group who have made near-heroic sacrifices over the past three years to make this event a reality. The main thing is that the church is now finished to a point where we can make full use of it, and we are proud of it..."[99] By the spring of 1967, with the continued sale of pulpwood to the Dryden mill and an additional grant from the Catholic Church Extension Society the Immaculate Conception Parish was, for the first time in its history, free of debt.

These positive new beginnings belied the uncertain future of the parish. In the late 1960s the C.P.R. closed its roundhouse in Ignace causing a good number of its permanent residents to leave. Bishop Jennings pondered whether an excellent priest like Father Campbell was more urgently needed in the developed areas of the diocese. He asked the Oblate Provincial if Ignace and its mission Upsala might be served once again by their priests in Sioux Lookout 264 km away.[100] "If your Fathers took it over", wrote Bishop Jennings, "I would like it to be still called a parish as I think it rather hurts people to be reduced, as it were, from a parish to a mission." The Oblates' manpower, however, was over-extended as it was with their responsibilities in Sioux Lookout and St Agnes Parish in Thunder Bay. By the fall of 1970 the Anglicans planned to close their Ignace church which had been established in 1912. The Roman Catholic Church was not alone it seemed in experiencing difficulties maintaining a presence in the town. As Father Bernard Campbell was about to leave Ignace to become pastor of Holy Saviour Parish in Marathon, his recommendation was to have the Immaculate Conception Parish served from Dryden on a fortnightly basis and then every Sunday from mid-May to the

Labour Day weekend to accommodate the influx of tourists.[101] As the 1970s began, serving the Roman Catholics of Ignace was not made any easier for the Bishop of Thunder Bay.

## The Red Lake Region

Situated on the southern and eastern extremities of Red Lake, 470 km northwest of Thunder Bay and approximately 150 km due north of Kenora and the Trans Canada Highway are the communities of Red Lake, Madsen, McKenzie Island, Balmertown and Cochenour. Apart from the missions of Pikangikum and North Spirit Lake, together they represent the most northerly reaches of the Thunder Bay Diocese. In 1925 gold was discovered in the region by prospector Lorne Howey. A year later gold rush fever swept over the Red Lake District attracting over 3,000 prospectors to the area. From that time, the Red Lake communities constituted the heartland of Ontario's gold belt and experienced the vicissitudes so characteristic of mining towns. Prior to 1947 they were accessible only by air and water transport. With the construction of Highway 105 in 1947 stretching 176 km north from Vermilion Bay on the Trans Canada Highway, the Red Lake District also emerged as a tourist centre attracting hundreds of anglers and hunters annually. In 1952 the town of Red Lake was the largest of the communities with a population of 2,200 and the only one with a Roman Catholic Church that comfortably seated 70 people.[102] The white wooden 20' x 24' St John The Apostle Church was built by a Jesuit missionary, Father Joseph-Charles Massicotte, s.j. in the summer of 1938 with funds donated by two American tourists visiting Northern Manitoba.[103] Father Massicotte served the people of the Red Lake region until 1942 when he became chaplain at Hospice Taché in St Boniface.

Roman Catholics of the Red Lake District formed the Association of St Francis in 1948 in order to secure a resident priest, to strengthen the bonds of Catholicity between the various communities and to raise funds for the maintenance of St John's Church.[104] As a scattered but growing community, Association members in Balmertown believed that they were "beyond the scope of a mission" and saw a desperate need for parish organization. They also realized that without the presence of a full time pastor many Roman Catholics would cease to practise their faith or would turn to other religious sects established in the area. They witnessed, for example, Catholic parents in Balmertown regularly sending their children to the Pentecostal Sunday

School. What is more, Roman Catholics married and later baptised their children in Protestant churches. "We need a priest", wrote Owen Matthews, a prominent member of the Association of St Francis in Balmertown, "a strong vigorous man, fearless and tireless, one who can stand a lot of defeats, one who can combat lassitude and indifference of the people, one who can withstand the discomforts and hard work which would be his lot in this district, in fact we need a veritable St Paul..."[105]

Owen Matthews was not overstating the challenge that the Red Lake communities would present to any priest. Nor were his expectations typical of Roman Catholics in the area. Father Ladislas Frytek, o.f.m. (b. 1915) a Franciscan missionary who served the white population of the Red Lake District from 1946–1953 observed "that the zeal of the few" far exceeded the indifference of the many.[106] His experiences reveal the scope of activities and responsibilities that came with being an itinerant priest visiting northern Ontario mining towns in the early 1950s.[107] Until 1951, he flew out of Winnipeg in a converted R.C.A.F. transport plane to Bissett, Manitoba, a gold-mining town 140 km due west of Red Lake. He divided his time - not always equally - between Bissett and the Red Lake District. During his two-week forays into Red Lake he celebrated three Sunday Masses - one in each of the communities of Red Lake, Cochenour and Balmertown.[108] Although the church in Red Lake was small it was not too small to accommodate those from the town wanting to attend Sunday mass. Father Frytek viewed St John's Church as a "mother's" church since it helped give birth to the Indian Church in Red Lake served by the Oblate missionary Eucharistie Benoit, o.m.i. and the Greek Catholic Church served by Father Figo.[109] In Cochenour and Balmertown services were held in private residences, halls or any convenient place where people could gather. In Balmertown he saw great potential for church construction since the President of the New Dickenson Mine was a Roman Catholic[110]. On weekdays, he travelled by boat or automobile to the various mine sites at Mackenzie Island and Madsen and visited the men in the bunkhouses. Because he was fluent in Polish, French and English he heard confessions and celebrated mass for the benefit of immigrant miners and their families. Moreover, he had the time and inclination to make physical improvements and to do repair work around St John's Church. With the help of parishioners, he made benches to replace chairs in the church, built a room in the church basement which served as a kitchen and bedroom and cleared the land of trees around the church to make way for a road and parking lot.[111] He was a man of boundless energy it seemed. Those who knew

Father Frytek had respect for his "deep faith" and for his warm and approachable personality.[112] Yet, some felt that the responsibility of ministering to the scattered Roman Catholic community in Red Lake was beyond the capabilities of an itinerant missionary priest. Just as the Franciscans gave up their service to Bissett which permitted Father Frytek to spend more time in Red Lake, he was transferred to Trail, B.C.[113]

Father Frytek's departure prompted Bishop Jennings to appeal to The Missionaries of Our Lady of La Salette to accept responsibility for the Red Lake District parishes. This order of missionary priests was founded in 1852 at Grenoble, France by Philibert de Bruillard, Bishop of Grenoble.[114] They did not establish a presence in the United States until 1893 but by the middle of the twentieth century their seminaries in Olivet, Illinois and later, Milwaukee Wisconsin, were graduating talented multi-lingual priests of Polish extraction. Father Benoit, o.m.i. was familiar with this congregation of missionaries and believed that because many of them studied in Rome they had an intimate knowledge of the European mentality.[115] Their response to Bishop Jennings' request was positive and immediate.[116] A prominent member of their congregation, Father John Zimmerman, m.s. (1890–1978), arrived in Red Lake on Friday, 9 October 1953 and became its first Roman Catholic canonical pastor.[117] He was German born but took his early theological training in Tournai, Belgium. Prior to World War I he studied at the Gregorian University in Rome and during the war continued these studies in Innsbruck, Austria where he received his doctorate in theology. Immediately after his ordination on 26 June 1917 he served in Germany and Italy until 1922 when he left for Saskatchewan where he ministered to a community of German-speaking Catholics. Prior to his posting in Red Lake he was Professor of Theology at the La Salette Seminary in Milwaukee. Father Zimmerman was highly valued as a pastor in both Canada and the United States because of his boundless energy, his deep commitment to the spiritual development of the people he served, and above all, for his remarkable fluency in German, French, Italian, Polish, and English. Needless to say, Bishop Jennings was relieved to know that the spiritual needs of Roman Catholics in the Red Lake District were in capable hands and that the Red Lake parish would experience "progress and development".[118]

There was little semblance of parish life in Red Lake when the diminutive Father Zimmerman arrived. The absence of account and announcement books, sacramental records and the transient nature of the population made the iden-

St John The Apostle Roman Catholic Church, Red Lake, Ontario. c. 1960
(Courtesy St John The Apostle Parish, Red Lake.)

tification of parishioners difficult.[119] Both Father Frytek and Father Zimmerman were astounded by the constant movement of single immigrant males in and out of the Red Lake District.[120] During the winter of 1953, he carefully took stock of the number of Roman Catholic families as he travelled through the district and discovered seventy-eight Polish, fifteen German and twelve Italian families. The women of these families (and the most faithful church-goers) spoke little or no English.[121] At 64, Father Zimmerman began the daunting task of developing a parish community in Red Lake. He appealed to Bishop Jennings to visit the area hoping that his presence would engender a spirit of unity and purpose among the Roman Catholic community.

Meanwhile, small steps were taken toward parish formation. A Catholic Women's League and a fund-raising committee were in the process of formation to assist in providing funds needed to construct a new church rectory. Prior to Holy Week of 1954, Father Zimmerman initiated a forty hour devotion service that ended the Saturday before Palm Sunday. He observed that a good number of Red Lake Roman Catholics who had not made their Easter Duty for over a decade did so in 1954.[122] Attendance at Sunday masses and holy days of obligation was increased by the introduction of an 8:30 P.M. evening mass. And, to Father Zimmerman's delight, three Protestant Lutherans, formerly of Germany, were taking religious instruction from him in preparation for their conversion to Roman Catholicism.[123] In July, construction had begun on the new rectory in time to provide suitable living quarters for Father Zimmerman and his young assistant from the La Salette congregation, Father Francis Kula, m.s.[124] Bishop Jennings made his long awaited visit to Red Lake in October where he confirmed 34, donated $500 on behalf of the diocese to St John Parish to offset costs for the new rectory and encouraged parishioners to organize a building committee to renovate their parish church.

While Fathers Zimmerman and Kula were struggling to develop a parish in Red Lake there was considerable pressure from the mining companies and from Bishop Jennings himself to build a new church and to erect a separate parish in Balmertown, 11 km east of Red Lake. It was tempting for Father Zimmerman to divert his valuable energies in Balmertown(the townsite for the Campbell and New Dickenson Mines) where he sensed a stronger commitment among Roman Catholics to their faith and a willingness of the mining companies to contribute generously to the construction of a new church and rectory. In 1955, a new church, St Francis Xavier, was built by the Roman Catholic community in Balmertown.[125] and blessed by Bishop Jennings on Sunday, 9 September 1956.[126] This would have been a more comfortable and convenient base for Father Zimmerman's ministry. But Red Lake, not Balmertown, was the centre of the district. He cautioned his bishop not to elevate Balmertown to the status of a parish prematurely. "The interdependence of Red Lake-Balmertown" wrote Father Zimmerman, "is still and will be for the immediate future rather beneficial than obstructive."[127] To develop the physical structures so necessary to parish life required the financial support and cooperation of all communities in the Red Lake area. Father Zimmerman argued that as soon as Balmertown became independent from Red Lake Balmertown's financial support for other projects in the district would not be forthcoming.

The parish-mission relationship between Red Lake and Balmertown, however, was short- lived. In the space of four years Father Leonard Karpinsky, m.s. of the the La Salette Congregation came to Balmertown as administrator of St Francis Xavier Church and by the spring of 1963 Bishop Jennings had canonically erected a new parish in Balmertown. "It is a great satisfaction that Balmertown has become a parish in the name of St Francis Xavier", wrote

St Francis Xavier Roman Catholic Church, 22 May 2002.
200 Dexter Road
Balmertown, Ontario.

Bishop Jennings, "and that with your work in the parish as administrator it has made such good progress in organization and in services to the people. It is a further satisfaction that you have your church and that it is paid for. Now as it becomes necessary that the priest spend more time in Balmertown looking after the affairs of the parish, there should be a good rectory, separate from the church...My wholehearted approval is given for such a project, and I trust it can be started no later than in 1964."[128]

During the 1960s the parishes of St Francis Xavier, Balmertown and St John's, Red Lake developed along different lines owing to their boundaries, the economies of the towns in which they were situated, and the nature and temperament of their parishioners. St Francis Xavier's boundaries were restricted to the Improvement District of Balmertown as well as Cochenour, 5 km north of Balmertown. The boundaries of St John's coincided with the Township of Red Lake with missions in Madsen, Mackenzie Island and Ear Falls, approximately 68 km south-east of Red Lake.[129] The population of Balmertown was heterogenous but relatively stable compared to the ever changing and fluctuating immigrant population of Red Lake.

St Theresa Roman Catholic Church, 22 May 2002.
Ear Falls, Ontario.
The first mass celebrated in the Ear Falls Chapel was on 11 August 1963 and it was blessed by Bishop E.Q. Jennings in May 1964.

Red Lake's numerically unstable cosmopolitan population made every aspect of pastoral work trying. The parish reports prepared by Father Zimmerman for St John's Parish provided Bishop Jennings with the insightful comments and frustrations of a pastor attempting to cope with a northern area of the diocese where "almost all nations of Europe" were represented.[130] His belief that a parish priest speak the language(s) of the people "to bring them to church and to the sacraments" was an unattainable goal in Red Lake for even a talented linguist like Father Zimmerman who spent countless hours preparing sermons in Polish, Italian and German. In the late 1950s significant numbers of Hungarians and Portuguese moved into Red Lake and Father Zimmerman expressed a deep sense of regret at not being able to reach these people. What is more, the remarkable fluency of Fathers Zimmerman and Kula in several languages spoken by their parishioners did not increase attendance from these groups beyond the most devout; most attended mass three times a year - at Christmas, Easter and the Feast of Corpus Christi.[131]

An unstable population coupled with the volatile nature of the gold-mining industry made the economic viability of the Red Lake parish and associated missions tenuous. Frequently, St John's Parish was unable to make its cathedraticum obligations to the diocese. The envelope system for Sunday collections instituted by Father Zimmerman in 1955 introduced some financial stability. As new immigrant families or single men moved through the parish on a yearly basis, however, the practice of making a financial contribution to support their pastor, the separate school or their bishop was rarely foremost in their minds.[132] "The Italians", wrote Father Zimmerman, "think that the Holy Father is rich enough to pay the salary of the bishops." When Bishop Jennings suggested in the mid-1960s that a larger and more comfortable church be built in Red Lake, Father Zimmerman and his parishioners were hesitant.[133] They looked woefully at the declining population of their town and the movement of the "best families" into Balmertown. To build a new church only to see it remain half empty had no appeal for Father Zimmerman or his parishioners. Bishop Jennings agreed that a new St John's Church would have to wait for better times.

### *Our Lady Queen of Poland Parish, Thunder Bay*

As the Missionary Fathers of La Salette were developing parishes in Red Lake and Balmertown, they also took charge of the newly established "Our Lady Queen of Poland" Parish, Port Arthur, Ontario in December 1955.[134] Father Peter Jaworski, m.s., a former provincial of the congregation, came to Port Arthur to lead approximately 827 Polish-speaking people (approximately 216 families) in parish formation and in the construction of their parish church.[135] Fund-raising and actual church construction was ten years in the making. Meanwhile, services were held at the Branch 19, Polish Alliance of Canada Hall.

Prior to the establishment of Our Lady Queen of Poland Parish, the Polish Catholics of Port Arthur were members of St Andrew's, St Anthony's or Corpus Christi parishes. Several Port Arthur Polish families made the long trek each Sunday to attend mass at St Casimir's (Polish) Church in Fort William's East End. It took time for these families to switch their loyalties to the newly emergent Polish parish in Port Arthur. When they did, they discovered some tension between the parish building committee and the pastor over whose responsibility it was to lead the congregation in fund-raising and church construction. Father Jaworski lamented to Bishop Jennings in 1958, for example, that all finances for the building campaign were in the hands of

St Mary Our Lady Queen of Poland Church, 24 July 2002.
93 Algoma Street North, Thunder Bay, Ontario.

the parish committee. This was reminiscent of the Holy Rosary Parish affair in Fort William during the 1920s and 1930s. The significant difference thirty years later in Port Arthur was that Bishop Jennings was ever present to interpret and present the universally accepted canonical relationship that had to exist between a pastor and parishioners and between a parish and the diocese of which it was a part. Father Jaworski's death in 1959 and the appointment of Father Joseph Ferus, m.s. as his successor gave Bishop Jennings an opportunity to do this.[136] As the Bishop's representative among the Polish Catholics of Port Arthur, Father Ferus, in consultation with the parish committee, would submit recommendations relating to the construction of the parish church to the Bishop for approval. To avoid misunderstandings that had erupted among the Polish Roman Catholics of Fort William and the Bishop of Sault Ste. Marie in 1932 over the ownership of church property, Bishop Jennings gently reminded Our Lady Queen of Poland parishioners that in Canada "church properties are acquired and held in the name of the diocese...What belongs to the parish belongs to the diocese."

More significant than the explanation of the legal relationship between a parish and a diocese was his eloquent credo as to why Our Lady Queen of Poland Parish was erected. To quote Bishop Jennings:

> It is my first wish that the beloved Polish people of Port Arthur should be all good Catholics; faithful to the proper worship of God, our Creator; faithful to participation in the Holy Sacrifice of the Mass; faithful to the reception of the Sacraments, without which we cannot have the life of God in our souls; faithful to prayer; and obedient to the commandments of God and His Holy Catholic Church...It is also my fervent wish that your parish should make the proper material progress, that it may soon succeed in providing itself with the building developments which are suitable to Divine worship, to the priestly work and priestly dignity of your pastor, to your own convenience and comfort in the practice of the Faith, and to the Christian education of your beloved children...

To assist in the realization of this vision for Port Arthur's Polish parish, Bishop Jennings made an unprecedented commitment that the Bishop of Thunder Bay would in perpetuity confide Our Lady Queen of Poland Parish to "priests of Polish ethnic origin and language."[137] Within five years of this pronouncement, through normal Sunday collections, regular bingos, special fund-raising projects and a significant bank loan, construction was completed on Our Lady Queen of Poland Church at 93 N. Algoma Street.[138] It was officially dedicated by Bishop E.Q. Jennings on Sunday, 22 August 1965 in time to com-

**Corpus Christi Roman Catholic Church, 1 June 2002.**
664 Red River Road, Thunder Bay, Ontario.

memorate the first millennium of the Polish nation (966 - 1966).

How had the Roman Catholic culture and presence in the vast area between Thunder Bay and the Lake of the Woods District changed after seventeen years as part of the new Diocese of Thunder Bay? First, parishes had been created in Red Lake, Balmertown, Sioux Lookout, Atikokan and Ignace where they did not exist before. The boundaries of each parish were clearly demarcated and encompassed vast areas. Each was responsible for several missions. If there was any one region that cast the Thunder Bay Diocese in the mould of "a mission diocese" it was the area between Thunder Bay and Lake of the Woods. Apart from Dryden and Ignace, it was the religious orders of priests that brought life to these parishes. In addition to the Jesuits who had served St Andrew's Parish in Port Arthur since its inception in 1882, The Missionaries of La Salette, The Scalabrinians, and the Missionary Oblates of Mary Immaculate (St Peter's Province) were securely woven into the fabric of the Thunder Bay Diocese. Their pastoral work in and outside of Thunder Bay significantly enhanced its unity and identity. With parish formation in this region also came the establishment of catholic education. It was the pastors of parishes in Atikokan, Dryden, Sioux Lookout and Red Lake for example, that took the initiative in establishing Roman Catholic

Our Lady of Loretto Roman Catholic Church. 21 June 2002
290 Grenville Avenue, Thunder Bay, Ontario.

Separate Schools in these towns. The future of each parish was fundamentally tied to the presence of separate schools in the area.

## *New Parishes in and east of Thunder Bay*

In contrast to the difficulties associated with the creation of Port Arthur's Mary Queen of Poland Parish and others in the small towns of northwestern Ontario, those that emerged in Thunder Bay and in the eastern portion of the diocese did so with relative ease. In response to the growing Roman Catholic population at the Lakehead after 1945, Bishop Dignan of Sault Ste. Marie canonically erected three new parishes just prior to the creation of the Fort William Diocese, namely, Corpus Christi and Our Lady of Loretto in Port Arthur (1950) and St Elizabeth in Fort William (1951).[139] The two new Port Arthur parishes were to alleviate the congestion at St Andrew's caused by a larger than capacity congregation consisting of approximately 850 families (4000 parishioners). Corpus Christi parish church and rectory were constructed in 1951 on Red River Road, 4 km west of St Andrew's. Once officially opened in January 1952 with its first pastor, Father Regis St James

St Margaret Roman Catholic Church, 31 July 2002.
88 Clayte Street, Thunder Bay, Ontario.

(1911-1976), it was to serve Catholics in one of the finest residential districts of Port Arthur.

The formation of Our Lady of Loretto Parish in the Current River area of Port Arthur took place over a longer period of time than that of Corpus Christi. It had its origins in the mid-1930s when a Jesuit missionary Alexander Macdonald, s.j. based at St Andrew's rectory, had a vision of creating a small church and a separate school in the area.[140] He recognized the head start made by the Protestants of Current River who already had a church with a resident minister "who proselytize[d] and use[d] every resource to win over our people, especially the children..." On behalf of the Sault Ste. Marie Diocese Father Macdonald purchased a Croatian Hall in 1937 and set about to convert it into a chapel.[141] The Jesuits realized that during the Great Depression, the Roman Catholics of Current River could not support a priest or build a church. At the time, the struggling ethnic Roman Catholic community was largely comprised of Ukrainians, Greek Catholics, Croatians, French, and Polish whose combined Sunday offering amounted to a little over $2.75.[142] By 1950, the population of Current River had grown significantly as major industries located near the area such as the Port Arthur Shipbuilding

Company, the Provincial and Abitibi paper mills and the grain elevators had reached peak employment levels. When Our Lady of Loretto Parish Church was constructed in 1954 it, like Corpus Christi, served a segment of Port Arthur's Roman Catholic population that previously attended St Andrew's.

St Margaret's was the third parish to be created in response to the needs of a growing population in the residential area of Brent Park in Port Arthur and as a relief to the increasing demands placed on St Andrew's church. The construction and opening of St Margaret's Roman Catholic School on Clayte Street in 1954 prompted Bishop Jennings to investigate the purchase of property owned by the Sisters of St Joseph adjacent to the school. "It would make another very fine little Catholic corner of Port Arthur" wrote Bishop Jennings "considering that there is such a splendid school already there."[143] The Fort William Diocese purchased one acre across from the school and, until a church could be built on the property, Sunday and some week-day masses and services, conducted by the Jesuits at St Andrew's, were held at St Margaret's School. In March 1957 Bishop Jennings blessed and dedicated a new church on the property to be known as St Margaret's chapel-of-ease "to provide a convenient centre of worship for the more distant members of the already larger than capacity congregation of St Andrew's."[144] Four years later, the chapel-of-ease was elevated to the status of a full-fledged parish with Father J.E. Roenicke as its first pastor.[145]

In Fort William, the growing parishes of St Patrick in central Fort William and St Agnes in Westfort William made the creation of a third territorial, English parish necessary.[146] St Elizabeth Parish (originally named Holy Ghost Parish) was formally erected on 2 May 1951 with the financial support of and in consultation with its two "mother" parishes. Prior to the formation of the Fort William Diocese the parish had been confided to Father Reginald A. Carroll (1918-1995), the property on which to construct the parish church on the corner of Sprague Street and Empire Avenue had been purchased, its boundaries had been established and construction on the church had begun. While construction was in progress, Father Carroll celebrated mass for the approximately 175 parish families in the newly constructed St Elizabeth school auditorium. He believed that the presence of the school would keep and attract Catholic families into the area.[147] By December 1952, when church construction had been completed, the number of young families with school-age children in the parish had risen to 225. When the spiritual and temporal dimensions of parish life are united in the common cause of liquidating the debt from

St Elizabeth Roman Catholic Church, 23 July 2002
766 Sprague Street, Thunder Bay, Ontario.

Annunciation of the Blessed Virgin Mary Parish Church 23 July 2002
Second Street, Nipigon, Ontario.

St Hilary Roman Catholic Church, 23 July 2002
Red Rock, Ontario.

**Holy Saviour Parish Church, 14 September 1999**
17 Stevens Avenue, Marathon, Ontario.

the construction of a new church, the resulting parish community that develops could not be more gratifying to the pastor and parishioners. This was part of St Elizabeth's parish experience for over fifteen years.

Parishes along the north shore of Lake Superior east of Thunder Bay emerged during the 1940s and 1950s as employment opportunities were provided by the national railways, hydroelectric power developments and the pulp and paper industry. For example, the Annunciation of the Blessed Virgin Mary Parish in Nipigon (110 km east of Thunder Bay) was erected by Bishop R.H. Dignan of Sault Ste. Marie on 19 June 1936 with Rev. John M. Leacy, former curate at Christ the King Church in Sudbury, as its first pastor.[148] Previously, the Roman Catholics of the town had gathered in a small church capable of seating 50 people to hear mass every third week celebrated by a Jesuit missionary based at St Andrew's Parish in Port Arthur. After the Second World War construction began on a major hydroelectric generating station

St Martin of Tours Parish Church, 14 September 1999.
110 Laurier Avenue, Terrace Bay.

Holy Angels Parish Church, 14 September 1999.
103 Superior Street, Schreiber.

(Pine Portage) on the Nipigon River to complement two that had already been built in 1920 (Cameron Falls) and 1930 (Alexander Dam). The town of Nipigon and the Annunciation Parish both grew resulting in the construction of a new Church of the Annunciation with attached "modern" living quarters for its parish priest, Father James J. Muldoon (1916-1997), in March 1949.[149] Each Sunday, Father Muldoon followed a similar routine to other parish priests outside of Thunder Bay in celebrating three masses (one in Nipigon, one in Red Rock and one in Beardmore) and travelling 201 km (126 miles). Four years later, his task was made a little easier when Bishop Jennings created a new parish in Red Rock (St Hilary) with Father John E. Roenicke (1918-1969) as pastor[150] and by having Jesuit missionary Alexander Rolland, s.j. (1904-1987) and later Father John McHugh, s.j. (1916-1993) temporarily serve the Beardmore mission from Macdiarmid.

The parishes of St Martin of Tours (Terrace Bay) and Holy Saviour (Marathon) were both canonically erected in April 1947[151] and both parishes received significant financial assistance from the pulp and paper companies that developed the town sites. The Longlac Pulp and Paper Company donated $8,500 toward the construction of St Martin of Tours Church which was completed in 1950.[152] Marathon Paper Mills of Canada owned the land on which Holy Saviour Church was built and provided free heat, water and electricity for the church until 1969. Both parishes were sheltered from downturns in the economy of a one industry town.[153]

Most of these emergent parishes in the diocese were eventually supported by subdivisions of the Catholic Women's League. Bishop Jennings recognized the pivotal role this organization had played in the spiritual and economic development of parishes with which he had been associated over the years. Accordingly, he called for the organization and establishment of a Diocesan Council of the C.W.L. In 1952, many parishes in the Fort William Diocese were without an active and established C.W.L. subdivision.[154] He attended all organizational meetings leading up to a convention organized by a C.W.L. organizing committee held in Fort William at the Royal Edward Hotel on 20 and 21 May 1953. Prior to the convention committee members[155] travelled to parishes east and west of Thunder Bay to organize subdivisions where they previously did not exist.[156] By the time the convention opened in Fort William twenty-two C.W.L. subdivisions had been formed. One hundred and thirty-two C.W.L. members from across the diocese attended. The high point of the convention took place on 20 May with the election of officers and their installation by Bishop Jennings.[157] The Diocesan Council of the Catholic Women's League became a significant bond of unity among all parishes in the Thunder Bay Diocese.

## *Bishop's Development Fund and the Quest for an Intercity Catholic High School*

Within five years of his installation, Bishop Jennings took the bold step of launching a diocesan fund-raising campaign. By 1957 the Roman Catholic population of the diocese had increased by 8 per cent and the number of priests serving this population increased by 26 per cent.[158] Thirteen new parish and mission churches had been erected and, through the efforts of separate school boards in northwestern Ontario, eleven new Roman Catholic schools had been built. The economic prosperity and sense of optimism that Canadians enjoyed in 1957 provided the appropriate climate in which to introduce the "Bishop's Development Fund". This fund was to be established through a voluntary subscription campaign organized in every parish of the diocese. The proceeds were to be used to care for the material and spiritual needs of the expanding Roman Catholic population in northwestern Ontario.[159] In a circular letter to parish priests in the diocese Bishop Jennings gave his rationale for the timing and purpose of the campaign.[160] "The financial needs are various", he wrote, "and if these needs are to be met at times when it is most advantageous it is necessary for the diocese to have the funds available for the required purposes."

What then, were the extraordinary needs of the diocese in 1957? Four objectives were set forth in the campaign literature: to construct a central catholic high school and college at the Lakehead for Roman Catholic students in Fort William, Port Arthur, and northwestern Ontario; to construct a new St Patrick's Cathedral; to provide financial assistance for the maintenance and construction of mission and parish churches; and to ensure the future financial viability of the Diocesan Seminary and Infirm Funds. To raise the funds necessary to achieve these goals Bishop Jennings engaged the services of Lawson Associates of New York on 10 May 1957 to direct a fund-raising campaign with the solicitation of pledges to take place in the fall of that year. A committee of prominent Roman Catholic businessmen volunteered in an advisory capacity to oversee fund-raising activities in each parish. Initially, Bishop Jennings envisioned the full participation of every parish since past experience had shown that the non-participation of even one parish would seriously jeopardize the success of the entire campaign. Several parishes postponed building projects or major renovations on their churches until the conclusion of the campaign.[161] Yet, he did exempt others from the campaign that had recently taken on the financial burden of constructing a new parish church or were in the process of doing so. Publicly he set $875,000 as the goal for the campaign; in private he hoped that a little over one million dollars would be raised.[162] At the conclusion of the six week campaign the amount pledged fell significantly short of his public or private expectations. By November 1957, $729,271 was received in pledges which, over a four year period, realized a net amount of $525,033 - 60 per cent of the original target and 50 per cent of what he had hoped for. Bishop Jennings' intent was to allocate portions of this amount to the cathedral, education, infirm and seminary funds and to return $144,385 to the parishes and missions in the diocese.[163]

Of all the projects for which the Bishop's Development Fund was intended to finance the construction of an intercity catholic high school was the most important. Since revenues from the general fund-raising campaign were insufficient to warrant construction in 1961, Bishop Jennings decided to launch yet another diocesan-wide appeal specifically for the high school. The proceeds accruing from this campaign were to be placed in the Lakehead Catholic Education Fund.[164] While the campaign was in progress, he decided to proceed with the planning of the new high school by seeking a staff from among the religious orders of priests in Canada. In all of this, there is no evidence in his correspondence that he consulted with the clergy and women religious of the diocese to arrive at a vision for the proposed new catholic high school or that he invited the opinions of prominent catholic businessmen on its efficacy. Instead, he articulated his vision and then sought their support for and involvement in its realization. A "central committee" for the proposed high school was formed together with several sub- committees designated to oversee such matters as fund-raising, grounds and maintenance and publicity.[165]

The intercity catholic high school was intended to replace St Patrick's Arpin Memorial High School located at the corner of Franklin and Donald Streets in Fort William which had been in operation since 1928. With a maximum capacity of 300, Bishop Jennings argued that the vast majority of students promoted to grade 9 from Roman Catholic elementary schools in Fort William and Port Arthur were denied the opportunity of continuing their catholic education. From 1952 to 1959 the total enrolment in the Fort William and Port Arthur separate schools increased by 70 and 75 per cent respectively. With a realistic 35 to 40 per cent transfer rate from the Thunder Bay separate schools to a Roman Catholic high school the existing facility was inadequate.

The sound academic training received by Arpin Memorial students during the 1940s and 1950s was both a justification for the continuance of the school and a legitimate promotional feature directed at parents to financially contribute to a new and enlarged facility. The Ontario Ministry of Education Inspector's Report of the school in 1960 for example, commented on the remarkable performance of Arpin Memorial students in writing Grade XIII external departmental examinations where out of a total of 139 papers written only 2 were graded as failures.[166] This, according to the ministry inspector, attested "to the quality of the teaching and the good work habits of the students." The same report concluded, however, that the overcrowding of the school and the large class sizes made additional accommodation mandatory.

Notwithstanding the high success rate of Arpin Memorial students on Ontario Grade XIII departmental examinations, it was a common practise throughout the 1950s for their students to leave the school after Grade XII and complete their Secondary School Honour Graduation Diploma (Grade XIII) at a public secondary collegiate institute. Students made this decision partly to take subjects not available at Arpin Memorial and partly because of the perception that instruction at the upper school level in a collegiate institute was superior. By 1961 Arpin Memorial was struggling to continue its Grade XIII program. In June of that year, seven students graduated with their Secondary Honour Graduation Diploma and, with the same number enrolled for the following September, a decision was made to discontinue Grade XIII. Four Sisters of St Joseph (including the principal) were left at St Patrick High School.[167] The principal argued that dropping Grade XIII would allow the remaining women religious on staff to concentrate on providing "a good basic Catholic education" from grades nine to twelve. Dropping Grade XIII was also a matter of finances. Teachers with specialist qualifications to teach upper school subjects were no longer forthcoming from the Sisters of St Joseph congregation. To hire qualified lay teachers was too expensive. Ironically, the school's enrolment reached its highest point in the fall of 1961.[168] Some have argued that eliminating Grade XIII had a negative impact on the school's future enrolment since Roman Catholic families in Fort William came to the conclusion that if their children could not complete their five-year academic program at St Patrick's perhaps it was prudent to have them enter a public secondary school where this was possible.

As a private high school financially supported and administered by St Patrick's Parish Arpin Memorial received no public funding. Teachers' salaries, utilities, maintenance, and administrative costs were paid out of modest student tuition fees, significant subsidization from St Patrick's Parish and, to a lesser extent, from five other parishes in Fort William. Since its student population came exclusively from Fort William, the Port Arthur parishes did not contribute financially to its operation. Throughout the 1950s families of students attending paid $50 per child in tuition. Presumably these fees were collected by the principal and turned over to St Patrick's Parish. Until 1953, the differential between fees collected and operating costs was borne entirely by St Patrick's Parish. Beginning in 1954, this differential widened significantly and it was at this point that the Fort William parishes of St Peter, St Dominic, St Agnes, St Casimir and St Elizabeth began to contribute a fixed amount from their annual revenues to the operation of the high school. In 1961, when Grade XIII was discontinued, its total operating budget was $45,300 of which 51.5 per cent was covered by student fees and 48.5 per cent by parish contributions.[169] As the school entered its fourth decade of operation it was filled to capacity and yet serious financial limitations called into question its ability to offer the wide range of academic, commercial and technical programmes that were quickly becoming the norm in Ontario high schools. This stark reality intensified Bishop Jennings' resolve to provide a new catholic high school for the Lakehead and for the Roman Catholic Diocese of Fort William.

Securing a teaching staff for the proposed intercity Catholic high school was one of Bishop Jennings' first priorities. To Provincials of recognized and established teaching orders of priests - the Resurrectionist Fathers, Basilian Fathers, Jesuits of the Upper Canada Province and the Missionary Oblates of Mary Immaculate, St Peter's Province - he made enthusiastic appeals for their participation in the project. He did this in part by emphasizing its dire need and by articulating his vision of the school hoping perhaps that this would ignite their interest. He emphasized that initially two or three priests from their congregation would be needed to administer the school and to set the highest standards of instruction. To allay any of their concerns about financing, he stressed that all fund-raising for the school's construction and operation would be the responsibility of the Bishop of Fort William. Although his letters were sincere, inviting and flattering, the Ressurectionst, Basilian and Jesuit Fathers could not accept his kind offer. Each year they received more offers from Canadian Bishops to teach in high schools and colleges than they were able to accept.[170] The Oblates, however, gave him a qualified acceptance. Their personnel shortages were no different than those of the Jesuits or Basilians. They staffed St Patrick's College at the University of Ottawa; every high school for which they assumed responsibility meant fewer Oblates for that school and a higher salary bill as more lay teachers were hired.[171] On the other hand, they held the Bishop of Fort William in high esteem.[172] If the Oblate Superior General in Rome approved and if a core staff of no more than three were assigned to the school no sooner than the 1962-1963 academic year, the Oblate Provincial would enter into a contract with the Bishop of Fort William.

Bishop Jennings' plan and vision for the intercity Catholic high school emerged as early as the summer of 1956 in his negotiations with City of Port Arthur officials to purchase a large tract of land on which to build the school.[173] It was later refined in his correspondence and conversations with the Oblates. Unlike Arpin Memorial, the new high school was intended to serve all Roman Catholic students at the Lakehead. In the long term he envisioned a campus consisting of a high school and a college with residence facilities for male and female students drawn primarily from northwestern Ontario.[174] The college, to be built after the high school, would be associated in some way with the neighbouring Lakehead College of Arts, Science and Technology. He believed it was essential to have a highly qualified staff in order that the highest academic standards be established from the outset.[175] Initially, students attending the high school would be taught in coeducational classes but in time Bishop Jennings believed instruction for boys and girls would be in separate classrooms with the boys taught by the Oblates and the girls by the Sisters of St Joseph.[176] Later, he admitted that a lay staff would eventually outnumber the religious.[177] He emphasized that the curriculum of the school should include traditional academic subjects as well as courses in home economics and technical subjects so as to accommodate a broad cross-section of students. The cost of such a school to accommodate 600-700 students was estimated to be $1.2 million.[178] Since the private school would not qualify for government grants, he planned to assess each parish in the diocese on a per family basis annually for financial support. Parish contributions would naturally be augmented by student fees. In 1960, Arpin Memorial raised its student fees from $50 to $75 per year. Notwithstanding this increase, the student enrolment in 1961 increased by 20 per cent. Bishop Jennings concluded from this that student fees in the new high school could be set at a higher rate without being a deterrent to maximum enrolment.

Bishop Jennings' initiative to provide a new catholic high school located in Thunder Bay came at a time when secondary education in Ontario was changing from exclusively academic institutions to inclusive schools providing students with opportunities to pursue purely academic studies as well as programmes in business and technology. As the secondary school population in Ontario grew rapidly in the mid-1950s so did the construction of composite high schools. In Thunder Bay alone six new "composite" high schools were built from 1959 to 1967 to augment two collegiate institutes and two technical high schools. What is more, his vision of the proposed catholic high school was not in tune with the new secondary school curriculum that was emerging in Ontario during the 1960s. Although he wanted course offerings to attract students with wide-ranging abilities, his concept of "composite" was a school with a home economics room and one shop devoted to industrial arts.[179] Public schools had been providing practical instruction in these areas since 1945. Arpin Memorial students routinely walked five blocks south to take these classes at Selkirk High School throughout the 1940s and 1950s.[180] A typical Ontario composite school in 1962 had several technical shops devoted to specialized instruction in auto mechanics, sheet metal, carpentry and electronics. Put simply, Bishop Jennings wanted to broaden the course offerings in the new high school to a level which had been commonplace in the public system for years. He had no intention of embracing the full academic, commercial and technical programmes as set forth in the Robarts Plan. In fact, his vision of a school where boys and girls would be taught in separate classrooms was in keeping with private school education throughout the province. His concept of this school had strains of the new philosophy that was emerging in Ontario and classical private catholic academic education that had a long and distinguished tradition in the province.

By the end of 1962, plans for the intercity catholic high school had progressed well beyond the conceptual stage. In the fall of 1959 thirty-seven acres of land west of Balmoral Street and adjacent to the Lakehead College of Arts, Science and Technology campus had been purchased from the City of Port Arthur by the Diocese of Fort William.[181] A year later, Bishop Jennings engaged the services of Mickelson, Fraser and Haywood architects to prepare conceptual drawings and specifications for the new high school.[182] During 1961 the land site was cleared; sewer, water and electrical services had been brought in; and the pilings were driven for the school's foundations.[183] When the architect's conceptual drawings were completed, the school's interior layout provided for 16 traditional classrooms, 3 laboratories, a shop, home economics room, a library, a cafeteria and a double gymnasium. In addition, the design illustrated a chapel to seat 100 and an auditorium to seat 600. By the end of 1962, $166,625 had been expended on the plans and property for the high school. The Missionary Oblates of Mary Immaculate, St Peter's Province had been given a tour of the site and were waiting to sign a formal contract with the Bishop to assume direction of the new high school.[184]

The major impediment to moving the project to conclusion was the disappointing returns from the fund-raising campaign. Although Bishop Jennings had set 1961 or 1962 as possible target dates for the commencement of construction, the realities of the campaign moved him away from these time lines to others less rigid. Unless $900,000 in cash and pledges was in hand he believed construction could not begin.[185] Proceeds ($187,740) from the high school campaign at the end of 1963 came nowhere near that amount. A national appeal to Canadian corporations failed to show that there was a source of funding outside the Lakehead waiting to be tapped to help support the advancement of catholic education in northwestern Ontario.[186] Funding a private catholic high school was not within the parameters of corporate Canada's giving policy. The reply of Canadian Oil Companies to Bishop Jennings' appeal letter was perhaps typical of most. "It has been our policy...not to make contributions to any one religious organization", wrote the company's president. "We have tried to contribute generously to large hospitals serving the general public and to university drives."[187] The one glimmer of hope was the unequivocal and selfless encouragement given the project by the Port Arthur pastors who, as the following letter suggests, presumed to speak on behalf of their parishioners.[188]

> As Dean of Port Arthur I have checked with the Pastors of St Andrew's, St Margaret's, Our Lady of Loretto, St Anthony's and of course Corpus Christi concerning the 20% you offered to the parishes from the campaign. As a result we unanimously relinquish all claim to any part of the funds for our own use and offer it for the use of the high school.
>
> We would like to report that there is a feeling of deep urgency on the part of the laity, akin to Your own, for the immediate construction of the high school. Much interest was evidenced in the present site and the work accomplished when I invited them to visit and view what has been done by You. We wish to extend our continued support and prayers for the success of this project dear to all hearts.

After seven years of fund-raising for the intercity catholic high school a total of $733,825.89 was raised. Given the escalation of building costs by 1965, this amount was insufficient to permit construction to begin. One can only imagine Bishop Jennings' disappointment in deciding not to proceed with an initiative begun in 1956 for the advancement of catholic education in his diocese. Nowhere in his private correspondence or in the local press is there a formal declaration on his part that he had terminated the project. From those that were associated with him on the project there is the impression that "he was a distant fellow to deal with" and that he kept things to himself. Some used the analogy that the high school project "was like a ship coming around the bend and just sank."[189]

Why did the intercity Catholic high school project fail? Those associated with catholic education in the province of Ontario during the 1960s viewed Bishop Jennings' initiative in this area to be courageous indeed.[190] The financial ramifications of such a project were so daunting that even those most committed to catholic education kept it at arms length. In Thunder Bay, the initial success and future viability of a private catholic high school depended on the continuing support of its parishes. During the 1960s, of the twelve Thunder Bay parishes ten had either established building funds for new churches or had just completed a building programme and were settling heavy debt loads with the Chancery. Even on a command performance at the behest of their bishop it is unlikely that the Thunder Bay parishes had the wherewithal to sustain a higher than ususal financial commitment to a new private catholic high school. The discontinuance of Grade XIII in 1961 at St Patrick Arpin Memorial High School and the gradual but steady decline of its enrolment in the 1960s made it painfully evident that catholic families, particularly in Port Arthur, were content with the education offered by the public high schools. In the final analysis, the failure of the private catholic high school campaign called into question the ability and desire of Thunder Bay's Roman Catholic community to support the extension of catholic education beyond the elementary school level.

In 1967 the existing St Patrick Arpin Memorial High School faced an uncertain future. In addition to a declining student population, the number of Sisters of St Joseph available to staff the school was diminishing with the result that more lay teachers had to be hired thus causing the operating costs to rise. Equally serious was the dilapidated state of the physical plant. Regular maintenance had been delayed for so long that it prompted the principal of

**St Patrick Cathedral Construction, June 1963**
In this photograph workers with Clayton Construction are positioning the pre-fabricated, pre-cast concrete beams in place. Although the design of the beams was done by Standard Pre-Cast Concrete of Toronto, their manufacture was done in Thunder Bay.

**St Patrick Cathedral**
211 S. Archibald Street, Thunder Bay, Ontario.

The Fort William architectural firm of McIntosh & Associates was awarded the commission for the design and construction management of St Patrick Cathedral in the fall of 1961. Clayton Company were the general contractors. Jean-Paul St Jacques was the design architect and project manager. In the 1960s, the exterior of the cathedral was considered modernistic while the interior followed the classic Gothic French cruciform plan. The catheral's shell is of pre-fabricated pre-cast concrete with Manitoba tyndal stone covering the exterior and interior walls. Demolition of the old St Patrick Cathedral took place on 1 October 1962. Construction of the new cathedral (which began in May 1963) took sixteen months to complete. Its seating capacity was between 1500 to 1800 people. The first mass celebrated in the new cathedral took place on 8 September 1964. The construction of the new St Patrick Rectory shown to the left of the cathedral in the above photograph began in November 1961 and was completed by 10 September 1962.

the school in 1967 to conclude that its day-to-day operations were placed in jeopardy.[191] Moreover, there was an urgent need to provide updated facilities such as a gymnasium, cafeteria and student counselling rooms. The soaring operating and maintenance costs coincided with the inability of St Patrick's Parish to be its major financial supporter. When construction of the new cathedral was completed in 1965, the parish faced a debt in excess of $900,000. Bishop Jennings had to make fundamental decisions about the future of the school.

The decisions he made in 1967 dramatically altered the relationship between St Patrick Arpin Memorial High School and St Patrick's Cathedral Parish. Early in that year, he created a seven member advisory St Patrick's High School Board with Rev. J. J. Muldoon as its moderator and administrator of the high school.[192] The purpose of this board was to manage the affairs of the school and, with the approval of the bishop, enter into contracts of employment with teachers.[193] Although the bishop was apprised of the board's deliberations and attended the occasional meeting to address specific issues, he maintained an arms-length approach to its operations. A major decision of the board in 1967 was to plan for the construction of a new gymnasium. In order to qualify for grants from the Ministry of Education, the Fort William Separate School Board would have to own the building.[194] The sale of the school to the Separate School Board was seriously considered by Bishop Jennings during the planning stages for the intercity Catholic high school. In 1959 its sale would have provided added revenue for the new high school project; in 1967 its transfer to the Separate School Board gave it a reprieve from closure.[195] Instruction for Grades IX and X would come under the aegis of the Board and for this they would receive Ministry of Education grants to offset maintenance costs and teachers' salaries. Its sale was accompanied by an arrangement whereby the St Patrick's High School Board would have "a favourable" lease back of the facilities necessary for the operation of Grades XI and XII. The High School Board received an infusion of $50,000 from the Lakehead Catholic Education Fund to carry out improvements to the school and the Board also solicited funds from Thunder Bay parishes for the continued operation of Grades XI and XII.[196] After thirty-nine years, the primary responsibility for St Patrick Arpin Memorial High School shifted from St Patrick Parish to the newly constituted St Patrick High School Board and the Fort William Catholic Separate School Board. It would be left to Bishop Jennings' successor to grapple with the remnants of private catholic secondary educa-

**St Patrick Cathedral Interior, September 1964.**
Although St Patrick Cathedral was constructed during the Vatican II years, its interior was more traditional than theatrical. A granite communion railing separated the nave from the sanctuary. Along the right side of the nave are six side altars and confessionals.
(St Patrick Cathedral Parish Archives)

Not clearly visible in this photograph is seating for parishioners to the extreme right of the sanctuary. To a limited extent the Vatican II concept that the seating of parishioners should surround the sanctuary is evident. The unadorned main altar is positioned so that the celebrant of the mass would not face those in attendance. The materials used in the interior-concrete block, stone, pre-cast concrete enhance the durability and longevity of the church.

**Coat of Arms of the Most Reverend Edward Quentin Jennings, D.D.**

**Right half (left to viewer):** The star, symbol of the Blessed Virgin Mary, Star of the Sea, recalls the Cathedral, dedicated to the Immaculate Conception, in the bishop's native city, Saint John, New Brunswick, and also the Cathedral of the Holy Rosary in the Archdiocese of Vancouver to which the bishop was first appointed as an auxiliary. The shamrock recalls St Patrick, patron of the Cathedral in Fort William. The "Chi-Ro", Greek monogram of Jesus Christ, Saviour, Leader, Teacher. **Left half (right to viewer):** The lily, symbol of St Joseph, patron of the Cathedral in Edmonton, Alberta, to which the bishop was attached when first appointed bishop. Abatros in flight recalls the bishop's service with the Royal Canadian Air Force in World War II. Maple Leaf recalls the bishop's service with the Canadian Expeditionary Force in World War I. **Motto:** Charitas Cum Fide (Charity with Faith) taken from the Epistle of St Paul to the Ephesians, Chapter VI, verse 23.

tion in Thunder Bay.

Bishop Jennings' commendable and courageous quest to establish an intercity Catholic high school died aborning and the fund-raising activities associated with it had long-term implications for the diocese. To the outside observer, the legacy of this fund-raising campaign was a vacant field off Balmoral Avenue and a wariness towards future diocesan fund-raising ventures. The dispersal of funds from the campaigns seemed to be shrouded in secrecy. When school construction on the intercity site failed to materialize, those who contributed at the parish level understandably asked: What happened to the money? No evidence exists in Bishop Jennings' papers that he communicated to pastors or to parishes the amount of money raised from one year to the next or that his plans for the intercity high school had been aborted or that the existing Arpin Memorial High School was facing a financial crisis during the 1960s. What he did leave behind, however, were detailed journals of cash disbursements accruing from the campaigns and of course, the annual Financial Statements of the Roman Catholic Bishop of Fort William. A careful analysis of these documents reveals that all funds raised through the Bishop's Development Fund (1957-1967) and the Lakehead Catholic Education Fund for the Catholic high school were in fact used for this purpose or to support Arpin Memorial High School.[197] In terms of public perception, it was an unfortunate juxtaposition of events that fund-raising for the new Catholic high school and the construction of St Patrick's Cathedral took place during the years 1962-1965. The failure of the one did not have any bearing on the completion of the other.

### *The Second Vatican Council, 1962–1965*

Amid the feverish activity of planning two diocesan fund-raising campaigns and the construction of St Patrick's Cathedral, Bishop Jennings was called upon, with all the bishops of the Roman Catholic Church, to attend the Second Vatican Council (1962-1965). This momentous event in the history of the Roman Catholic Church was the brainchild of Pope John XXIII (1881–1963). He defined its immediate task as renewing (*aggiornamento*) the religious life of the Church and bringing up to date its teaching, discipline, and organization, with the unity of all Christians as the ultimate goal.[198] Initially, neither Pope John XXIII nor the bishops of the church had any idea how long the Second Vatican Council would last. "I presumed", wrote Bishop

Alexander Carter of Sault Ste. Marie, "that we would go to Rome, make some minor modifications to the Pre-Conciliar documents, approve them, then end up in a blaze of glory and come home."[199] As it turned out four fall sessions were held in each year from 1962 to 1965. The documents and decisions emanating from these deliberations were to alter the character and practise of Roman Catholicism for the balance of the twentieth century and beyond.

It is difficult to ascertain the impact of Vatican II's theology and principles on Bishop Jennings' thinking and decisions. The construction of St Patrick's Cathedral in 1963 and 1964 and the activities of the intercity Catholic high school project limited his Vatican Council attendance to the first and last sessions.[200] His leadership and administrative styles were such that his presence in the diocese was mandatory while these two projects were in progress. He did not have a chancellor or auxiliary bishop to assume administrative responsibilities. In fact, he returned to the diocese from Rome in November, 1962 to award the contract for the cathedral's construction.[201] Therefore, his impressions of and insights into some of the most important Vatican Council deliberations were gleaned from official documents and transcripts rather than from the personal interventions of his fellow bishops at the council sessions and the informal commentary and analysis offered by recognized theologians. The tempo of his daily routine during the first session of the Council was so lively that he wished he was a much younger man.[202] In addition to the formal deliberations of the Council held at St Peter's in Rome, he attended some of the Sunday study sessions arranged specifically for Canadian Bishops held in the hall of the Jesuit Gregorian University where lectures were given by leading theologians and Scripture scholars.[203] From these formal and informal meetings, he stood in awe of the cultural diversity of the Roman Catholic Church which manifested itself in the free, open and democratic participation of over 2,500 "conciliar fathers" with voting rights from around the world. The votes that took place on positions initially espoused at Vatican II revealed a profound separation between the majority (1800-1900) who wished to rethink the church's role in the modern world and a minority (300) who wished to maintain the status quo. When the documents were revised, however, they were approved almost unanimously.[204]

Although Bishop Jennings was among those who favoured change there is no evidence to suggest that the spirit of Vatican II dominated his last years as Bishop of Thunder Bay. When he returned from the conclusion of the first session in December of 1962 he did not hold study sessions or meetings with the clergy and laity of the diocese to summarize and interpret the positions and developments of the Second Vatican Council. Rather, in circular letters he guided his clergy through significant changes approved by Canadian Bishops such as the proclaiming of the lessons, epistles and gospels in the vernacular.[205] During this period of self-reflection and momentous change for the Roman Catholic Church, he sided with those of his fellow bishops who advocated patience and prudence to avoid a sometimes clumsy rapidity associated with the implementation of liturgical reforms. He was prepared to wait upon events knowing that the changes heralded by the Second Vatican Council would be implemented over a long period of time and perhaps unevenly from diocese to diocese and from parish to parish.

The establishment of a Diocesan Senate of Priests was one reform recommended by the Second Vatican Council through the decrees on the *Bishop's Pastoral Office* and the *Ministry of Life of Priests* acted on by Bishop Jennings in concert with the clergy of the Thunder Bay Diocese. The notion of a Senate of Priests was one avenue through which a bishop might decentralize the decision-making process relating to issues affecting the entire diocese. Discussions on the formation of a Priests' Senate began at the annual clergy retreat held at Avila Centre on 27-28 May 1968.[206] In their deliberations they benefited from the examination of models already established in the Sault Ste. Marie and Toronto Dioceses. The purpose of this body was to promote "the spiritual, material and intellectual welfare of priests" and to "plan for changing pastoral needs and the welfare of the Diocese."[207] The Senate of the Thunder Bay Diocese was to consist of seven priests, five to be elected by the priests in the diocese and two priests from religious congregations to be appointed by the bishop. In July, 1968 elections took place[208] and throughout the fall the Thunder Bay Diocesan Senate of Priests met to recommend changes to priests' salaries, mass stipends and stole fees, health and disability insurance, subsidization of low income parishes and missions and the cathedraticum. On the basis of these deliberations Bishop Jennings published the "Official Financial Regulations"that would govern the diocese beginning in 1969.

Although Bishop Jennings sometimes wished that he had assumed the responsibilities as the first Bishop of Thunder Bay at a younger age, his record of accomplishments would compare favourably with those of his younger peers. In the space of seventeen years, he canonically erected ten parishes, blessed fourteen new churches and sixteen separate schools. In addition, he initiated the construction of a new cathedral for the diocese. One only has to peruse the detailed records he kept of his three hundred Confirmation visits to every parish and several of the most isolated missions of the diocese including Pekangikum and North Spirit Lake to realize that he did not view holidays as a constant in his life. In the fall of 1969, at age 73, he made a decision to retire. After Vatican II it became customary for Roman Catholic Bishops to offer their resignations to the Holy Father any time after age 70 and certainly no later than 75. Accordingly, in August 1969, he submitted his resignation to Pope Paul VI through the Apostolic Delegate to Canada, the Most Reverend Emanuele Clarizio[209]. A month later it was accepted but he remained on as Apostolic Administrator of the diocese until such time as his successor was appointed. As was the custom at the time, Bishop Jennings was transferred as Bishop of the Titular Episcopal See of Assidona, a non-existent diocese preserved in the records of the church. Later, he was known simply as the Former Bishop of Thunder Bay. As Apostolic Administrator, he was responsible for officially changing the name of the diocese from the Diocese of Fort William (*Dioecesis Arcis Gulielmi*) to the Diocese of Thunder Bay (*Dioecesis Sinus Tonitralis*) on 17 April 1970 to coincide with the amalgamation of the former cities of Fort William and Port Arthur into the new municipality of Thunder Bay that year.[210] Once Bishop Jennings' successor was named, he retired and remained in Thunder Bay until his death on 22 October 1980.

## NOTES

[1] *DTBA*, 2.011/1, Bishop E.Q. Jennings Papers, official birth certificate. See also National Archives of Canada (NAC). RG 150 (1992-93/166) Canadian Expeditionary Force Service Files, 1262039, Edward Quentin Jennings, Box 4822, Sequence 24.

[2] *Ibid.*, 2.011/13 newspaper file. See also Father Edward Purcell, *Unsung Heroes of War: Our Catholic Chaplains* (Edmonton: Cruachan Enterprises, 1998), pp. 54-59.

[3] *NAC*, RG 150, Edward Quentin Jennings Service file. He was honourably discharged from the Canadian Expeditionary force on 10 May 1919.

[4] *DTBA*, 2.011/2, Certificate of Ordination.

[5] *Catholic Year Book, 1951 and Ecclesiastical Directory*, (Winnipeg: The Catholic Press Company, 1951), p. xix. Prior to his appointment as the first Bishop of Kamloops, Father Edward Jennings was consecrated Titular Bishop of Sala, Auxiliary of Vancouver on 11 June 1941.

[6] *DTBA*, Bishop E.Q. Jennings Papers, 2.01/1, The Most Rev. Idelbrando Antoniutti to +Dignan, 18 May 1952.

[7] *Ibid.*, + Antoniutti to +EQJ, 6 May 1952.

[8] Area of the Fort William Diocese is calculated on the basis of geographical limits as set forth in Bill No. 6, "An Act respecting The Roman Catholic Bishop of Fort William" given third and final reading in the Ontario Legislature on 8 March 1955. See also *DTBA*, 1.02, J. E. Hamilton to Chancellor T. Zuydwijk, s.j., 25 September 1978.

[9] *Ibid.*, +EQJ to +Antoniutti, 20 May 1952.

[10] *Ibid.*, +EQJ to +Antoniutti, 8 July 1952.

[11] *Ibid.*, +Antoniutti to +EQJ, 23 July 1952. For coverage of E.Q. Jennings' installation ceremony see *DTJ*, 26 August 1952.

[12] *Ibid.*, 1.03, +Dignan to +EQJ, 21 May 1952.

[13] *Ibid.*, +Dignan to +EQJ, 5 June 1952.

[14] *Ibid.*, 1.04, Joseph Robert to +EQJ, 1 September 1953.

[15] *Ibid.*, 2.01/1, "DECREE concerning the division of the dioceses of St Boniface and Sault Ste. Marie and the erection of the new diocese of FORT WILLIAM", Rome, 29 April 1952.

[16] *Ibid.*, 2.011/11, +EQJ Installation Address, 26 August 1952.

[17] *Ibid.*, 2.011/4, Rev. P.J. McGuire to +EQJ, 7 August 1952.

[18] *DSSMA*, John A. Dyke to +Scollard, 18 and 23 October 1929.

[19] *Archives de la Société Historique de St Boniface* (SHSB), Box 16, file 314, Fr. Alexander Rolland, s.j., to +Georges Cabana, 5 August 1942.

[20] *Ibid.*, Box 18, file 364, Rev. E. Maurice, o.m.i. to +Cabana, 20 November 1951.

[21] *SHSB*, Box 10, file 166. According to Father Dallaire's calculations Atikokan had approximately 70 to 100 Roman Catholics. See Gaston Carrière, ed., *Dictionnaire Biographique des Oblats de Marie Immaculée au Canada, III*, 304.

[22] *Ibid.*, Box 11, file 211, Rev. J. Blais to +Arthur Beliveau, 6 and 10 February 1931.

[23] *Deschâtelets Archives* (DA), L 681, Rev. L. Gauthier, o.m.i. to Rev. J. Magnan, o.m.i., 10 September 1931. Prior to chapel construction, occasional services were held in an old O

&M (Ontario and Minnesota) "shack."

[24] *Ibid.,* L 931, Report of Atikokan Pastoral Visit, 4 June 1942.

[25] *SHSB,* Box 18, file 364, Rev. Édouard Maurice, o.m.i. to +Cabana, 8 February 1950. See also Gaston Carrière, ed., *Dictionnaire Biographique des Oblats de Marie Immaculée au Canada,* III, 321.

[26] *DTBA,* 4.01/28, +EQJ to +Percival Caza, 24 November 1952.

[27] *Ibid.,4.02,* Rev. Stanislas Gauvin to +EQJ, 13 August 1952.

[28] *Ibid.,* 8.19, Gauvin to +EQJ, 6 January 1953.

[29] *Ibid.,* 8.19, Rev. R. Audet to +EQJ, 14 May 1953.

[30] *Ibid.,* 4.01/28, +EQJ to +Paul Emile Cardinal Léger, 7 September 1954.

[31] *Ibid.,* 4.01, Father Lawrence Carl Wittig was born in Kitchener Ontario (Berlin) on 14 July 1909 and ordained to the Holy Priesthood on 15 June 1935 in Sacred Heart Church, Sault Ste. Marie by The Most Rev. R.H. Dignan. He devoted forty-one years to the service of parishes in the Dioceses of Sault Ste. Marie and Thunder Bay. After serving the Atikokan parish for five years he became assistant pastor of Our Lady of Loretto Parish in Port Arthur.

[32] See Port Arthur *News-Chronicle,* 7 December 1953, p. 3.

[33] Father Stelio Fongaro, "The Venerable John Baptist Scalabrinian, Bishop and Founder: A Portrait", (http://www.Scalabrinian.org), p. 1.

[34] *DTBA.,* 5.07, Rev. Salvatore DeVita, c.s. to +EQJ, 3 April 1967.

[35] *Ibid.,* 5.07, Very Reverend Corrado Martellozzo, Provincial Superior to +EQJ, 6 March 1954.

[36] *Ibid.,* 5.07. Rev. Armando Pierini to +EQJ, 5 March 1958. Father Gragnani was born in Italy in 1911 and ordained in 1934. After his ordination he was sent to the United States where he ministered to Italian migrants in Chicago and Kansas City, Missouri. Prior to his arrival in Atikokan he had been pastor in Eveleth, Minnesota. Father Anthony Carrano was born in New Haven Connecticut in 1921 and ordained in 1954. He had been Assistant Pastor in Chicago, Kansas City and Eveleth.

[37] *Ibid.,* 3.02/36, Atikokan Parish Reports, 1959-1969. Coldstream, 8 km outside of Atikokan had 29 Catholic families while Sapawe had 20.

[38] *Ibid.,* Rev. Julio Gragnani to +EQJ, 25 April 1960. See also Atikokan Parish Reports, 3.02/36,1960 - 1967,

[39] *Ibid.,* Rev. Gragnani to +EQJ, 18 July 1966.

[40] *Ibid.,* 3.02/36, Rev. Mario Spada, c.s., Parish Report, 15 February 1970.

[41] *Ibid.,* Atikokan Parish Reports, 20 January 1963.

[42] *Ibid.,* 8.19, Rev. J. Gragnani to +EQJ, 6 February 1963.

[43] *Ibid.,* 507, Rev. Florian Girometta, c.s., Provincial to +EQJ, 29 May 1959.

[44] *Ibid., 8.29,* Rev. B. Campbell to +EQJ, 2 May 1962.

[45] *Ibid.,* 5.07, Girometta, c.s. to + EQJ, 14 and 21 July 1960.

[46] *Ibid.,* 5.07. Rev. Salvatore DeVita, c.s. (Provincial) to +EQJ, 12 January 1966; Devita to +EQJ, 7 October 1966; DeVita to +EQJ, 27 May 1968.

[47] *Ibid.,* 3.02/21, St Anthony Parish Reports, 1955-1969.

[48] *Ibid.,* 5.07, +EQJ to DeVita, 16 July 1968

⁴⁹*Ibid.*, 5.07, +EQJ to DeVita, 26 October 1968. Father Umberto Rizzi, c.s. (Pastor) and Father Lino Santi, c.s. (Assistant pastor) became the first Scalabrinian team at St Anthony's. See *Ibid.*, 5.07, Rev. Adam A. Torresan, c.s. (Provincial) to +EQJ, 12 September 1969.

⁵⁰For a detailed history of Sioux Lookout see *Tracks Beside the Water: Sioux Lookout* (Sioux Lookout: Sioux Lookout and District Historical Society, 1982).

⁵¹George Farlinger established the Patricia Lumber Company in 1909 which supplied railway ties to the C.N.R.

⁵²Gaston Carrière, *Dictionnaire biographique des Oblats de Marie-Immaculée au Canada*, III, 25.

⁵³*DA*, L 4461, P47L, 18, "Oblate Mission: A Bell of History" (n.d.)

⁵⁴Gaston Carrière, ed., *Dictionnaire biographique des Oblats, III*, 86-87.

⁵⁵*SHSB*, box 13, file 249, Parishioners of Sacred Heart Church to + Beliveau, 6 January 1915.

⁵⁶*Ibid.*, Mother M. St Teresa, Superior General, Loretto Abbey, Toronto, to Bishop Emile Yelle, 11 July 1936. The Institute of the Blessed Virgin Mary (Loretto Sisters) was founded at Saint-Omer, France in 1609 by the Venerable Mary Ward and established a presence in Toronto Canada in 1847.

⁵⁷*Ibid.*, J. L. Moran to +Yelle, 17 February 1938.

⁵⁸*Ibid.*, box 16, file 303, W. W. Dawson to +Cabana, 10 December 1947.

⁵⁹*Ibid.*, +Cabana to Fr. L.P. Brunet, 19 April 1948.

⁶⁰See http://www.consolata.ismico.org. Today, the Consolata Missionaries Institute numbers 2,200 priests, brothers and sisters who serve in thirty countries mainly in North and South America, Europe, and Africa.

⁶¹Father Luigi Amadio, telephone conversation with author, 22 May 2001. Father Luigi Amadio was born in Sault Ste Marie, Ontario in 1916. In 1922 he was taken to Italy by his parents where he was educated. He was ordained to the holy priesthood in 1939 and returned to Canada in 1947 as a member of the Consolata Missionary Order.

⁶²*Ibid.*, +Cabana to Rev. L. Amadio, 5 May 1951.

⁶³*DTBA*, 8.40, Rev. G. Bonaudo, i.m.c. (Superior) to +EQJ, 15 February 1955.

⁶⁴*Ibid.*, 8.40, +EQJ to Very Rev. Fergus O'Grady, o.m.i., 20 June 1955.

⁶⁵*DA*, L 4461, +EQJ to Rev. L.O. O'Grady, o.m.i., Provincial, 18 November 1954.

⁶⁶*Ibid.*, L 4461, P47L, 6, Rev. Fergus O'Grady, o.m.i. (Provincial) to +EQJ, 14 February 1955; Rev. L.K. Poupore, o.m.i. (Provincial) to +EQJ, 3 August 1956; DTBA, 8.40, O'Grady to +EQJ, 14 December 1954; 5.06, Poupore to +EQJ, 20 July 1956.

⁶⁷*Ibid.*, 8.40, +EQJ to O'Grady, 9 May 1955.

⁶⁸*DTBA*, 8.40, Rev. Denis Shea to +EQJ, 22 October 1956.

⁶⁹*Ibid.*, Letter to Sacred Heart Parish from building committee, 21 October 1967.

⁷⁰*Ibid.*, Father Don Pruner, o.m.i. to +EQJ, 23 May 1968. "Work on the new church began in May, 1968, and the first block was laid by Father Don Pruner, o.m.i. on June 20th, 1968. The first mass was celebrated on Holy Thursday, April 3, 1969."

⁷¹*DA*, L4451, +EQJ to Rev. G.E. Cousneau, o.m.i., 17 March 1965.

⁷²*DTBA*, 5.17, Rev. A. J. Hogan to +EQJ, 29 June 1964; 2 July 1965.

⁷³*Ibid.*, 3.01/3, St Agnes Parish Report, 7 February 1966; 7 February 1967. In 1966, Father Davis estimated that 104,000 communions had been distributed.

[74] A pulp and paper mill was present in the town of Dryden as early as 1906 when the Gordon Bros. Pulp and Paper Co was created. Since then the industry continued to grow under various corporate names: Dryden Pulp and Paper Co.; Dryden Paper Co.(1918); Anglo-Canadian Paper Mills Ltd., (1953); Reed Paper Group (1960); Great Lakes Forest Products (1979) and most recently Weyerhauser (1999).

[75] *SHSB*, Box 10, file 186, Report of the Dryden Mission, 1923; *DTBA*, 8.23, Joseph Bellavance, "Historical codex of St Joseph's Parish, Dryden, Ont., 1925-1934", p. 2.

[76] *DTBA*, 8.32, "Codex Historicus de la Paroisse de St Joseph, Dryden, Ont." Joseph Bellavance, ptre curé, 11 July 1925. p. 2.

[77] *SHSB*, Box 10, file 185, Fr. J. Bellavance to Archbishop A. Beliveau, 26 September 1925.

[78] *Ibid.*, Box 10, file 185, J. L. Skillen to Archbishop Beliveau, 20 May 1928; see also Box 18, file 366, Pastoral Visit Report, 28 May 1934.

[79] *Ibid.*, Box 18, file 371, Dryden Parish Report. Father Dugal was appointed pastor on 25 July 1942 and also given responsibility for the mission churches in Eagle River and Ignace and the Roman Catholic Cemetery in Dryden.

[80] *DTBA*, 4.01/21, Biographical details of Father Marcel Dugal taken from *The Canadian Register* on the occasion of his twenty-fifth anniversary as an ordained priest, 19 August 1960.

[81] *SHSB*, Box 19, file 371, Rev. Dugal to +Georges Cabana, 2 November 1943; See also the *Dryden Observer,* 13 August 1943.

[82] *Ibid.*, Rev. Dugal to +Cabana, 30 August 1950; 19 April 1951; +Cabana to Rev. Dugal, 24 April 1951.

[83] *DTBA*, 8.23, Rev. Dugal to +EQJ, 24 January 1959.

[84] *Ibid.*, +EQJ to O'Grady, 25 April 1955.

[85] See Elinor Barr, "Holy Corner: The Role of Religion in Ignace", The Thunder Bay Historical Museum Society, *Papers and Records,* XXV(1997), 2-17.

[86] *SHSB*, box 18, file 366, Rev. R.G. Bélanger to Rev. A. Decosse, 30 September 1936.

[87] *DTBA*, 8.23, Joseph Bellavance, "Historical Codex of St Joseph's Parish, Dryden, Ont., 1925-1934", 19 July 1925, p. 3.

[88] *SHSB.*, box 10, file 185, "An Account of Missionary Work, July 28th to August 5th, 1935. Ignace, Ontario."

[89] *Ibid.*, box 18, file 366, Father Rudolphe G. Bélanger to Msgr. L. Primeau, o.m.i., 10 December 1935.

[90] *Ibid.*, box 18, file 358, Immaculate Conception, Ignace, Ontario Mission Report, 1 May 1951, Parish of Sacred Heart, Sioux Lookout by Father Louis Amadio, i.m.c."

[91] *DTBA*, 8.29, (Mrs.) Wm. Smyk to +EQJ, 8 February 1954; +EQJ to Mrs. Smyk, 12 February 1954.

[92] *Ibid.*, Rev. D.M. Brennan, o.m.i. to +EQJ, 22 April 1958. Father Brennan estimated that the average Sunday collection over 30 Sundays in 1958 amounted to $31.12. His successor, Father Bernard Campbell estimated that during the 1960s the average Sunday collection totalled $15.00. Father Campbell telephone conversation with author, 8 January 2002.

[93] *Ibid.*, +EQJ to Rev. D.M. Brennan, o.m.i., 8 April 1957.

[94] *Ibid.*, Rev. B.A. Campbell to +EQJ, 9 December 1960.

[95] *Ibid.,* Rev. Campbell to +EQJ, 22 March 1963.
[96] *Ibid.,* Campbell to +EQJ, 3 January 1961.
[97] *Ibid.,* Campbell to +EQJ, 17 January 1963.
[98] *Ibid.,* Campbell to +EQJ, 5 May 1964; 28 April 1967. The Dryden Paper Company entered into a four-year contract with the Ignace Parish to supply 100 cords of wood annually cut from their licensed timber limits. The men of the parish would cut the wood and hire a logging truck to transport the wood to the mill site. For this, the parish would raise $1200-$1300 each year the contract was in effect. Father Bernard Campbell, telephone conversation with author, 8 January 2002.
[99] *Ibid.,* Campbell to +EQJ, 24 November 1966.
[100] *DA,* L 4461, P47L, 25, +EQJ to Rev. Lorne MacDonald, o.m.i, 1 September 1969.
[101] *DTBA,* Rev. B. Campbell to +Norman J. Gallagher, 13 October 1970.
[102] *Ibid.,* 8.37, Rev. L. Frytek, o.f.m. to +EQJ, 22 January 1953. *DA,* L 996, M27L, Fr. E. Benoit, o.m.i. to Rev. J. Magnan, o.m.i., 24 October 1965.
[103] For a short biography of Father Massicotte, s.j. see John Richthammer "Fr. Muskrat and the first church at Red Lake", in *Northwestern Ontario Catholic (NWOC),* 1999 (February), p. 6.
[104] *Ibid.,* 8.37, Owen Matthews to +EQJ, 28 September 1952.
[105] *SHSB,* Box 17, file 328, Owen Matthews to +Georges Cabana, 13 November 1949.
[106] *DTBA,* 8.21, Rev. L. Frytek to +EQJ, 23 July 1953.
[107] Rev. Ladislas Frytek, O.F.M., telephone conversation with author, 12 April 2001. Father Frytek was born in 1915 and ordained a Franciscan priest on Vancouver Island in 1945. At 86 he is pastor of Our Lady of Lourdes, a French and English Parish in Coquitlam, British Columbia.
[108] *SHSB,* Box 17, file 328, Rev. L. Frytek, O.F.M., to +Georges Cabana, 15 July 1951.
[109] *DTBA,* 8.37, Father L. Frytek to +EQJ. 16 April 1953.
[110] *SHSB,* Box 10, file 167, Mission Report, 1949.
[111] *DTBA,* Father L. Frytek to +EQJ, 27 August 1953.
[112] *Ibid.,* Dr. W. Desmond Poland to +Georges Cabana, 21 June 1951.
[113] *Ibid.,* 8.37, Rev. Frytek to +EQJ, 27 August 1953.
[114] Donald Paradis, m.s., *The Missionaries of La Salette: From France to North America* (Hartford, 1992), pp. 2-3.
[115] *DA,* L 996, M27L, 3, Fr. E. Benoit, o.m.i. to Rev. I Tourigny, o.m.i., 4 September 1958
[116] *DTBA.,* 8.37,Rev. Peter Jaworski, m.s. to +EQJ, 31 August 1953.
[117] *Ibid.,* 8.37, Fr. John Zimmerman, m.s., "St John The Apostle Parish, Red Lake", Codex Historicus, p. 7.; See also 5.04/6, Father J. Gurka, m.s. to +O'Mara, 1 February 1978.
[118] *Ibid.,* 8.37, +EQJ to Very Rev. Stanley, Provincial, La Salette Fathers, 12 October 1953; +EQJ to Dr. W. Desmond Poland, 16 September 1953.
[119] *Ibid.,* 8.37, Rev. John Zimmerman, m.s. to +EQJ, 11 November 1953.
[120] *Ibid.,* 3.02/77, Red Lake Parish Reports, 1952, 1954.
[121] *Ibid.,* 3.02/77, Red Lake Parish Report, 13 January 1954.
[122] *Ibid.,* 8.37, Father Zimmerman to +EQJ, 21 April 1954.
[123] *Ibid.,* Father Zimmerman to +EQJ, 28 January 1954.

[124]*Ibid.*, 8.37, Rev. Michael Bielak, m.s. to +EQJ, 25 August 1954. Father Francis Kula, m.s. was assigned to Red Lake to assist Father John Zimmerman in his work. Father Kula, a Canadian born member of the La Salette Congregation, was recently ordained. He studied at the Gregorian University in Rome and had a working knowledge of Italian and French. He was fluent in Polish and English.

[125]*Ibid.*, 8.21, F.A. Fell to +EQJ, 26 February 1955. Fell was the General Manager of New Dickenson Mines Ltd. in Balmertoown. He viewed the addition of a new Roman Catholic Church as a welcomed addition to the mining townsite. St Francis Xavier Church was officially blessed by Bishop Jennings on 8 September 1956 on his pastoral visit to the Red Lake District.

[126]*Ibid.*, 8.37, "St John The Apostle Parish", *Codex Historicus*, p. 24.

[127]*Ibid.*, Fr. Zimmerman to +EQJ, 6 April 1960.

[128]*Ibid.*, +EQJ to Rev. Leonard Karpinski, m.s., 29 May 1963.

[129]*Ibid.*, Fr. Zimmerman to +EQJ, 20 September 1961.

[130]*Ibid.*, 3.02/77, St John Parish Reports, Red Lake and Missions, 19 January 1960.

[131]*Ibid.*, 24 January 1963.

[132]*Ibid.*, Rev. John Zimmerman to +EQJ, 20 December 1960. See also 3.02/77, Parish Report, 24 January 1963.

[133]*Ibid.*, Fr. Zimmerman to +EQJ, 6 December 1966.

[134]*Ibid.*, 5.04/6, Rev. Peter Jaworski, m.s., to +EQJ, 24 November 1955. Prior to his arrival in Port Arthur, Father Jaworski served as the Provincial of his order and had been known to Bishop Jennings as the "former efficient and energetic" Pastor of the Blessed Virgin Queen of Poland parish in Beauséjour, Manitoba. As the La Salette Provincial he was responsible for assigning two priests to the communities of Red Lake and Balmertown.

[135]*Ibid.*, 3.02/13, Our Lady Queen of Poland Parish Report, 3 February 1956.

[136]*Ibid.*, 8.06, +EQJ to the Parishioners, Our Lady Queen of Poland Parish, 7 June 1959.

[137]*Ibid.*, 8.06, "Declaration of Intention, Edward Q. Jennings, Bishop of Fort William, 8 August 1960."

[138]*Ibid.*, 8.06, Rev. Thad Galuszka, m.s. to +EQJ, 19 August 1964.

[139]DSSMA, Greg Humbert, ed., *Sources: Ralph Hubert Dignan*

[140]*ASJUC*, C-410, file 10, A. Macdonald to J.W. Swain, s.j., 17 July 1936.

[141]*Ibid.*, W. McMannus, SJ to Provincial, 29 June 1937.

[142]*Ibid.*, Charles J. Carroll, s.j. to Provincial, 6 May 1939.

[143]*DTBA*, 5.17, +EQJ to Rev. Mother St Bride, 1 July 1955. Sister St Bride was the Superior-General of the Sisters of St Joseph, Sault Ste. Marie based in North Bay, Ontario.

[144]*Ibid.*, Memo by EQJ on establishment of St Margaret's Chapel-of-Ease, 3 March 1957.

[145]*Ibid.*, 8.15, Joseph P. Monaghan, s.j. to +EQJ, 16 January 1961. In the year of its creation, St Margaret's Parish had 909 parishioners representing 211 families. The new church rectory was blessed and dedicated by Bishop Jennings in November 1967.

[146]*DSSMA*, Greg Humbert, ed., *Sources: Ralph Hubert Dignan*, p. 295.

[147]*Ibid.*, Rev. R.A. Carroll to +Dignan, 2 November 1951.

[148]DSSMA, R.H. Dignan, *The Journal*, pp. 76-77.

[149]*Ibid.*, 20 March 1949, p. 274.

[150] *DTBA*, 8.34, Rev. J. J. Muldoon to +EQJ, 25 July 1952; +EQJ to Rev. J. J. Muldoon, 18 July 1953.

[151] *DSSMA*, R.H. Dignan, The Journal, pp. 259-260.

[152] *Ibid.*, p. 291; Rev. John Reonicke to +Dignan, 19 December 1950.

[153] *DTBA*, 8.33, Rev. A. Greengrass to +EQJ, 26 October 1952; S.B. Black to Rev. A. Greengrass, 18 June 1969.

[154] *Ibid.*, 14.01, Minutes of the Fort William Diocesan C.W.L. Council, 12 October 1952, pp. 1-4.

[155] *Ibid.*, Members of the committee included Mrs. F.H. Carroll, Mrs. L.A. Greene and Mrs. E.J. Payette, p. 1.

[156] *Ibid.*, pp. 1-2. C.W.L. subdivisions did not exist in the following parishes: Corpus Christi (Port Arthur), St Anthony's (Port Arthur), St Peter's (Fort William), St Casimir's (Fort William), St Dominic (Fort William) St Elizabeth (Fort William), Armstrong, Ont., Fort Frances, Ont., Rainy River, Ont., Terrace Bay, Ont., Marathon, Ont., Baird, Ont.

[157] *Ibid.*, 20 May 1953, p. 21.

[158] *Ibid.*, "Our Responsibility: Bishop's Development Fund", 1957.

[159] *DTJ*, 28 August 1957.

[160] *DTBA.*, 3.01/3, +EQJ Circular Letter No. 4/57, 13 May 1957.

[161] *Ibid.*, 3.02/44, St Joseph's Parish, Dryden, Rev. M. Dugal to +EQJ, 3 January 1958; 8.26, St Mary's Parish, Fort Frances, +EQJ to Rev. Louis Aubin, o.m.i., 4 March 1957.

[162] John J. Stapleton, "Feasibility Study re: Expansion of Catholic Secondary Education in Thunder Bay", pp. 12-13. Fund-raising goals were based on the premise that 12,500 parishioners in the 28 parishes and missions in the diocese would make pledges to the campaign. Lawson Associates, however, were able to identify 9,746 potential prospects. Two parishes - St Joseph's in Dryden and Our Lady Queen of Poland in Port Arthur - had undertaken major fund- raising campaigns of their own to build new churches and did not participate in the diocesan campaign. Nevertheless, this would not account for the approximate 2,500 differential in prospective donors.

[163] *Ibid.*, p. 14.

[164] *Ibid.*, p.15. From 1961-1966 Bishop Jennings engaged the services of Niewenhous, Sunday and Company to direct fund-raising for the Lakehead Catholic Education Fund. Their contract with the Bishop was to raise $750,000 over a three-year period between 1962 and 1965.

[165] Members of the Central Committee were Bishop Jennings (chair), Rt. Rev. A.J. Hogan, Rev. C.J. Bathhurst, s.j., Rev. Sister Mary (Principal of St Patrick Arpin Memorial, 1959), F.H. Black, G. Marostica, W.J. Weiler.

[166] *DTBA*, 10.02/3, A.S. McKague to Sister Mary, Principal, Arpin Memorial High School, 30 November 1960.

[167] *Ibid.*, Sister Mary to +EQJ, 13 June 1961.

[168] J. Stapleton, "Feasibility Study re: Expansion of Catholic Secondary Education", p. 10.

[169] *DTBA*, 3.01/1, St Patrick Parish Annual Reports, 1952-1961.

[170] *Ibid.*, 10.02/2, Very Rev. G.B. Flahiff, c.s.B, Superior-General, Basilian Fathers, to +EQJ, 9 March 1961; +EQJ to Flahiff, 24 February 1961; 5.03, +EQJ to Very Rev.

Gordon George, s.j., Provincial Superior, 16 August 1958; Gordon to +EQJ, 6 October 1958.

[171] *Ibid.*, 5.06, Rev. L.K. Poupore, o.m.i. to +EQJ, 4 June 1961.

[172] *Ibid.*, 8.40, Father Dennis Shea, o.m.i. to +EQJ, 21 February 1961.

[173] *Ibid.*, 3.05/1, +EQJ to Arthur H. Evans, City Clerk, City of Port Arthur, 24 July 1956.

[174] *Ibid.*, 3.05/1, +EQJ to A.H. Evans, 24 October 1956.

[175] Archives Deschâtelets, L4451, Gerald Cousineau, o.m.i. to Rev. Don Pruner, o.m.i., 15 January 1963.

[176] *DTBA.*, 10.02/3, Minutes, Central Committee of Intercity Catholic High School, 28 April 1959.

[177] *DA*, L4451, +EQJ to Rev. L.K. Poupore, o.m.i., 7 February 1962.

[178] *Ibid.*, 10.02/4, "Brief: Proposed Intercity Catholic high school, Fort William-Port Arthur", 25 January 1961/

[179] *Ibid.*, 10.02/3, 16 April 1959.

[180] Armand Danis, interview by author, 13 June 2001, tape recording, Archives of the Roman Catholic Diocese of Thunder Bay.

[181] *Ibid.*, 3.05/1, A.H. Evans to J.F.W. Ross, City Solicitor, 8 October 1957; +EQJ to Evans, 28 November 1959. See also Thunder Bay Archives, 4658, Deed 6238, October 7, 1958. The Roman Catholic Bishop of Fort William paid $150 per acre for the first 28 acres ($4200) and later paid $7,973 for an additional 7.973 acres.

[182] *Ibid.*, 10.02/3, F.R. Fraser to +EQJ, 16 February 1960.

[183] *Ibid.*, 3.02, The Roman Catholic Bishop of Fort William Financial Statements as at 31 December 1962 reveal that $166,624.60 had been expended on the high school project.

[184] *DA*, L4451, Rev. Gerald E. Cousineau, o.m.i., to +EQJ, 4 March 1963.

[185] *DTBA*, +EQJ to G.B. Weiler, 2 January 1961.

[186] *Ibid.*, 10.02, +EQJ to Harold Foley, 6 August 1960. Companies with operations in northwestern Ontario such as Great Lakes Paper, Abitibi Power and Paper, Ontario and Minnesota Paper Co., St Lawrence Corporation, New Dickenson Mines Ltd., were approached with little success.

[187] *Ibid.*, W.H. Read to +EQJ, 7 November 1961.

[188] *Ibid.*, 2.011/5, Very Rev. F.R. St James, V.F., to +EQJ, 23 November 1962.

[189] Dr. Thomas Kane, telephone conversation with author, 15 June 2001. Dr. Kane was a member of the Building and Grounds Committee for the Inter-City High School Project which, to his recollection, met on three occasions.

[190] *DTBA*, 10.02/4, Rev. V. Priester to +EQJ, 23 February 1961. Rev. Priester was Executive Director of the English Catholic Education Association of Ontario.

[191] *Ibid., 10.02/9,* Brief: St Patrick Arpin Memorial High School, 1967.

[192] *Ibid.*, 10.02/8, +EQJ to Frank Sabatini, 23 February 1967; +EQJ to Rev. J.J. Muldoon, 23 February 1967. The members of the board were Rev. J.J. Muldoon (Moderator and Administrator of the high school), M. Earle McCabe, Bernard I. Black, James Currie, William Desimone and Frank Leonard. Mr. Leonard had to resign since he was in a conflict of interest postion as an inspector with the Ontario Ministry of Education.

[193] *Ibid.*, R.T. Greer to +EQJ, 8 April 1967.

[194] *Ibid.*, M. Earle McCabe to +EQJ, 8 August 1967.

[195] *Ibid.*, +EQJ to R.T. Greer, 17 October 1967.

[196] *Ibid.*, +EQJ to Rev. J. J. Muldoon, 20 March 1967.

[197] *Ibid.*, 10.02/15, Stapleton Report, p. 18. From 1957 to 1970 a total of $731,199.51 was raised (from the two campaigns) for the intercity high school. During this same period funds were spent on improvements to the intercity property ($301,462.44), on campaign expenses ($108,018.79), on the operation of Arpin Memorial ($206,831.67), on a rebate to St Patrick Parish after 1967($4,867.99) with the balance ($112,645) left in the Lakehead Catholic Education Fund.

[198] For a summary of the Second Vatican Council sessions and its consequences see F.L. Cross and E.A. Livingstone, eds., *The Oxford Dictionary of the Christian Church,* pp. 1682-1683.

[199] See Alex Carter, *Alex Carter: A Canadian Bishop's Memoirs* (North Bay: Tomiko Publications, 1994), p. 167.

[200] *DTBA,* 3.04/4, Circular Letter No. 3, 1963; Circular Letter No. 5, 1 September 1965.

[201] Jean-Paul St Jacques, interview by author, tape recording, 14 June 2001, Archives of the Roman Catholic Diocese of Thunder Bay.

[202] *DTJ,* 13 December 1962.

[203] *Ibid.*, See also Alex Carter, *Memoirs,* p. 170.

[204] The Most Rev. John A. O'Mara, telephone conversation with author, 15 July 2002.

[205] *DTBA,* 3.01/4, Circular Letter No. 3, 30 April 1964.

[206] *Ibid.*, 4.04, "Meeting of Diocesan Priests, 29 May 1968: Prologue"

[207] *Ibid.*, +EQJ to Rev. St James, 9 July 1968.

[208] *Ibid.*, Fathers F.R. St James, Roy Carey, George Bourguignon, R.A. Carroll, J. Stankewicz, Aimée Lizée, O.M.I, and Michael J. Estok, s.j. were the elected and appointed members of the first Thunder Bay Diocese Senate of Priests.

[209] *DTBA,* 2.011/5, +EQJ to +Emanuele Clarizio, 21 August 1969; +Clarizio to +EQJ, 16 September 1969.

[210] *Ibid.*, 2.011/5, +Clarizio to +EQJ, 9 April 1979; +EQJ to +Clarizio, 16 April 1970 (telegram). See also the Thunder Bay *Times-Journal,* and Thunder Bay *Times-News,* 17 April 1970.

The Most Reverend Norman J. Gallagher, D.D., C.D. November 1963.
Auxiliary Bishop to the Military Vicar of the Canadian Armed Forces.
After a twenty-one year career in the R.C.A.F., Father Norman Gallagher became the first padre ever to be consecrated a Roman Catholic Bishop in Canada.
(Courtesy Archives of the Chaplain General, National Defense Headquarters, Ottawa)

CHAPTER FOUR

# BISHOP NORMAN J. GALLAGHER

The selection of episcopal candidates to succeed a retiring or a deceased bishop is based on a time-honoured tradition within the Roman Catholic Church.[1] In the years immediately following Vatican II, a lengthy consultative process took place among the bishops of an ecclesiastical province, the priests, women religious, representatives of the laity from the diocese concerned, and the Pro-Nuncio of the country prior to the final appointment of a new bishop by the Holy Father.[2] In March 1970 the bishops of the Ecclesiastical Province of Toronto received a list of episcopal candidates (with no mention of the sponsor) giving their dates of birth and ordination and in some instances, noteworthy academic credentials and administrative experience.[3] Interestingly, the name put forward by the Vatican for "serious consideration" as Thunder Bay's new bishop was a priest from the Sault Ste Marie Diocese whose name did not appear on the list. Knowing that there was opposition in some quarters of the Thunder Bay Diocese to the appointment of a bishop from its eastern mother diocese[4], the Apostolic Pro-Nuncio asked Bishop Jennings to test the waters vis-à-vis this initial selection. On the basis of confidential written opinions of representative priests and laymen received from Bishop Jennings[5], the Vatican withdrew the name of their original candidate and looked to the ranks of auxiliary bishops in Canada and appointed the

The Most Reverend Norman J. Gallagher, D.D., C.D.
Second Bishop of Thunder Bay, 15 April 1970–28 December 1976

Most Reverend Norman Joseph Gallagher, Auxiliary to the Archbishop of Montréal, as the second Bishop of Thunder Bay.

Bishop Gallagher's tenure at the helm of the Thunder Bay Diocese was brief but memorable. He had much in common with his predecessor. Both were born of anglophone parents but became bilingual through their formal education and associations. Both were among a select group of Canadian priests who had volunteered for active military service and had been elevated to the episcopate. In a diocese like Thunder Bay that was perceived as having a western orientation, it seemed appropriate that the religious careers of both were formed in western Canada. To their superiors and to those who knew them personally, they both demonstrated a capacity for hard work. Bishop Gallagher, however, did not have the luxury of a buoyant economy in which to administer the affairs of the diocese as did his predecessor. The 1970s were years of rampant inflation, high interest rates, labour unrest, and high unemployment. It was in this economic climate that he had to struggle with an enormous cathedral debt, small parishes east and west of Thunder Bay struggling to survive economically and the increasing deficits from the private sector of St Patrick Arpin Memorial High School. He dealt with these problems and the overall financial administration of the diocese prudently without resorting to a fund-raising campaign. Regretfully, his failing health over the five and a half years he was Bishop of Thunder Bay dampened his enthusiasm and efforts to achieve a unified pastoral ministry throughout the diocese based on the reforms of the Second Vatican Council.

Norman Joseph Gallagher, son of James Gallagher and Marion McPhee, was born in Coatbridge, Scotland in the Archdiocese of Glasgow on 24 May 1917.[6] Little is known of his family in Scotland except that his father was a blast furnace keeper and that Norman was one of eight children. In 1923, he moved with his family to Canada where they first settled on a farm in Saskatchewan and within a year took up residence in the town of Swift Current. His Catholic education began in the town's separate elementary school under the direction of a French order of women religious, the Sisters of Charity of St Louis (s.c.s.i.). He then proceeded to Swift Current Collegiate and graduated in 1934. At the height of the depression, he wanted to continue his studies at a Catholic college. Two choices presented themselves: the Jesuit Campion College in Regina or the Collège Mathieu in Gravelbourg, 103 km south-east of Moose Jaw.[7] Since the latter was less expensive, Norman Gallagher enrolled in a classical education program where French was the sole language of instruction. In 1937, he graduated with a Bachelor of Arts degree granted by the University of Ottawa. He continued his theological studies at the Collège Mathieu Grand Séminaire (Séminaire Mazenod) and was ordained to the priesthood by the third Bishop of Gravelbourg, the Most Reverend Joseph Guy on 24 March 1941 for the Diocese of Gravelbourg. Shortly thereafter he served for three months as curate of the Gull Lake Parish, 51 km south-west of Swift Current.[8]

The Second World War had a profound impact on the religious career of Father Norman Gallagher. On 14 October 1941 he enlisted as an Active Auxiliary chaplain in the Royal Canadian Air Force and then transferred to the Active Reserve Force on 7 April 1942.[9] There is no evidence in his early papers or correspondence to suggest why or under what circumstances he was drawn to this apostolate over traditional pastoral work in rural Saskatchewan. Perhaps like many young men in Canada he responded to a call to serve his country during a time of war. Whatever the reason, at 25, he began a long and distinguished career as a chaplain in the Royal Canadian Air Force. After having served in various units in Canada, his first posting overseas was at the picturesque resort town of Bournemouth on the English Channel approximately 150 km southwest of London. Early in the war Bournemouth became the reception centre for air force personnel from Canada, Australia, and New Zealand. By the time the British Commonwealth Air Training Plan had become fully operative, Bournemouth received 25,000 to 30,000 servicemen annually. Here, the role of Roman Catholic chaplains like Father Gallagher was to administer the sacraments and to promote and maintain high morale among soldiers preparing to enter the main theatre of war in Europe. On 6 June 1944, together with chaplains from most other Christian denominations and four other Roman Catholic chaplains, he landed on the beaches of Normandy, France with the 2$^{nd}$ Tactical R.C.A.F. Unit. During the liberation of France, chaplains occasionally had the luxury of celebrating Mass in French parish churches but most often Mass was said in a tent. It was during the last years of the war that Father Gallagher recorded some of his experiences as a padre which reveal a dimension of the war given scant attention by historians. This was one of his recollections of the daily ritual of celebrating Mass:

> The daily Mass in No. 39 Wing took place in the large tent which also served as a cinema for the airmen. The movie followed the Mass. I always began with a handful present, but long before the Mass ended, I often had a full house. At first, it was the

Catholic boys who were slipping in to get a good seat for the movie but soon the effort became ecumenical and my congregation ran the gamut of the various persuasions of our Wing. After the liberation of Paris and Brussels, however, the side distractions were a bit more enticing and we lost a great deal of our sense of togetherness. But, at no time did attendance at Mass and the sacraments flag appreciably.

After the war Father Gallagher was expected to return to the Diocese of Gravelbourg to continue his pastoral ministry in the small parishes and missions of Saskatchewan.[10] The intervention, however, of the Most Reverend Maurice Roy, Archbishop of Quebec and Military Vicar of the Canadian Armed Forces was to change all that. The confidential assessment reports of Father Gallagher's twenty months service overseas strongly suggest that he had found his niche in the chaplaincy service of the Canadian Armed Forces.[11] "His work overseas has been of the highest order", wrote one of his superiors. "Although he has achieved the highest possible popularity with both Catholic and non-Catholic personnel, this popularity was not bought at the expense of priestly dignity." Through his loyalty, tact and good judgement, he had succeeded in maintaining morale among the Canadian soldiers with whom he had come in contact. On the basis of these reports, Archbishop Roy was convinced that Father Gallagher's talents could be used most profitably in the post-war chaplaincy service. Accordingly, he made a plea to Bishop Marcel Lemieux that Father Gallagher be relieved of his responsibilities in the Gravelbourg Diocese.[12] Reluctantly, the Bishop of Gravelbourg agreed. On 1 January 1949, Father Gallagher was promoted to the rank of Squadron Leader (S/L) and became Command Chaplain of Air Transport Command.[13] For the next thirteen years, he served as Wing Commander and Command Chaplain with the Canadian Armed Forces setting up and supervising Roman Catholic chaplaincy services in Canada, Europe, and in any trouble spot in the world where Canadian forces were present to act as peacekeepers.

By the early 1960s the Canadian chaplaincy service had grown to such an extent that it was becoming increasingly difficult for Archbishop Roy of Quebec to oversee its administration without neglecting important duties within his own diocese and the Ecclesiastical Province of Quebec.[14] His request for an auxiliary bishop to the Military Vicar of Canada was granted by the Vatican with the appointment of Father Norman Gallagher to that position in June 1963.[15] This appointment had historical significance for the Roman Catholic Church in Canada. It was the first time that the assistance of an auxiliary bishop was granted to the Military Vicar in Canada. Moreover, after a twenty-one year career in the R.C.A.F. Father Gallagher became the first padre ever to be consecrated a Roman Catholic Bishop in Canada and, as such, Archbishop Roy hoped that the expression of trust and confidence placed in a member of the military would be appreciated by all those belonging to the Canadian Armed Forces.[16] Bishop Gallagher thus became the principal channel of communication between Roman Catholic Armed Forces chaplains and the church itself. His episcopal consecration took place in Ottawa's Notre-Dame Cathedral by the Most Reverend Sebastiano Baggio, Apostolic Delegate to Canada on 12 September 1963.[17]

As Auxiliary Bishop to the Military Vicar of the Canadian Armed Forces and as a participant in the Vatican II sessions, Bishop Gallagher came in frequent contact with Canadian bishops and was reasonably well-known among them. The Archdiocese of Montréal desperately needed an auxiliary with Bishop Gallagher's diplomatic skills and understanding of Canada's two founding cultures to work alongside His Eminence, Paul-Emile Cardinal Léger. Accordingly, in August 1966, he was appointed Auxiliary to the Archbishop of Montréal[18] (and later to Archbishop Paul Grégoire) and was made Director of the Office for English-language affairs. For the next four years, as well as being the pastor of St Patrick's Parish in Montréal (situated on Dorchester Boulevard, now René Lévesque Boulevard), he coordinated the ministry and apostolate directed to the anglophone faithful of the Montréal Diocese. His experiences as an auxiliary bishop in both Ottawa and Montréal made him a likely candidate to fill one of several Canadian dioceses that were without a bishop in 1970. The following extract taken from the *Memoirs* of the Most Reverend Alexander Carter (1909-2002), former Bishop of Sault Ste. Marie, presents a humourous prelude to Bishop Gallagher's next episcopal appointment:[19]

> As was the custom during our annual Plenary Assembly of the CCCB [Canadian Conference of Catholic Bishops], the Apostolic Delegate held a reception for the Bishops. My brother Emmett [Carter] and I attended, along with Archbishop Philip Pocock, Bishop Norman Gallagher, who was then Auxiliary Bishop of Montreal, and Bishop William Power of Antigonish. After the reception we had a slight delay. As we were leaving, the Apostolic Delegate asked Bishop Gallagher to wait a few minutes because he wanted to discuss something with him. The rest of us waited in the car. Knowing that there were one or two dioceses vacant and awaiting the appointment of a new Bishop, we decided to question Bishop Gallagher about this private conversation. When he arrived we pestered him, trying to find out what the Delegate had to say.

After many teasing questions about which diocese he would be going to, Gallagher said, "Well, I was not going to tell you, but since you insist - as I was leaving, the Apostolic Delegate pulled me aside and began asking me about Bishop Carter. I asked the Delegate "Which one?" He answered, "The nice one," and I said to him, "Oh, I didn't know there were three!" With that we all exploded with laughter and no further questions were asked of our quick-witted friend.

One of the vacant dioceses to which Bishop Alexander Carter referred was Thunder Bay. The Most Reverend Norman Gallagher[20] was appointed to succeed Bishop Jennings on 15 April 1970.[21]

Shortly after Bishop Gallagher's appointment a small committee was formed under the chairmanship of Bishop Jennings to plan for the enthronement and installation ceremonies of the second Bishop of Thunder Bay to be held in the new St Patrick's Cathedral on Tuesday, 26 May 1970.[22] The ceremony was characterised by a simple, dignified solemnity. Attendance was not limited as was the case with his predecessor's in 1952 by a small sanctuary. In a remarkable display of unity and solidarity among Canadian bishops, thirty attended from across the country led by Archbishop Philip F. Pocock of the Ecclesiastical Province of Toronto, Archbishop Maurice Baudoux of St Boniface and George Cardinal Flahiff of Winnipeg. Seventy religious and diocesan priests, eighty women religious and twelve hundred members of the laity filled the cathedral and participated in the ceremony with Archbishop Pocock as the enthroning prelate. "This evening the Diocese of Thunder Bay" remarked Archbishop Pocock, "with its vast territory, endowed by God with a rugged beauty and a wealth of natural resources, blessed by a people who by their character, their hospitality, their optimism and their strong and vigorous faith reflect the image of the land itself, welcomes its second Bishop, Norman Joseph Gallagher."[23] As he symbolically took possession of his new diocese by occupying the episcopal throne in the cathedral, Bishop Gallagher was welcomed with a chorus of encomium. George Cardinal Flahiff referred to him as "a loyal and dedicated man of peace." "The qualities I have found in Bishop Gallagher" observed Archbishop Pocock, "are great warmth of heart, charity and love. He has prudence, tact, good judgement, common sense and wit. I call all of this wisdom." Although Archbishop Paul Grégoire of Montréal did not attend the installation he remembered Bishop Gallagher this way: "You are a man of patience...You speak little but always to the point...The man who controls his tongue controls his whole being, says the epistle of St James."

His response to all of this was one of humble gratitude. In particular, he recognized the character and values of his predecessor in saying: "...I name with affection and respect Bishop Jennings and I ask God to give me a little of his charity and much of his humility." Above all, his enthronement address reflected his faith in the values and principles that emerged from the Second Vatican Council. "What is the Church?" was the fundamental question in the minds and hearts of all who attended the historical Vatican II deliberations. Bishop Gallagher, together with most other bishops, had embraced the following view of the post-Vatican II Roman Catholic Church:[24]

> All of you here present are the living reality of what the Church really is. If we the clergy exist it is to serve you from whom we have come and amongst whom we must work...It is my conviction that no renewal is possible in the Church until we fully realize that the Church is people, and the renewal of people must start in their hearts...The echoes of history surround the founding of the church in this area. The faith has been maintained and developed at great human sacrifice. Let us ask God that in the seventies we may be blessed by God to build a better world together with our fellow citizens of all denominations, colours or creeds.

Within three weeks of his installation, Bishop Gallagher set out to visit each pastor and parish in Thunder Bay itself and in the western and eastern regions of the Thunder Bay Diocese – a total of thirty-nine parishes. Travel to the parishes west of Thunder Bay by automobile took the better part of a week. Those east of the city along the north shore of Lake Superior, although less arduous and shorter by 160 km, involved a 220 km side trip north along highway 527 to Armstrong and then along the northern portion of the Trans-Canada Highway 11 to Beardmore, Macdiarmid and Jellicoe. What had he learned from this tour? First, he was genuinely impressed with the deep faith and stability of the priests, most of whom had become comfortable in their respective parishes for well over a decade. Many welcomed a change. The unique geography, history and culture of the diocese led him to conclude further that "a unified pastoral ministry" would be difficult to attain.[25] Much of the western portion of the diocese was in a different time zone from its eastern counterpart. This area had once been a part of the Archdiocese of St Boniface and its parishes had been served by Oblates of Mary Immaculate, Manitoba Province, with their provincials residing in Winnipeg. "Because the clergy and the people in that area are in the Central Time Zone", concluded Bishop Gallagher, "they are inclined to 'think' western and have more in common with Winnipeg than with Thunder Bay." The eastern portion of the diocese on the other hand (formerly a part of the Sault Ste. Marie Diocese), with its English language parishes and its Italian, Polish, and Slovak national parishes where the liturgy was carried out in their native tongue were in tune with the Ontario mentality. Parishes in all regions of the diocese understandably looked to their bishop as a symbol of unity.

Bishops Norman Gallagher and E.Q. Jennings before him were ideal personages around which pastors and parishes in the diocese could rally. The bilingual designation of the Thunder Bay Diocese was more a courtesy to the clergy than a benefit for the laity. As mentioned previously, both bishops were comfortable speaking and corresponding in French. The French language had been an integral part of Bishop Jennings' education in his native province of New Brunswick. When Oblate pastors from Kenora, Fort Frances, and Rainy River wrote to him in French he responded in kind. In deference to their bishop's first language, subsequent correspondence was in English. And yet, it was comforting for them to know that when complex problems or issues demanded precise explanation Bishop Jennings welcomed and understood their verbal or written communications in French. Similarly, it was in Gravelbourg, Saskatchewan that Norman Gallagher became bilingual and where he came to appreciate the coexistence of Canada's two founding cultures.[26] It was his ability to speak both French and English that made him so effective as a chaplain with the Canadian Armed Forces.[27] His years as an auxiliary bishop with the Military Vicariate and in Montréal enhanced his credibility among the francophone Oblates in the Thunder Bay Diocese several of whom were his instructors at the Oblate Collège Mathieu and Seminary in Gravelbourg Saskatchewan.[28] That both Bishop Jennings and Gallagher voluntarily joined the Canadian Armed Forces gave them a respect among the clergy and laity of the diocese that comes from selfless devotion to one's country. Geography, language, and culture were obstacles to the realization of a unified pastoral ministry which Bishops Norman Gallagher and Edward Quentin Jennings were partially able to overcome on the strength of their pastoral and episcopal experiences.

## *Responding to Vatican II*

The gradual implementation of the reforms espoused by the Second Vatican Council at the parish level had the potential of uniting the various regions of the diocese. The annual parish report form submitted to the chancery office by pastors was significantly altered by Bishop Gallagher after careful study and consultation with the clergy to reflect "a true pastoral picture of the parish..."[29] The first part of the report placed particular emphasis on regular pastoral visitations by priests to families in the parish. Equally important was the responsibility of the parish priest to regularly visit Separate and Public Schools, to lead liturgical celebrations in the schools and to speak to teachers individually or in groups. Most of the report concentrated on the "Church's Mission of Sanctification" through the sacraments. Questions such as How often have you had Penitential Celebrations in your parish? Do you have Preparation for Marriage Courses? Do you have a Parish Council? In what manner do you find yourself involved in Ecumenical activities? led parish priests to re-examine their ministry in the light of Vatican II decrees. By example and understanding Bishop Gallagher attempted to move them toward a new pastoral ministry. It was a daunting task indeed. In particular, liturgical reforms such as celebrating Mass in the vernacular facing the congregation and delivering homilies at all masses including those of marriage and the deceased were viewed by many priests with apprehension. Although the Canadian Conference of Catholic Bishops provided the English texts for the various parts of the Mass, these texts were altered and fine-tuned over two or three years.

As expected, some priests made the transition willingly and quickly. For example, Father Charles Ruest, o.m.i. (1908-1981), an Oblate Missionary in the Kenora District, suggested that Saulteau translations of the Eucharistic prayers and Sunday missal prepared by Father Joseph Arsène Brachet, o.m.i. (1886-1982) be used for the benefit of Indian people attending Mass at his missions.[30] Others, however, took several years to feel confident in the daily celebration of the new Mass and a few did not change until the demands of their congregation and their bishop made it mandatory.

The new liturgy necessitated a corresponding change in the physical appearance of the sanctuary. The unadorned but imposing Altar of Sacrifice was to be the focal point of the Mass at the front of the sanctuary. Altar railings were gradually removed. Microphones on the altar and at the lectern became commonplace. A hymn board, visible to the entire congregation with number references to the Catholic Book of Worship, had become mandatory by 1973. At some masses, songs sung by the congregation were accompanied by musicians in or close to the sanctuary strumming guitars. Altar girls as well as altar boys served on the altar. The involvement of the laity as lectors, ushers, extraordinary ministers of the Eucharist, and as lay visitors to distribute communion to the sick were now more prominent and their roles in the service were slowly evolving and being refined. Prior to the distribution of communion the laity and clergy extended to each other the sign of peace. The majority of Catholics welcomed and accepted these changes. In some parishes in the diocese, however, letters of protest and deep concern were addressed to parish priests and Bishop Gallagher. How these liturgical reforms were coordinated throughout the diocese is not clear. What is clear is that the efforts of pastors and laity and the financial resources of the parishes were continually directed to their implementation.

The liturgical reforms ushered in by the Second Vatican Council were so fundamental that their introduction, though gradual, was assured. This was not the case from one diocese to another with reforms such as the enhanced role of the laity in the church and ecumenism. Ecumenism, a movement in the Church towards the recovery of the unity of all believers in Christ, transcending differences of creed, ritual, and polity", in fact, pre-dated Vatican II. During the 1940s for example, many national Councils of Churches were formed including the Canadian Council of Churches in 1944 where Roman Catholic priests participated as "observers". By 1948, these councils had formed themselves into the World Council of Churches. The Vatican II *Decree on Ecumenism* described members of other communions as "separated brethren" rather than outside the church. After 1965, Roman Catholic Bishops around the world, in varying degrees, emulated the openness and liberal views of Pope John XXIII and his successor, Pope Paul VI, to bring all Christians together in dialogue.

Bishop Norman Gallagher had embraced the notion of ecumenism early in his religious career. This was amply demonstrated during his years as a R.C.A.F. chaplain. One of his closest colleagues and friends in the chaplaincy service was a United Church of Canada padre W/C Rev. William Rodger whom he had considered as "one of the finest Christians" he had come to know.[31] Their churches often stood side by side on R.C.A.F. bases in Europe. His wit and humour were revealed one day when a ferocious windstorm hit the base at Grotenquin, France. So severe was the storm that the roof was completely torn off the Roman Catholic Church while miraculously, the neighbouring United church remained in tact. To Bill Rodger Father Gallagher remarked: "That proves God is a Protestant".[32] Within months of his arrival in Thunder Bay Bishop Gallagher began attending the Thunder Bay Council of Clergy meetings together with several members of the diocesan clergy.[33] On several occasions, a Roman Catholic priest was elected chairman of the organization. All understood that it was an association of clergy and not of churches.[34] In a circular letter to the priests of the Thunder Bay Diocese he commended their genuine efforts to meet with members of other Christian denominations at the personal level and in organizations. "It is just such human contacts that respect for persons is engendered", remarked Bishop Gallagher. "It is said that 'priests need priests' but I think we could add to that the thinking of Pope Paul VI that Christians need Christians. I am convinced that it is in scripture and social action that the roots of ecumenism will find their beginnings."[35]

During the first decade after Vatican II it was scripture more than social action that provided common ground for ecumenical activities among Christian clergy in northwestern Ontario. Without promptings or encouragement from their bishop several parishes and missionaries initiated activities and reforms that were clearly ecumenical. St Andrew's Parish in Thunder Bay for example, was ideally located in the Waverly Park area to participate in ecumenical services with neighbouring Trinity United, St Paul's United, and First Baptist churches. On 22 February 1970 it hosted an inter-faith service with the Trinity United Church Congregation and the Shaarey Shomagim Synagogue. In the spring of that year, St Andrew's was again the venue for a city-wide "Service for Christian Unity" sponsored by the Thunder Bay Council of Clergy. This ecumenical meeting inaugurated the week of Prayer for Christian Unity being promoted in all parts of Canada by the Canadian Catholic Conference and the Canadian Council of Churches.[36] In the Red Lake District, Father Chester Urzedowski, m.s. was secretary to the Red Lake District Ministerial Association. The Association wanted to organize a Christmas Centennial Program for elementary school students in four centres, namely, Red Lake, Madsen, Cochenour, and Ear Falls. On some of the Indian Reserves such as the Whitedog near Kenora, Ontario, where the missionaries or clergy worked in close association with one another, ecumenical activities were also grounded in scripture. The Anglican Bishop invited the Roman Catholic children of the Whitedog Reserve to participate in a bible study conducted by an Anglican priest, Father Peter Brown. Father Charles Ruest, O.M.I., an Oblate Missionary, held Father Brown in such high regard that he welcomed the Anglican Bishop's invitation.[37] Throughout northwestern Ontario, all members of the Christian clergy collaborated, particularly during the Christmas and Easter seasons, in presenting the Christian message in local newspapers and wherever possible, on radio.[38]

There was a limit, however, to scripture engaging Christian clergy in ecu-

**Waverley Park in Thunder Bay, 1984.**
St Andrew's Church (upper left) situated in close proximity to First Bapist Church (red brick, upper left), Trinity United (grey stone), and St Paul's United (red brick tower visible in lower left), made arrangements for regular ecumenical services after Vatican II convenient.

menical activities. Some Protestant clergy in the Kenora Ministerial Association for example, frequently "exchanged pulpits" particularly during the Unity Octave (18 - 25 January). After Vatican II, they were anxious to extend this practice to the Roman Catholic Churches as well.[39] The Oblates at Notre Dame du Portage Parish were reluctant to accept invitations to preach in the Anglican, United, or Presbyterian churches except for marriages or funerals. For his part Bishop Gallagher viewed pulpit exchanges "quite in order and even desirable" provided they were not part of a Eucharistic celebration.[40] As Auxiliary Bishop of Montréal, he had accepted invitations to preach in the Baptist and United Churches. The Eucharist is the focal point of a Roman Catholic service as opposed to sermons and hymns in Protestant churches. Whether the Vatican II deliberations brought the Roman Catholic Church and other Christian denominations closer to a mutual understanding of this fundamental tenant of the Roman Catholic faith is a moot point. Bishop Gallagher argued therefore, that a failure to clearly spell out the Catholic position on the Eucharist would render a disservice to the cause of ecumenism.[41] And although the ecumenical movement since Vatican II had diminished mutual suspicions among Christians, he argued that at the diocesan and parish levels it had not moved much beyond the point of pleasant human relationships.

There was no better evidence of this than in the Thunder Bay Diocese. As Bishop Gallagher reviewed the annual pastoral reports from parishes, comments in response to the question, In what manner do you find yourself engaged in Ecumenical activities? were meagre indeed. He concluded that until Christians in general and Roman Catholics in particular developed a thorough grounding in their faith, progress toward the realization of the ideal of ecumenism would continue to be restricted to the existence of Ministerial Associations, the sharing of physical facilities when needed, and the cooperation of clergy and laity in staging annual ecumenical services.

The distinction between clergy and laity within the Roman Catholic Church itself, which historically had been more pronounced than in the Protestant Churches, changed dramatically after Vatican II. In some Canadian parishes prior to Vatican II, including several within the Thunder Bay Diocese, advisory groups, boards of directors, or boards of trustees had been formed to work with the pastor mainly in the financial administration of the parish.[42] This involvement of the laity in parish affairs was formalized and emphasized in several Vatican II documents[43] and manifested itself in the formation of parish councils. Parish councils, whether elected or appointed, were to include representative members of the parish. As a group, they were to share responsibility with the pastor for the temporal direction of the parish. This did not diminish the pre-eminent position of the pastor. According to Canon Law, the pastor was to preside over the parish council proceedings and ratify their recommendations prior to implementation.[44] In theory at least, the parish council's role was mainly advisory and consultative.

Within the Diocese of Thunder Bay parish councils emerged unevenly from parish to parish. The initiative came from the people and pastor. Understandably, not all parishes were at the same level of maturity with a willingness and consciousness to recognize the need and importance of change. And not all pastors were comfortable with sharing responsibilities for parish affairs. Bishop Gallagher recognized the reluctance on their part to initiate a parish council.[45] "I find it much more expedient to make decisions on my own", he wrote. "But I feel that the full theology of 'The Church' cannot develop until we encourage and foster the development of all members in the Body of Christ". During the early 1970s Bishop Gallagher received draft constitutions from parishes across the diocese requesting his comments and suggested revisions. Most viewed the shared responsibility between pastor and parish council this way: "It is understood that the Parish Council shall have responsibility for the financial and material administration of the affairs of the parish and that in religious, social or education matters it shall act in an advisory capacity to the pastor." In each case, he was careful to point out that the role and responsibilities of the pastor in any area not be overshadowed by the parish council. For example, he recommended in several instances that the pastor be made an "ex officio" member of the finance committee.[46] In some parishes, councils were formed but remained inactive for years. In others, parish councils were a remote possibility. By 1975, out of thirty-nine parishes twenty-one had active parish councils.

Early in 1971 Bishop Gallagher introduced several administrative changes that were intended to promote unity within the diocese and at the same time, to enhance the efficiency of its operation. At a regular meeting of the Priests' Senate held at the Corpus Christi Rectory, he announced his intention to move some priests who had requested a transfer. Accordingly, 21 February 1971 was designated as moving day. Some priests such as Father Reginald Carroll who had been at St Elizabeth's Parish since its inception in 1951 moved to St Joseph's Parish in Dryden. Father William J. Fenlon from St Mary's Church, Fort Frances was transferred to Our Lady of Loretto Parish in Thunder Bay.

Although Bishop Gallagher realized that moves such as these were difficult and sometimes painful, he was committed to this practice as a future diocesan policy.[47] Those who had spent several years in the smaller and remote parishes would be given an opportunity to serve and administer parishes in Thunder Bay. The movement of priests throughout the diocese would give them an appreciation of its unique problems and characteristics. To help support the poorer parishes Bishop Gallagher raised the annual levy on the "have" parishes from one per cent to two per cent. This form of subsidization of the "have not" parishes was intended to create a sense of collective responsibility among all parishes in the diocese.[48] Construction of new parish churches, the renovation of existing facilities, and the need to support missionary activity required the transfer of more funds to the Diocese through the cathedraticum than the $30,000 received in 1969. Parishes were raising more money but the total received through the 10 per cent cathedraticum to the diocese was not yielding a corresponding increase. Financial advisors to Bishop Gallagher estimated that based on the $1M total income of all parishes in 1971, the cathedraticum receipts should have been $100,000. Accordingly, Bishop Gallagher streamlined the Annual Parish Financial Report Form to accurately reflect all parish income.[49] Within the space of three years the cathedraticum had reached $90,000. In matters of theology Bishop Gallagher was a liberal; in matters of finance he was a fiscal conservative.

Responsibility for the cathedral debt was also shared among all parishes in the diocese. At the end of 1970, St Patrick's Cathedral Parish was shouldering a debt of $810,000. It had been paying $50,000 annually since 1965 on interest and paying little if anything on the principal. Until the debt became manageable the parish could not make the necessary physical changes to the Cathedral necessitated by the liturgical reforms of Vatican II.[50] Bishop Gallagher sought the advice of his fellow Ontario Bishops on how best to deal with this problem. On their recommendation, he instituted a cathedral assessment on each parish of six per cent. "The Cathedral is the mother church of the diocese", argued Bishop Gallagher, "and should be a symbol of our unity. This unity will be exemplified when the parishes of the diocese rally to the overwhelming needs of the cathedral parish in a temporary measure to alleviate its crushing financial burden. This can and should be done without creating a financial campaign atmosphere." The Cathedral Parish continued to pay $50,000 annually in interest and their cathedraticum payment was applied to the principal.[51] The assessment of six per cent did not apply to the Cathedral

Parish. Needless to say, the added assessment on top of the ten per cent cathedraticum was not popular particularly among the smaller parishes east and west of Thunder Bay struggling to reduce their own capital debts at a time when church attendance and financial contributions were declining.[52] Bishop Gallagher attempted to make the cathedral assessment more palatable to all parishes by demonstrating the financial sacrifice and generosity evident from several quarters including the Thunder Bay Chancery, the Cathedral Parish and the Hamilton Diocese who together contributed $60,000 to the cathedral debt leaving a balance at the end of 1972 of $740,000. Bishop Gallagher's initiative on the cathedral debt resulted in the burning of the cathedral mortgage in 1982.[53] The transfer of priests, the subsidization of low income parishes, and the cathedral assessment in addition to the traditional cathedraticum, each in its own way, helped focus the attention of pastors and parishes on the well-being of the diocese as well as on the individual parish.

In addition to encouraging priests to look beyond the development of their own parishes and to understand and appreciate the problems facing the entire diocese, he welcomed initiatives that broadened and renewed their intellectual growth. What was it that the laity expected from a Roman Catholic priest after the Second Vatican Council? asked Bishop Gallagher. He believed that they expected a priest to be learned in moral theology and scripture and above all, to demonstrate personal integrity.[54] In his mind no one in a community had less surveillance in the performance of their duty than the parish priest. He likened personal integrity to a "golfer in the rough" who swings at the ball, misses, and counts the stroke. During the 1960s St Augustine's Seminary in Toronto operated the Kehoe Renewal Centre for priests. Prior to Bishop Gallagher's arrival in Thunder Bay several priests from the diocese had participated in seminars offered by the centre. The main factor deterring a parish priest from attending seminars offered by the Kehoe Renewal Centre was finding a substitute priest. To get around this problem, the Senate of Priests organized what came to be known as "Kehoe on Wheels" whereby several times a year a teacher from Kehoe would come to the diocese and offer seminars on the new catechism or new developments in dogmatic and moral theology and scripture.[55] Together with interested priests from the diocese, Bishop Gallagher attended these sessions faithfully.

Neither the creation of new parishes nor the construction of new parish churches were commonplace during the 1970s. With the exception of three small missions serving native communities and an emerging Croatian Catholic

**Holy Family Roman Catholic Church, 13 July 2002.**
2055 Rosslyn Road, Thunder Bay.
On 13 June 1965 Bishop Jennings blessed the Holy Family Parish Rectory and outdoor shrine on Rosslyn Road. Construction began on Holy Family Church on 21 November 1969 in what was then Neebing Township, a semi-rural area west of Fort William.

**St Benedict Roman Catholic Church, 27 July 2002.**
St Benedict Church is situated on Highway 61 south of Thunder Bay in Blake Township. It was once a mission attached to St Patrick Cathedral Parish and is now a mission of Holy Family Parish. Mass is celebrated at 1:30 P.M. the third Sunday of each month.

Our Lady of Fatima Roman Catholic Church, 21 May 2002.
Vermilion Bay, Ontario(on Highway 17 west of Dryden)

Nestor Falls Chapel, 23 May 2002.

**St Isidore Roman Catholic Church, 30 July 2002.**
On 28 June 1917 Bishop David Scollard of Sault Ste Marie and Father Louis Lafortune, s.j. visited Dorion, a hamlet 20 km east of Thunder Bay and met with twelve Roman Catholic families to plan the completion of their new chapel. St Isidore Church is located on the Dorion Loop Road. Before the church was built, the Jesuit priests would travel by train to Dorion and say Mass at someone's home. A year after Bishop Scollard's visit and under the leadership of Father Paquin, s.j. (who designed the church), construction began. Parishioners voluntarily donated their time in the construction of the church. It was completed in 1922. Today, St Isidore Church is a mission of the Annunciation of the Blessed Virgin Mary Parish in Nipigon, Ontario.

Assumption of the Blessed Virgin Mary (Croation) Catholic Church, 4 July 2002
479 Oliver Road, Thunder Bay.

community in Thunder Bay's north ward, most of the parishes in the diocese had been established prior to 1970. In the late 1960s, the Roman Catholic Church at Mission Road in Fort William was too small and had fallen into such a state of disrepair that the Jesuits responsible for St Anne's Mission proposed that a new church be built.[56] Father William Maurice, s.j. (b. 1908) gave assurances that the entire cost of church construction (approx. $25,000) would be borne by the Roman Catholics of the Fort William Indian Band. Bishop Jennings agreed to its construction and it was officially opened and dedicated on 6 July 1969. Two years later, on 10 December 1971, Bishop Gallagher canonically elevated three Indian Missions to parish status, namely, St Anne's on Mission Road,[57] Fort William, St Francis Xavier, Heron Bay, and Sacred Heart, Gull Bay.[58] St Francis Xavier at Heron Bay became the most easterly parish in the diocese. In Thunder Bay North, Rev. Julius Balog was granted permission to establish the "Thunder Bay Croatian Congregation" with "the status and autonomy of a Community of Catholic people united with their priest and their bishop."[59] Prior to the construction or acquisition of a church, they rented facilities from St Andrew's Parish for their services.

## Paul Bruyère (1902–1976)

The elevation of the former missions of St Anne, Heron Bay and Gull Bay to parish status was a significant step taken by Bishop Gallagher empowering native people in northwestern Ontario to take responsibility for their own spiritual development. This fundamental change in the native apostolate was given further emphasis with the ordination of Paul Bruyère to the Permanent Diaconate. Paul Bruyère was born on the Manitoba Fort Alexander Indian Reserve on 30 April 1902.[60] All of his formal education was taken at the Fort Alexander Residential School where he completed studies to the end of grade 8. At 15, he left home and was hired as a seasonal labourer on farms in the summer and fall and as a trapper and logger in winter. "...Ever since I was 15 years old", recalled Paul Bruyère, "I was with the white people, studying and learning their way of living. So today, to me a white man is another one of God's creatures with a soul like mine and his blood is as red as mine." Paul married on 8 February 1932 and through the course of the marriage he and his wife raised twelve children. In subsequent years Paul experienced problems with alcohol abuse and he credited the support of his wife in helping him through the crisis. In 1944 the family moved from Fort Alexander to Fort Frances where Paul worked with the Matthew Saw Mill Company. His fellow workers demonstrated confidence in his leadership abilities by electing him vice president and then president of the Saw-Mill and Bush Worker's Union Local 2601 during the 1950s.

It was in 1952 that Paul Bruyère began spending many weekends and holidays away from his family assisting Father Charles Comeau, o.m.i., pastor at Our Lady of Lourdes Parish on the Couchiching Reserve and resident missionary at the Indian Residential School in Fort Frances.[61] Paul assumed the role of a lay missionary and catechist in the Kenora, Fort Frances, and Red Lake Indian missions. When he retired in 1967 he became a full-time catechist and began offering religion and marriage preparation courses to native adults.[62] In addition, he organized Alcoholics Anonymous groups for Indians living on reserves. He travelled to North Spirit Lake and Sandy Lake, the most northerly native communities in the diocese, to conduct retreats.

Why did Paul Bruyère devote so much of his life as a lay missionary?

> I wish to work as Lay Missionary, because I want to do my duty as [a] Christian or

Catholic. As [a] lay man, I wish to fulfill my role in the Church of Christ. As I understand in my Baptism I became a Child of God, a Disciple of Christ and entered His Holy Priesthood. According to St Paul; I do it to help to spread the Good News of Christ to my fellow Indians and others for their Salvation and for the Glory of God. And this is where my happiness is. If I love my fellow-men, I can say I love God. And I have made my personal vow before God to do this till I am called to meet My Master.

After nineteen years as a lay missionary, Paul Bruyère requested that he be ordained a permanent deacon.[63] In response, Bishop Gallagher was cautious and at times, hesitant. He candidly admitted that this hesitancy was inexplicable.[64] Accordingly, he sought the advise of fellow bishops and of priests who were familiar with Paul Bruyère's work as a lay missionary. With varying degrees of enthusiasm all recommended that he be ordained to the permanent diaconate. Priests and missionaries who had been associated with him in some way recognized that he had special qualities and talents that enabled him to make Catholic

Bishop Norman Gallagher congratulates Paul Bruyère on his ordination to the Permanent Diaconate at St Anne's Church, Fort William First Nations Reserve, 14 September 1974. Looking on is Father James J. Farrell, s.j. (centre), Superior of Ontario Jesuit Missions.

doctrine and values understandable to the native people.[65] In this sense, his Indian mentality and perfect knowledge of the Indian language were fundamental. Moreover, his sense of humour endeared him to his people. Others were impressed with "his diplomacy and wisdom."[66] Above all, he was perceived as "open, ready to learn, and ...a man of deep faith and piety..."[67]

The bishops consulted saw no canonical difficulty in ordaining Paul Bruyère to the permanent diaconate.[68] They all questioned, however, what training he would require prior to ordination. Their recommendations ranged from having him enrol in a course for married deacons at Toronto's St Augustine's Seminary to working with a good parish team in order to obtain enough knowledge of elementary theology and scripture to taking a correspondence programme with some tutorial work over a one year period. All agreed that Paul Bruyère's lack of formal education beyond grade 8 should not stand in the way of his ordination.

In the summer of 1974, Bishop Gallagher decided to ordain Paul Bruyère to the permanent diaconate. "After praying on it and consulting many of those with whom you have worked as a catechist..." wrote Bishop Gallagher, "I now wish to confirm to you in writing that I am hereby calling you to Ordination as a permanent Deacon in the Roman Catholic Church...I am ordaining you, Paul, in order that you may serve the Indian people even more than before. Also, you will, God-willing, be the first of several to follow in this work."[69] On 14 September 1974 Paul Bruyère was ordained to the Permanent Diaconate at St Anne's Church on the Fort William First Nations Reserve in the presence of priests from the Oblates of Mary Immaculate congregation and the Jesuit order. He enjoyed the distinction of being the first Indian to be ordained as a permanent deacon in Canada. Paul Bruyère was held in such high regard by the Canadian Oblates that he was asked to attend the beautification of their founder, St Eugene de Mazenod, in Rome in 1975.

## *Closure of St Patrick Arpin Memorial High School*

The financial constraints facing the diocese during the early 1970s called into question its continued support for the private sector (grades 11 and 12) of Arpin Memorial High School. When Bishop Gallagher came to Thunder Bay enrolment at the school was in serious decline.[70] Its peak enrolment of 331 in 1960 had diminished by 55 per cent in September 1970. Of the students that did attend the school, only half remained to complete their secondary school graduation diploma. Deficits for its operation continued to soar and were covered by contributions from Thunder Bay parishes in 1971 and 1972.[71] The financial woes of the school moved Bishop Gallagher to request all Thunder Bay parish priests, either by school visitations or from the pulpit, to encourage Grade 8 students in the separate school system to continue their education at St Patrick's High School.[72] "It is important for them, important for Arpin Memorial, and important for the future of Catholic Secondary Education in this region", wrote Bishop Gallagher. The economic viability of Catholic high schools like Arpin Memorial, however, rested with the policies of the provincial government. The full funding of Roman Catholic schools to the end of Grade 13 was the subject of a brief presented by the Ontario Separate School Trustees' Association to the Government of Ontario on 26 May 1969. On the eve of the 1971 Ontario provincial election, the Davis Government announced that it would not support the extension argument on the grounds that it was too costly, that it would be divisive, and that it would invite other religious denominations to demand similar favours. Although the Ontario Roman Catholic Bishops publicly presented cogent arguments against the government's position, the people of Ontario demonstrated their confidence in the Davis Government with a resounding victory for the Conservative Party at the polls on 21 October 1971. This political victory put a period on the hope that additional provincial funding would ensure the continuance of the only Roman Catholic high school in the Thunder Bay Diocese. Moreover, there is no evidence to suggest that the intervention of parish priests or the bishop from the pulpit or in the classroom had any impact on stemming the tide of the school's declining enrolment.

The future of Arpin Memorial High School was now in the hands of Bishop Gallagher. He alone had the final authority for the flow of funds from the parishes and the Lakehead Catholic Education Fund to Arpin Memorial to absorb deficits incurred in the operation of grades 11 and 12. On 9 December 1971 he convened a meeting of all Thunder Bay parish priests in the St Patrick High School cafeteria to discuss the future of the school.[73] The frank and open discussion that ensued revealed that all were united on the need for Catholic secondary education in Thunder Bay; they were divided on how best to achieve that end in a city where the vast majority of Catholic high school students attended public high schools. The North Ward priests favoured the broader concept of establishing publicly funded Catholic intermediate schools while the South Ward priests (several of whom were former graduates of St Patrick High School) argued in favour of keeping the school open with financial subsidization from their parishes. Of these eight parishes, only four were in a position to make substantial contributions. After much prayer and reflection, Bishop Gallagher informed the chair of St Patrick's High School Board that the diocese could no longer financially support Arpin Memorial and hence it would close at the end of June, 1972 .[74] "But we must be men of hope," concluded Bishop Gallagher. "This setback is partial, not total...Let us walk in faith, knowing that now more than ever we need understanding, unity and above all, perseverance." The closure of St Patrick Arpin Memorial High School in June 1972 made way for its transformation into a junior high school with instruction offered to the end of grade 10.[75] The Diocese sold the school to the Lakehead District Separate School Board for $184,197[76]. In 1973, a wing was added to provide a new library, music, and industrial arts facilities. A year later, a second intermediate school, St Ignatius, built in 1967 but expanded in 1972 provided a similar range of programmes for students in the North Ward. Both schools became the new foundation for Catholic high school education in Thunder Bay.

Bishop Gallagher's failing health prevented him from being an active participant in this new era of Catholic education in the diocese. In fact, visible signs of the onset of health problems coincided with his arrival in Thunder Bay. Those closest to him – Father Georges Bourguignon and his Vicar General, Father Regis St James – urged him to seek medical attention at the Tri- Service Military Hospital, Ottawa. He left for Ottawa on 2 November 1970 and gave Father St James authority to act on his behalf on urgent matters in the diocese that might arise in his absence.[77] He had no idea how long he would be absent from the diocese and confided to his Vicar General that although he was grateful for his help he was concerned that too much responsibility was placed on his shoulders too soon.[78] After four weeks in hospital Bishop Gallagher was becoming restless and admitted that he found it difficult to "leave everything in God's hands." Just before Christmas of 1970 he was diagnosed with Parkinson's Disease.[79] The medication prescribed allowed him to carry out normally the religious and administrative duties as bishop. One of the early effects of the disease was that it often caused his voice to fade out. Moreover, confirmation tours throughout the diocese exhausted him. As the Parkinson's Disease progressed the trembling in his hands became worse and he accepted fewer invitations to formal social occasions throughout the diocese.[80] His health deteriorated further in April 1975 when he entered St Michael's Hospital, Toronto for surgery to alleviate internal bleeding caused by stomach ulcers.[81] While in Toronto, he had a visit from the Pro-Nuncio to Canada, Archbishop Guido Del Mestri. Their conversations led them to conclude that, given the state of his health, he could continue on as Bishop of Thunder Bay but with the assistance of an auxiliary bishop or a coadjutor bishop "with right to succession".[82] From April to July of 1975, Bishop Gallagher often confided to his priests that because of his illness he was "letting them down" and that he was not able to preach as a bishop should.[83] Most of the diocesan administrative affairs during these months devolved on his Vicar General and Chancellor. Deciding which category of bishop to have at his side became a pressing issue in July 1975. In his own mind, Bishop Gallagher's preference was for an auxiliary bishop for which the selection criteria would be less stringent and whose appointment would not necessarily lead to becoming the Ordinary of the Diocese.

To confirm this decision, he invited the views of his priests. After a meeting with the Senate of Priests in early July[84], each received a letter asking whether they preferred an auxiliary bishop or a coadjutor bishop with "right to succession".[85] He asked further if this bishop should come from inside or outside the diocese and whether it made any difference if he was a "religious" or "diocesan" priest. He contacted his brother bishops in Ontario for names of suitable candidates.[86] In response to Bishop Gallagher's letter the overwhelming majority of priests preferred an auxiliary bishop.[87] They were not too concerned whether or not he came from the ranks of diocesan or religious priests but instead believed that the person selected should be the best man for the job. "These informations are very helpful indeed", wrote Archbishop Del Mestri, "and...are indicative of the maturity of their views. The fact that only six out of twenty-nine have opted for a choice coming from within the diocese is certainly to be kept in mind."[88]

No sooner had Bishop Gallagher received valuable advice from his priests and settled on a definite course of action than he was forced to return to hospital for further treatment. This prompted him to have a change of heart in requesting a coadjutor instead of an auxiliary bishop.[89] "I hope all of this is not confusing the issue" wrote Bishop Gallagher apologetically to the Pro-Nuncio, "simplifying what we are all attempting to do, which is to find the best man, who, in God's wisdom can be found to carry on the task of Bishop of Thunder Bay." This was Bishop Gallagher's "time on the cross." Prior to returning to hospital in early August of 1975, he confided to Archbishop Del Mestri that "some of my days are a bit dark and I feel myself slipping. But then on other days I bounce back and all is hope and promise." By the fall of 1975 there was little hope or promise for Bishop Gallagher.[90] He was confined to St Joseph's Hospital in Thunder Bay and was gravely ill. He received the Sacrament of Anointing of the Sick which was administered by Father St James. Bishop Gallagher died on 28 December 1975. He was 58. Over a thousand people gathered in St Patrick's Cathedral on Friday, 2 January 1976 to attend the funeral Mass in his honour. Archbishop Philip Pocock of Toronto, enthroning prelate at Bishop Gallagher's installation in May, 1970 was the principal celebrant assisted by Cardinal Maurice Roy of Quebec City and Cardinal George Flahiff of Winnipeg. The presence of Archbishop Angelo Palmas, the newly appointed apostolic Pro-Nuncio to Canada, together with twenty-five bishops from across Canada added to the solemnity of the occasion.

What was the legacy of Bishop Norman Gallagher to the Diocese of Thunder Bay? His contributions cannot be found in the physical structures within the diocese but rather in the thinking and theological renewal of the clergy which he fashioned by example and by discussions he had with each one of them. Prominent notice was given to his passing in *L'Église de Montréal* and the following assessment of the impression he left on the minds and hearts of those who knew him in Montréal would apply equally to those in the Thunder Bay Diocese: "Although Bishop Gallagher spent only a few years in Montreal...he will be remembered for his wise leadership, his warm and friendly relations with people from all walks of life, for his ability to convey deep theological insights in simple language, and for his witty sense of humour." This generalization found universal acceptance among the clergy of Thunder Bay. An Anglican clergyman's first encounter with Bishop Gallagher was at a Thunder Bay Council of Clergy meeting and he felt nervous sitting beside a Roman Catholic bishop. Bishop Gallagher's humility and quiet humour immediately set the young Anglican clergyman at ease.[91] Bishop Gallagher developed a bond of trust and affection with the Catholic priests in the diocese by treating them as equals and by taking them into his confidence. That he would consult them on the important issue of requesting an auxiliary bishop was a poignant example of this. Above all, he led them in the process of theological renewal. Through his circular letters, personal correspondence, individual conversations, and sermons he encouraged them to reconsider their previously held views on forms of Penance, the native deaconate program, teenage marriages, and ecumenism. "Your leadership", wrote a Jesuit priest, "has been for me a source of calm and consolation."[92] The 1970s were years of momentous change for the Roman Catholic Church. Bishop Gallagher led the priests and laity in the diocese to embrace these changes as an opportunity to renew their faith.

## Notes

[1] *DTBA*, 2.01/26, Coadjutor Archbishop of Toronto, Philip F. Pocock to the Archbishop of Kingston and the Bishops of the Ecclesiatical Provinces of Kingston and Toronto, 7 January 1970. Procedure followed is contained in the Decree of the Sacred Consistorial Congregation, 19 March 1919, Vol. 1, p. 194.

[2] See George C. Salamon, o.m.i. and J.N. Davidson, comps. *History of Notre Dame Du Portage Parish: Rat Portage* (Kenora), 1982, p. 25; *ASJUC*, Jesuit Newsletter, v. 44, 5, 1 May 1969. Both sources make reference to a questionnaire prepared by the Diocese of Thunder Bay Senate of Priests sent to priests, women religious and lay people in the diocese. "What are the qualities you expect to find in a Bishop as a man, as a priest?" was one of the questions posed.

[3] *Ibid.*, 2.01/26, +Philip F. Pocock to +Jennings, 9 March 1970.

[4] *Ibid.*, +Emanuele Clarizio to +EQJ, 13 March 1970 (Personal).

[5] *Ibid.*, +EQJ to +Clarizio, 21 March 1970.

[6] *Ibid.*, 2.011/11, Bishop Norman Gallagher Papers, birth certificate and Landing Card, Canada Immigration, April 29, 1923. St John New Brunswick.

[7] Msgr.Bourguignon, interview by author, tape recording, 29 January 2001, Archives of the Roman Catholic Diocese of Thunder Bay. During the 1930s the Collège Mathieu was affiliated with the University of Ottawa administered by the Oblates of Mary Immaculate.

[8] Archives of the Chaplain General (ACG), National Defence Headquarters, Ottawa. Norman Gallagher file, "Consecration Address", 22 September 1963, p. 3.

[9] National Archives of Canada (NA). Access to Information Division. Military Personnel File of Norman J. Gallagher. See also Jacques Castonguay, *Unsung Mission: History of the Chaplaincy Service (RC) of the RCAF.* trans. Lieutenant Michael Hoare (Montreal: Institute De Pastorale, 1968), pp. 90-91.

[10] *NA*, +NJG Military Service File, Memorandum from L.A. Costello, W/C to DPC, 13 June 1945.

[11] *Ibid.*, Confidential Assessment Reports of Fr. Norman Gallagher, 28 January, 8 February and 17 September, 1945.

[12] *DTBA*, 2.012/8, Bishop Norman Gallagher Papers, +Maurice Roy to +M. Lemieux, (Bishop of Gravelbourg), 12 July 1946 (copy).

[13] *NA*, Norman J. Gallagher Military Service File.

[14] *DTBA*, 2.012/8, +Maurice Roy to Cardinal Carlo Confalonieri, Secretary of the Sacred Consistorial Congregation, 10 September 1962. (copy).

[15] *Ibid.*, Apostolic Nuncio in France to Wing Commander Father Norman Joseph Gallagher, 12 June 1963.

[16] *Ibid.*, +Maurice Roy to Hon. Paul Hellyer, Minister of National Defence, 10 July 1963.

[17] *ACG*, "Consecration Address", 22 September 1963, p. 5.

[18] *Ibid.*, +Sergio Pignedoli, Apostolic Delegate to Canada to +Norman Gallagher, 30 August 1966.

[19] Alex Carter, *Memoirs*, p. 230.

[20] *DTBA*, 2.012/8, +Clarizio to +EQJ, 15 April 1970 (personal)

21 *Ibid.*, +Clarizio to +EQJ, 16 September 1969.
22 *Ibid.*, Msgr. George Bourguignon interview, 29 January 2001. In addition to Bishop Jennings, Father George Bourguignon, Father Reg Carroll, Louis Salini and Earle McCabe served on the installation and enthronement committee.
23 *Ibid.*, 2.012/19, Bishop Norman Gallagher Papers, Enthronement Address by Archbishop Philip Pocock, 26 May 1970.
24 *Ibid.*, 2.012/6, Enthronement Speech given by Bishop Norman Gallagher, 26 May 1970, St Patrick Cathedral, Thunder Bay, Ont.
25 *Ibid.*, 1.07, Quinquennial Report, 4 September 1974.
26 *ACG.* Bishop Norman J. Gallagher file, "Consecration Address", 22 September 1963.
27 *NA,* Norman J. Gallagher Military Service file.
28 *DTBA.*, Bourguignon interview, 19 January 2001.
29 *Ibid.*, 3.04, Rev. G. Bourguignon (Chancellor) to Priests of the Diocese, 19 April 1912.
30 *Ibid.*, 8.321, Rev. C. Ruest, o.m.i. to +EQJ, 20 March 1965. Saulteaux is the language of an Aboriginal people formerly living on the north shore of Sault Ste Marie and now living in the Kenora District and in Manitoba.
31 *ACG.* Bishop Norman J. Gallagher file, "Consecration Address", 22 September 1963. See also *DTBA*, 3.04, Rev. William Rodger to Rev. George Bourguignon, 15 December 1976.
32 See Douglas Harvey, *The Tumbling Mirth: Remembering the Air Force* (Toronto: McClelland and Stewart, 1976), pp. 84-86.
33 *DTBA.*, 1.05, Thunder Bay Council of Clergy Minutes, 9 September 1970.
34 *Ibid.*, 8.32, +Norman Gallagher to Rev. I. Blanchette, o.m.i., 14 December 1972.
35 *Ibid.*, 3.01/10, +Norman Gallagher Circular Letter, 1 March 1973.
36 *ASJUC,* Newsletter, March 1973.
37 *DTBA.*, 8.323, Rev. Charles Ruest, o.m.i. to +NJG, 31 January 1975.
38 *Ibid., 1.05,* +NJG to Rev. J. Keating, 18 September 1973.
39 *Ibid.*, 8.32, Rev. J. Jalbert, o.m.i., to +NJG, 14 December 1972.
40 *Ibid.*, 8.23, +NJG to Rev. I. Blanchette, o.m.i., 14 December 1972.
41 *Ibid.*, 105, +NJG to J. Keating, 18 September 1973.
42 St Patrick Cathedral Parish for example had a board of directors during the 1950s and 1960s. As early as 1925, Father Bellavance of St Joseph's Parish, Dryden referred to his advisors as a "parish council."
43 See for example "The Constitution on the Liturgy" (1963), "The Constitution of the Church" (1964) and "The Decree on the Apostolate of the Laity" (1965).
44 James A. Coriden, et. al. ed., *The Code of Canon Law: A Text and Commentary,* pp. 430-432.
45 *DTBA,* 3.01/8, +Gallagher Circular Letter, 4 January 1972.
46 *Ibid.*, 8.05, +NJG to Rev. W.J. Fenlon, 23 April 1971.
47 *Ibid.*, 3.01/7, +Gallagher Circular Letter, 29 January 1971.
48 *Ibid.*, 3.01/9, +Gallagher Circular Letter, 12 December 1972.
49 *Ibid.*, Bourguignon interview, 29 January 2001.
50 *Ibid.*, 8.01, +NJG to John Off, 27 April 1972.

[51] *Ibid.*, 8.01, +NJG to Rev. R. St James, 12 December 1972.

[52] *Ibid., 3.04,* Rev. B.A. Campbell to Rev. G. Bourguignon, 9 December 1972.

[53] Ibid., 8.01, St Patrick Cathedral Parish Council Minutes, 13 April 1982.

[54] *Ibid.,* +Norman J. Gallagher, tape recording, "Address to seminarians at the Grande Séminaire de Montréal on priestly formation", c. 1969. See Ted Honderich, ed., The Oxford Companion to Philosophy (Oxford: Oxford University Press, 1995), p. 410.

[55] *Ibid.*, Bourguignon interview, 29 January 2001.

[56] *Ibid.*, 8.09, Rev. William Maurice to +EQJ, 18 August 1968.

[57] *Ibid.,* +NJG to Rev. W. Maurice, s.j., 10 December 1971.

[58] *Ibid.,* +NJG to Rev. L. Brennan, s.j., 10 December 1971; 8.181,+Gallagher to Rev. Brian Tiffin,s.j., 10 December 1971

[59] *Ibid.,* 8.31, +Norman Gallagher to Rev. Julius Balong, 27 May 1974.

[60] *Ibid.,* 4.02, Paul Bruyère file, Fr. Charles Ruest, o.m.i. to +Gallagher, 7 March 1972 with Paul Bruyère CV attached; see also Paul Bruyère autobiography, 15 March 1971.

[61] Maurice Gilbert, o.m.i. and Normand Martel, o.m.i., *Dictionnaire biographique des Oblats de Marie Immaculé au Canada, IV,* 67-68.

[62] *DTBA*, 4.02, Fr. Roger Bazin to +NJG, 30 June 1971.

[63] *Ibid.,* Paul Bruyère to +NJG, 7 June 1971.

[64] *Ibid.,* +NJG to Rev. Michael Murray, S.J., 31 May 1974 (confidential)

[65] Ibid., Fr. Charles Ruest, o.m.i. to +NJG, 7 March 1972.

[66] *Ibid.,* Fr. C.E. Comeau, o.m.i. to +NJG, 7 April 1971.

[67] *Ibid.,* Fr. Firmin Michiels to +NJG, 24 June 1971.

[68] *Ibid.,* +Alexander Carter to +NJG, 9 July 1971; +J.N. MacNeil to +NJG, 15 July 1971; +Maurice Baudoux to +NJG, 20 July 1971.

[69] *Ibid.,* +NJG to Paul Bruyère,26 June and 15 August 1975.

[70] J. Stapleton, "Feasibility Study Re Expansion of Catholic Secondary Education in Thunder Bay", pp. 21-22.

[71] *Ibid.,* In 1970 the deficit for the private sector of the school was $31,720 and was projected to climb to $65,000, $72,000 and $80,000 over the next three years. See also *DTBA,* 3.04, Rev. G. Bourguignon to Rev. R.J. van Berkel, 4 March 1972.

[72] *DTBA.,* 3.01/7, +Gallagher Circular Letter, 1 March 1971.

[73] *Ibid.,* +Gallagher Circular Letter, 14 December 1971 (confidential); Bourguignon interview, 29 January 2001.

[74] *Ibid.,* 10.2/11, +NJG to Romeo Lovis, 14 December 1971.

[75] *Ibid.,* Guy O'Brien to +NJG, 30 March 1972.

[76] *Ibid.,* Guy O'Brien to +NJG, 11 October 1972.

[77] *Ibid.*, 4.01, Fr. St James file, +NJG to Very Rev. F.R. St James, V.G., 27 October 1970 (personal & confidential).

[78] *Ibid.*, 4.01, +NGJ to Fr. St James, 9 November 1970.

[79] *Ibid.*, Bourguignon interview, 29 January 2001.

[80] Guy O'Brien, interview by author, tape recording, 29 April 2002, Archives of the Roman

Catholic Diocese of Thunder Bay.

[81] *Ibid.*, 3.01/14, Rev. George Bourguignon to priests of the Diocese, 7 April 1975.

[82] *Ibid.*, 3.01/15, +NJG Circular Letter, 8 July 1975 (confidential); 3.01/16, +NJG to Dr. J.T. Marotta, 7 July 1975 (Personal & Confidential).

[83] *Ibid.*, Rev. J. Gurka, m.s. to +NJG, 11 July 1975.

[84] *Ibid.*, 3.01, +NJG to Most Rev. Guido Del Mestri, 11 July 1975.

[85] *Ibid.*, +NJG to Priests of the Diocese, 8 July 1975. (Confidential)

[86] *Ibid.*, +NJG to Archbishop Philip F. Pocock, 8 July 1975.

[87] *Ibid.*, +NJG to +Del Mestri, 29 July 1975. Bishop Gallagher received 29 replies to his letter. 23 preferred an auxiliary, 2 a coadjutor, and 4 had no preference.

[88] *Ibid.*, +Del Mestri to +NJG, 1 August 1975. (personal)

[89] *Ibid.*, +NJG to +Pocock, 7 August 1975; +NJG to +Del Mestri, 16 August 1975.

[90] *Ibid.*, 3.04, Rev. George Bourguignon to Archbishop Joseph MacNeil (Edmonton), 26 August 1975.

[91] *Ibid.*, 2.012/21, Rev. Canon Alvin J. Thomson to Msgr. George Bourguignon, 10 January 1976.

[92] *Ibid.*, 2.012/25, Rev. A.C. Schretlen, s.j. to +NJG, 18 July 1975.

**Coat of Arms of the Most Reverend John A. O'Mara, D.D.**

The left side of the shield represents the Diocese of Thunder Bay. The upper part is a black field bearing a bright bolt of lightning to represent Thunder. The lower part is composed of a silver field bearing two blue wavy bars to represent Bay. The right side shows the personal crest of the O'Mara family, with one lion removed. In its place an eagle's head has been substituted to honour St John the Evangelist, the bishop's baptismal patron. The uniting of the personal coat of arms with that of the Diocese signifies the spiritual unity of the bishop with his See. The motto "The Ministry of Reconciliation" is taken from the second letter of St Paul to the Corinthians and expresses both an ideal and a program of life. On this special copy of Bishop O'Mara's Coat of Arms appear the names of Deacons and their wives (Ministers of Service) from the Permanent Diaconate Programme of 1987.

CHAPTER FIVE

# BISHOP JOHN A. O'MARA

The Most Rev. Norman Gallagher's death left the Thunder Bay Diocese without a bishop for six months. Whatever responsibilities are accorded a Vicar General, they cease when an episcopal see becomes vacant with the death, resignation, or transfer of a bishop. In January 1976, therefore, the Apostolic Pro-Nuncio appointed Father Regis St James as Vicar Capitular.[1] As Apostolic Administrator of the diocese, Father St James was notified on 20 May of the appointment of Bishop Gallagher's successor. "It is my duty to inform you" wrote the Most Reverend Angelo Palmas, "that the Holy Father has appointed as Bishop of Thunder Bay, Msgr. John A. O'Mara. The news concerning this nomination will be published during the Consistory to be held in Rome, on Monday May 24...I wish on behalf of the church, to express to you my deep sentiments of gratitude for the work you have accomplished in a very zealous and devoted way during the vacancy of your diocese."[2] A month later, Father St James travelled to Toronto to attend the episcopal ordination of Thunder Bay's new bishop on 29 June 1976 at St Michael's Cathedral, Toronto. Early that morning, Father St James died in his sleep. To avoid the appointment of another Vicar Capitular for a period of three weeks, Bishop O'Mara was advised to take canonical possession of his diocese earlier than planned.[3] His official installation as Bishop of Thunder Bay was some-

The Most Reverend John A. O'Mara, D.D.
Third Bishop of Thunder Bay, 2 July 1976–2 February 1994
(DTBA)

what unconventional in that it proceeded his serving as principal celebrant at the concelebrated funeral mass for Father St James on 2 July in St Patrick's Cathedral.[4] That evening, Monsignor George Bourguignon, Chancellor of the Diocese, read the letter from the Apostolic Pro-Nuncio to the assembled congregation authorizing the installation of the Most Rev. John A. O'Mara as the Bishop of Thunder Bay. As previously planned, the ceremonial installation took place on Wednesday, 21 July.

The installing prelate, Archbishop Philip F. Pocock of Toronto, remarked that he knew of no priest whose talents and experience had better prepared him to be a residential bishop than Bishop O'Mara.[5] John Aloysius O'Mara was born in Buffalo, New York on 17 November 1924, the second of six children born to John Aloysius O'Mara Sr. and Anna Theresa Schenck.[6] The O'Mara family had been engaged as fruit farmers in the St Catharines area since the 1860s.[7] John O'Mara Sr. and his family moved to Buffalo, New York where they opened a grocery business in 1916. When John Jr. reached school age he attended St Joseph Elementary School and the Jesuit Canisius High School in Buffalo. By 1940, the O'Mara grocery business in Buffalo was failing and John's father returned to the fruit farming business in St Catharines. At 15, John O'Mara Jr. continued his secondary education at Toronto's St Michael's College School graduating in 1942. After spending one year studying engineering at the University of Toronto and another out of school, he entered St Augustine Seminary, Toronto in 1944 spending the next seven years studying philosophy and theology where his formation as a priest took place in a traditional cloistered environment. He was ordained to the priesthood for the Archdiocese of Toronto on 1 June 1951. Two years later he earned a Licentiate in Canon Law (J.C.L.) from St Thomas University (Angelicum), Rome.

For the next twenty years Father O'Mara's religious career was divided between pastoral and administrative duties in the Archdiocese of Toronto. In the fall of 1953, he was appointed assistant chancellor of the Archdiocese of Toronto and the following year was made secretary to His Eminence James Charles Cardinal McGuigan. At the relatively young age of thirty, he was named a Prelate of the Papal Household with the title Monsignor. He was appointed Pastor of St Margaret Mary Parish, Woodbridge, Ontario which in 1957 had approximately forty families.[8] "It was there that I learned to be a priest", recalled Bishop O'Mara. "It was the first time I had a lot of involvement with people in a pastoral sense, with baptisms, funerals and marriages, people who were struggling to live their lives in a Christian sense." In addition to his responsibilities as a parish priest he accompanied Cardinal McGuigan to the Second Vatican Council (1962-1965) where he attended each session and had access to all conciliar documents. From 1969 to1975 he was Rector of St Augustine's Seminary in Toronto when it became a charter member of the Toronto School of Theology (TST). It and its member schools later entered into a Memorandum of Agreement with the University of Toronto making possible the conjoint granting of basic and advanced degrees in theology. Since the main currents of Anglican, Protestant and Roman Catholic traditions were represented at the TST, seminarians from St Augustine's Seminary were part of a rich environment for ecumenical education in a pluralistic age within a major North American University. Monsignor O'Mara did some teaching in canon law at St Augustine's but most of his time was spent in organizational matters leading to the formation of the TST and in the administration of the seminary. During his last two years as Rector at St Augustine's he also assumed the role of Pastor at St Lawrence Parish, Scarborough. By the time he had come to Thunder Bay, Bishop O'Mara's administrative experience within the Roman Catholic Church was conducted at some of the highest levels and his theological and pastoral outlook was firmly grounded in the teachings and principles of the Second Vatican Council.

*Catholic Secondary Education*

Bishop O'Mara came from an educational environment in southern Ontario where private Catholic secondary schools were the norm. The absence of a Catholic high school in northwestern Ontario prompted him, together with the Lakehead District Roman Catholic School Board, to explore how and under what conditions southern Ontario communities successfully operated a Catholic high school. To this end, they commissioned the Dean at the Faculty of Education at Lakehead University to prepare a feasibility study on the expansion of Catholic secondary education in Thunder Bay and to recommend a plan for its implementation.[9] When the study was completed in 1981, it revealed that during the 1970s the number of Catholic secondary schools (with programmes to grade thirteen) in Ontario had increased significantly and that enrolment in these schools was on the incline. The organizational key to the success of these schools was based on "the partnership concept" whereby a separate school board whose jurisdiction already extended to the end of grade ten entered into an agreement with a private body established by a bishop to operate grades eleven to thirteen of a private school. The most successful partnerships were those which had the full support of their bishop, parish priests, separate school board, catholic teachers and parents.

After discussions with the Board's director, Bishop O'Mara appointed the Thunder Bay Catholic Education Advisory Commission made up of prominent educators and business people with a mandate to study all aspects of the question of providing Catholic secondary education in Thunder Bay.[10] Recommendations of the commission were to be premised on the understanding that the standard of education to be provided would be equal to that offered by the public secondary schools in the city and that all arrangements made would meet the requirements of the Ontario Ministry of Education. Moreover, its investigations were to be made with an "open mind" and without "preconceived notions with respect to structures and organizational patterns." The first task of the Commission was to determine the degree of support for the extension of Catholic education in Thunder Bay beyond grade ten.

The model presented by the Commission to the Thunder Bay parish priests, Catholic ratepayers, and parents was "the partnership concept".[11] It concluded that the most practical way of proceeding would be to gradually phase-in the conversion of the two existing intermediate schools (St Patrick and St Ignatius) over a five-year period into two grades nine to thirteen schools under the jurisdiction of the Separate School Board and a Private Board of Governors appointed by the Bishop of Thunder Bay. This plan was deemed workable if the separate school system could retain a significant number of its enrolled intermediate students thus permitting the addition of senior grades one year at a time in each school. The proposal was placed before Catholic parents and ratepayers in the fall of 1982. Over seventy per cent of those surveyed rejected it on the grounds that the $750 annual tuition fee to be paid by each student enrolled in the senior grades was not affordable.[12] Given this response the Lakehead District Roman Catholic School Board recommended to Bishop O'Mara that the expansion of Catholic secondary education be postponed to at least 1984, that both the model and time-frame for this expansion be carefully re-examined and that a public relations programme be undertaken by the diocesan clergy and separate school board to increase the awareness of all Catholics concerning the value of catholic secondary education.

The philosophical underpinnings of a Catholic secondary education had been eloquently expressed by a variety of thinkers belonging to religious teaching orders and congregations of priests over the years. A recent example was that provided by Father Pedro Arrupe, s.j., Superior General of the Society of Jesus from 1965 to 1991. He expressed the importance of a Christian secondary education this way:[13]

> ...Secondary education gives us access to the minds and hearts of great numbers of young men and women at a privileged moment of their lives. They are already capable of a coherent and rational assimilation of human values illuminated by Christian faith. At the same time, their personality has not yet acquired traits that are so set that they resist healthy formation. It is especially during the years of secondary education that the mind-set of young people is systematically formed: consequently, it is the moment in which they can and should achieve a harmonious synthesis of faith and modern culture...The ideal of our schools is not to produce little academic monsters, dehumanized and introverted. Neither is it to produce pious faithful, allergic to the world in which they live, incapable of responding to it systematically. Our idea is much closer to the unsurpassed model of the Greeks, in its Christian version: balanced, serene, and constant, open to whatever is human...

Additional arguments are given in the Vatican II "Declaration on Christian Education"(28 October 1965).[14] According to this document all Christians had a right to a Christian education which, in its view, developed the maturity of the human person. It argued further that it was incumbent on all parish priests to promote Christian education particularly for the young who "are the hope of the church."[15] Ideally, a community would emerge in a Catholic school "animated by a spirit of liberty and charity based on the Gospel." The Catholic school was an institution open to modern developments preparing its pupils to actively participate in society. By living "an exemplary and apostolic life" they would become "a saving leaven in the community."[16] Little evidence exists to suggest that any of these ideas did or did not form the basis of homilies delivered by priests within the diocese in 1983 and 1984 or that negative public opinion on the desirability of secondary Catholic education had diminished since 1982. Whatever the level of support among the clergy or laity, Bishop O'Mara and the newly formed Thunder Bay Secondary Education Advisory Commission did not waiver in their resolve to pursue the "partnership concept".

The determination to forge ahead with the introduction of grades eleven to thirteen under a private board was based largely on the incremental gains the separate school system had made in Ontario since the mid-1970s. In 1978 for example, a new per pupil weighting factor was introduced for separate school boards offering grade nine and ten programmes resulting in grant enhancements.[17] Additional grants were also provided for those boards offering religious education courses in grades eleven and twelve. The ratification of Canada's new constitution in 1982 with its Charter of Rights and Freedoms created a favourable political climate for a government to recognize the efforts of Roman Catholics to extend publicly funded Catholic education beyond grade ten. In the early 1980s Ontario Bishops, trustees, and administrators were confident that the extension of Catholic education through the partnership model was a stopgap measure until full funding of Catholic separate schools became a reality.

This partnership concept was reflected in most phases of establishing the administrative framework for the private sector of catholic secondary education in Thunder Bay during 1983 and 1984. On the recommendation of the bishop and the Advisory Commission the Lakehead District Roman Catholic School Board agreed to accept responsibility for the administration, management and supervision of the private sector as far as the laws of the Province would allow.[18] The private school was to be named St Patrick Secondary School and the principal of the school was the same individual appointed by the Separate School Board to be principal of St Patrick Intermediate School.[19] The principal made an official request of the Ontario Ministry of Education to register St Patrick Secondary School as a private school in keeping with the Education Act with the authorization to issue Ontario Secondary Diplomas to graduating students. A teacher (whose salary was borne by the Thunder Bay Diocese) from the separate school system was seconded to facilitate the implementation of catholic secondary education programmes beyond grade ten at St Ignatius and St Patrick intermediate schools.[20] To fund the programme the diocese made an initial commitment of $50,000 annually that came from the various parishes in Thunder Bay.[21] In addition, the diocese accessed $200,000 which was in the Education Fund created by Bishop Jennings for capital educational expenditures during the 1960s. Teachers' salaries represented the most significant expenditure for the private school. Tuition fees of $750 per student paid for a fraction of these costs. The Bishop of Thunder Bay and the Separate School Board looked to the generosity of their teachers to accept greater work loads, larger classes and additional responsibilities for extracurricular activities.

Just as the Catholic School Board and the Diocese of Thunder Bay were finalizing administrative arrangements for the introduction of grade eleven at St Patrick Secondary School, Premier William Davis announced on 12 June

1984 that beginning in the fall of 1985, the Government of Ontario would "grant Roman Catholic schools equality of status and financing with the province's public education system".[22] Understandably, all Bishops in the province rejoiced at the announcement. "In Thunder Bay the Diocese will sponsor Grade 11 in September and Grade 12 next year", wrote Bishop O'Mara to the Premier. "So we are just one year ahead of the Provincial Plan. However, your announcement of future funding for these classes, as well as funding for Grades 9 and 10, has lifted the heavy burden of double taxation from the shoulders of our people."[23] When the fifty-two students took their places in St Patrick Secondary School in September 1984 they had paid their tuition fees and were part of the short-lived private Catholic school in Thunder Bay under the direction of a Board of Governors subject to the final authority of the Bishop of Thunder Bay.[24] Upon graduation from Grade twelve they were among the first to receive their diplomas from a Catholic high school funded by the Province of Ontario. A new chapter in Thunder Bay Catholic secondary education had begun.

An essential feature of the government's legislation to support Catholic high schools in Ontario was the provision that surplus public high schools would be transferred to separate school boards. In June 1987 one south ward Thunder Bay public high school (Selkirk Collegiate and Vocational Institute) was transferred to the Catholic School Board. A fully composite 1,000 student capacity high school was also needed for the north ward of the city. The transfer of such a facility was met with some resistance by several newly elected trustees to the public board, by north ward ratepayers, and by the Ontario Secondary School Teachers' Federation. Several schools were offered but none met the criteria set by the Catholic Board. In response to this recalcitrant posture of the public board, the Catholic trustees applied to the Ontario Education Ministry in 1989 to build a new composite high school on a parcel of land adjacent to Avila Centre transferred to them by the Roman Catholic Diocese of Thunder Bay.[25] The public discussion of this initiative was a deliberate ploy on the part of the Catholic board to gain political leverage in their negotiations to hasten the transfer of a suitable high school surplus to the needs of the public board.[26] In 1990 negotiations between the two boards resulted in the transfer of Lakeview High School. With two fully composite high schools the Lakehead District Roman Catholic School Board was able to begin the process of providing a comprehensive secondary Catholic education to students in Thunder Bay. For a ten year period after the passage of Bill 30 in 1985 which gave force to the extension of full funding to Ontario Catholic high schools, there was a provision that non-Catholic surplus secondary school teachers in the public system would be transferred to Catholic high schools and that, if space permitted, Catholic high schools would admit all students (non-Catholic included). Hence, an "ironic tension" was created between the passage of Bill 30 and the distinctive character of separate schools in Ontario.[27] Would Catholic high schools be able to create a Catholic ethos with the presence of non-Catholic teachers? Was Bill 30 a "blessing or a curse" for Catholic high schools in Ontario? A response to these problems would continue to engage Ontario bishops in debate and discussion well after the passage of Bill 30.

*"In the light of the past, together we build for the future."*

There was little in the way of new church construction in the Thunder Bay Diocese during the 1970s. The following two decades, however, witnessed the building of several "second generation" parish churches. By the dawn of the new millennium most churches within the diocese had either been rebuilt or had undergone extensive renovations. The financing of these building projects was the responsibility of individual parishes. Some were able to handle expenditures of this magnitude better than others. During the 1950s and 1960s when interest rates were at a low ebb, Bishop Jennings permitted pastors to borrow (on the credit of the diocese) a set amount from a chartered bank. By 1980, however, when interest rates were high, there was a need for a diocesan plan to coordinate building projects and to make its collective financial resources available to all parishes. Bishop O'Mara established a diocesan building fund comprised of surplus parish funds credited to individual parishes but deposited with the diocese. The diocese paid parishes interest on their deposits. These funds were available to all parishes building new churches or engaging in renovations at interest rates significantly lower than those available at financial institutions.

Building a new church is a singular event in a parish's history. For centuries, Roman Catholics offered their talents and financial resources to create beautiful and prayerful places to hear the Word of God and to celebrate the Sacraments. A sense of belonging and community developed among those who participated in the church's physical creation. The church itself gave both unity and continuity to the institution of the parish. For some, the process of building a "second generation" church seemed to threaten that unity and link with the past. Bishop O'Mara's challenge during these years was to allay the fears of these people and to suggest that adapting to change did not necessarily mean a break with tradition. The experiences of St Agnes (1982), St Dominic (1983), Notre Dame Du Portage (Kenora, 1983), Immaculate Conception (Ignace, 1984), St John The Apostle (Red Lake, 1986) and St Anthony (1992) parishes in renovating and building new churches demonstrated a new level of maturity within the Thunder Bay Diocese as its bishop made decisions in concert with pastors and parishioners. Above all, parishes accepted some responsibility for each others' development.

The imposing concrete foundation and all brick two tower structure of St Agnes Church at the corner of Brown and Mary Streets in Thunder Bay belied its structural weaknesses. When it was built in 1914 a locally manufactured red brick of inferior quality was used and over time there was visible evidence of serious surface disintegration. More serious perhaps was the assessment of architects and structural engineers in 1965 that the front sections of the church (north and south towers) had "settled" unevenly over time causing weaknesses in the load bearing walls.[28] The church was not considered to be unsafe but any attempt to correct these structural problems would, in the opinion of architects, be too costly. Finances permitting, they recommended that a new church be built.

Twelve years elapsed between the recognition that a new church was needed and an agreement in principle to rebuild once sufficient funds were available.[29] At St Agnes the process of church-building was, from the beginning, a cooperative effort involving parishioners, the Oblate Fathers, and Bishop O'Mara. When a building committee was formed in 1979, Bishop O'Mara was invited to attend one of the meetings to offer several suggestions and guidelines that might be followed in the planning and design stage.[30] A year later, the committee presented the 1700 families in the parish with a plan and status report. They were informed that the building fund stood at $300,000, that a door-to-door campaign would be organized to raise an additional $200,000, and that the parish would borrow $300,000 from the diocese. The last mass celebrated in the old St Agnes Church was on 31 May 1981. The following month the demolition of the old church took place and construction of the new began. During this time Sunday Masses were celebrated at First Church United on the corner of Kingsway and Brock Streets; weddings and funeral services were held at St Elizabeth Church or St Patrick Cathedral.[31] The official blessing and dedication

**St Agnes Roman Catholic Church, 26 April 2002**
1019 Brown Street, Thunder Bay, Ontario.

This church replaced the original built on the same site in 1914. Mounted in the bell tower is the bell which had originally been part of the St Rose of Lima Catholic Church at Silver Islet during the late 1870s. To the right of the entrance is the church hall. The new church was dedicated by the Most Rev. John O'Mara on 6 June 1982.

**Foyer of St Agnes Roman Catholic Church, 4 July 2002**
The foyer of the church is dominated by the impressive tiffany lamp structure that adorns the ceiling. Inset into the lighting fixture are some of the stained glass windows from the original church built in 1914. Taken together the windows reflect the Marian theme. The large foyer provides a convenient meeting place for parishioners to gather for conversation after Mass and other church services.

**St Agnes Church interior, 4 July 2002**
The interior of this church is one of several in the diocese which reflects the ideals of Vatican II. A seamless transition exists between the sanctuary and the congregation. Here, the organ and choir are situated at the front in close proximity to the sanctuary.

**St Agnes Church Sanctuary, 4 July 2002.**
To the immediate right of the sanctuary is a Casavant Frères organ (made in St Hyacinthe, P.Q. in 1930) from the original St Agnes Church. This "miniature" Casavant was normally found in chapels or large homes. In late 1981 the organ was dismantled, stored off-site, and reassembled once the new church was built. Together with the stained glass windows in the foyer and confessional, the Casavant organ represents a physcial link with the original St Agnes Church built in 1914.

of the church took place on 6 June 1982. "The new St Agnes church is a beautiful modern building with simple graceful lines", commented Bishop O'Mara. "...It is compact, well planned ...with facilities for a wide spectrum of parish events. It will be a lasting monument to your Faith, your Hope and your Love in the Risen Christ."[32] In the space of seven years, St Agnes Parish paid off their indebtedness to the diocese.

The methodical and uncomplicated approach taken by St Agnes' parishioners to the construction of their new church was not an experience shared by St Dominic (Italian) Parish. Decisions to build their new church away from the original site and to reconstitute it as a national and territorial parish led to controversy. A new church had long been the dream of parishioners and their pastor Rev. Daniel China.[33] By the 1970s the original structure was in need of expensive repairs. No matter how many renovations had been made since its construction in 1912, it never shed its rustic frontier appearance and never matched the simple elegance of the neighbouring St Peter's Slovak and St Mary's Ukrainian Catholic Churches. What is more, mass attendance waned as Italian families moved out of Fort William's East End to newer subdivisions of the city. As early as 1956 the plan was to purchase properties around the church, demolish the existing structure, and rebuild on the original site at the corner of McLaughlin and Connolly Streets. This process had been followed by the neighbouring St Casimir's Polish Roman Catholic Church in 1953. By 1970, however, a parish building committee had been formed and it re-examined where a new St Dominic Church might be built. The notion of remaining at the existing location was abandoned in favour of another site on Simpson Street which was close to the church but still in the city's East End.[34] Then in 1974 it was decided to move out of the East End entirely to a 1.5 acre site purchased on the corner of Redwood Avenue and Spruce Court in Thunder Bay's new Northwood sub-division.[35] During the 1960s and 1970s former St Dominic parishioners residing in the Northwood subdivision attended Sunday Mass at St Patrick's Cathedral or at St Agnes Church. The committee argued that the future stability and growth of St Dominic Parish depended on the relocation of its church to the Northwood area.

Bishop O'Mara's predecessor, Bishop Norman Gallagher, had serious reservations about the Northwood site.[36] What percentage of St Dominic parishioners were for or against the new location? If a new wave of Italian immigrants settled in Thunder Bay would they take up residence in the East End or in the Northwood subdivision? Bishop Gallagher was prophetic in asking if the character of the "National Italian Parish" as it was known in the early 1970s would be destroyed with a move to the new location. Although he approved the land purchase in Northwood, he insisted that construction not begin until a "convincing consensus" on the Northwood site was achieved.[37] Meanwhile, services were held at St Dominic's on McLaughlin Street and the parish continued to augment the building fund[38] in the hope that time, prayer, and rational thought would lead to a consensus on the proposed new site.

When he came to Thunder Bay in 1976, Bishop O'Mara was appraised of the deteriorating physical condition of St Dominic Church, the contributions parishioners had made over the years to a building fund[39] and the debate they were having over a new site. By 1978 there was some urgency to begin the process of parish formation in Northwood and to provide a church for over one thousand Roman Catholic families living in the area – one-third of whom were of Italian descent. It was common practice in Canada and elsewhere in North America for bishops to join a personal (national) parish to a territorial one.[40] Canon Law (Canon 518), for example, provides that "as a general rule, a parish is to be territorial, that is, to embrace all Christ's faithful of a given territory. Where it is useful, however, personal parishes are to be established, determined by reason of the rite, language or nationality of the faithful of a certain territory, or on some other basis." If a new St Dominic Church was to be located in Northwood, it would, out of economic necessity, have to serve as the national "Chiesa Italiana" for Thunder Bay South as well as the territorial church for the Northwood subdivision.

To create such a parish much depended on Father China. He was a senior priest in the diocese who had been pastor of St Dominic's for twenty-five years. As such, he was perceived as the acknowledged leader of the Italian community in Thunder Bay south. His vision of the new church was fundamentally at odds with that of his bishop. He believed it should be strictly a national Italian church under the patronage of "St Dominic Savio" with an open invitation to other Catholics to attend. In their first meeting on 29 March 1978, however, Father China deferred to Bishop O'Mara's view and that of the Senate of Priests and the Diocesan Consultors for a dual purpose parish. Moreover, he agreed to be its pastor and, with the assistance of an associate, begin the process of forming a new parish community. His first challenge was to convene a meeting of St Dominic parishioners on 30 October 1978 to galvanize support for a new church in Northwood.[41]

The respect and affection Father China enjoyed among his parishioners was not enough to convince them to embrace this concept. The twenty-five members attending the meeting rejected outright the idea of twinning a territorial parish with their national parish.[42] He took this as a lack of confidence in his leadership and seriously considered resignation. In addition, he admitted that his energies were diminishing and his health was failing and that the responsibility of organizing a new parish came too late in his life. Shortly after this crucial meeting, he became seriously ill and entered McKellar Hospital for emergency surgery. Early in 1979, his prognosis was uncertain and Bishop O'Mara decided to proceed with the organization of a new Northwood parish.

Although it was initially established without the involvement of Father China or St Dominic parishioners, its name and first pastor were carefully chosen by Bishop O'Mara to assuage their discontent and to invite their support and participation.[43] On 19 January 1979, St Patrick Cathedral Parish was divided and a new parish was erected in Northwood under the patronage of St Joseph which had been the original name of Fort William's "Chiesa Italiana" until 1936 when Bishop Dignan of Sault Ste. Marie renamed it St Dominic. Father Ralph DiGiacinto (b.1937), an Italian-speaking priest, was transferred from Holy Saviour Parish in Marathon to become its first pastor. The boundaries of the parish were clearly set and, until the new church was built, Masses (one in Italian and two in English) were to be celebrated each weekend at St Francis School.

For both Bishop O'Mara and Father Ralph DiGiacinto the task in the spring of 1979 was to draw the East End and Northwood parishioners together in an effort to build a new church. Bishop O'Mara had meetings with St Dominic's new church committee to discuss the eventual closure of the old St Dominic Church and the possibility of building a new church on property purchased on behalf of St Dominic Parish west of Northwood Plaza.[44] Later, he invited them to participate in the inaugural meeting of the building committee for the new church.[45] More difficult for Bishop O'Mara perhaps, was the consideration of Father China's future. By the spring of 1979, he seemed to have fully recovered from the major surgery he had had a year earlier and was aware of the bishop's meeting with St Dominic's parishioners. Even though he might have had a change of heart on a decision he had made to withdraw from the responsibility of leading the new parish in Northwood, his advancing years and failing health put a period on any reversal of that decision.[46] Yet, for Father China to remain on the sidelines while a new Thunder Bay South Italian church was built was perhaps a thought too brutal to contemplate. The most Bishop O'Mara could offer was that he remain at the original St Dominic's until the new church was built and then perhaps be transferred to a new parish outside of Thunder Bay or to St Joseph's Manor as chaplain. Father China's preference was to retire in Italy. Whatever the decision, he was given the assurance of financial security in retirement provided by the Diocese of Thunder Bay.

Father China's status in the spring of 1980 prompted several members of St Dominic's new church committee to travel to Ottawa to appeal to The Most Reverend Angelo Palmas, Apostolic Pro-Nuncio, for a national Italian church to be built in Northwood under the patronage of St Dominic with Father China as its pastor.[47] Not surprisingly, the Pro-Nuncio implored them to work closely with their bishop to accommodate the needs of all Catholics in Northwood.[48] Both Bishop O'Mara and The Most Reverend Angelo Palmas exhibited genuine empathy for St Dominic parishioners as they attempted to have their aspirations met. A small but influential and vocal minority did not want their church moved out of the East End. Others argued that if the Slovaks, Polish and Ukrainians had successfully established and maintained national parishes in Thunder Bay then why not the Italians.[49] They claimed that St Dominic Parish traditionally had served native Italians who relied on attending services and receiving the Sacraments in their language. For the "neo-Canadians of Italian origin" their request seemed a just recompense for the half million dollars that had been raised since 1952 for a new church.

Bishop O'Mara was more than willing to accommodate St Dominic parishioners on the name of the new church. In March 1980 it was changed to "The Church of Saints Joseph and St Dominic" to reflect its dual function of serving the Italian community of Thunder Bay south and the people of Northwood.[50] By the fall of that year, however, the building committees of St Dominic Church and the Church of Saints Joseph and Dominic had found common ground in their desire to build one church as the visible expression of their shared beliefs as Roman Catholics.[51] Accordingly, they recommended to their bishop that the new parish in Northwood be named simply St Dominic to ensure a sense of continuity for the Italian community of the south ward and to reflect the customs and traditions of that parish which had evolved since 1912. Bishop O'Mara wasted little time in acceding to their request. On 12 November 1980 he issued a formal decree that the old St Dominic parish at 700 McLaughlin Street was suppressed, that the new parish in Northwood would henceforth be known as St Dominic and become the Italian national parish for Thunder Bay

**St Dominic (Italian) Roman Catholic Church, 26 April 2002**
130 Redwood Avenue, Thunder Bay, Ontario.
Dedicated by the Most Rev. John A. O'Mara, 7 May 1983.

south and the territorial parish for Northwood and that "all monies, securities and all other assets from the old St Dominic Parish and the new parish in Northwood be transferred to the new St Dominic Parish."[52] Father China remained at St Dominic Church on McLaughlin Street to tend to the pastoral needs of those wishing to attend services there.

At the crucial moment when the East End and Northwood communities had a firm resolve to work jointly toward construction of a new church, Bishop O'Mara sensed the need for a pastoral team experienced in parish formation and church construction to bring the St Dominic venture to a successful conclusion. He found this team in the Scalabrinian Fathers. In April 1981 he had been in conversation with their Provincial Superior in Chicago and requested that he assign two priests to St Dominic Parish. The Scalabrinians had already served with distinction in the diocese since 1958 and had responsibility for St Anthony's Parish since 1968. The Very Rev. A. J. Calandra, c.s. responded favourably to Bishop O'Mara's request and offered Father Umberto Rizzi, c.s. as pastor of St Dominic Parish who officially began his duties on 14 May 1981. "May I again assure your Excellency", wrote the Scalabrinian Provincial "that we have had much experience dealing with parishes that are a mixture of Canadians and newly arrived immigrants. We make no distinctions, we serve all with equal love and zeal."[53] With responsibility for St Anthony and St Dominic Parishes, the apostolates for seamen and chaplaincy work to migrant workers, the Scalabrinians had established a centre for service in the Thunder Bay Diocese.[54] In the case of St Dominic Parish, they lived up to their reputation in leading a vibrant congregation in parish formation and in the construction of a new church which was officially opened on 7 May 1983.[55]

The successful completion of St Dominic Italian national and territorial parish in Thunder Bay's Northwood subdivision was suggestive to the Thunder Bay north pastors.[56] Jumbo Gardens, a new subdivision in the north end of the city and west of the expressway, had grown rapidly since the mid-1960s. By 1987 house construction in the area showed no signs of abatement. A significant number of the 4000 homes already constructed there were owned by Roman Catholics of Italian descent who previously had been members of St Anthony's parish. The 10km distance of St Anthony's church from the new subdivision and its limited seating capacity were sufficient reasons for keeping them from attending Sunday Mass. Accordingly, the north ward pastors suggested that a new St Anthony's Church might be built in Jumbo

Gardens. The non-Italian parishioners attending St Anthony Church situated on a corner lot in the downtown core of Thunder Bay north with limited parking could attend nearby St Andrew's Church as could the Portuguese community that made up a small portion (100 families) of St Anthony's parish. Canadians of Italian descent would more than likely constitute the majority of those attending the proposed new church. This scenario involved the closure and sale of the old St Anthony church.

Bishop O'Mara did not dispute the need for a new parish in the Jumbo Gardens area but saw its growth and development as being distinct from St Anthony's.[57] His wish was that the link between St Anthony and the new church would be the administration of both by the Scalabrinian congregation. He announced that beginning on 8 November 1987 mass would be celebrated by the Scalabrinians each Sunday morning at 10:30 A.M. in Holy Cross School on Brittanny Drive. At some future date he hoped that a church - St Francis of Assisi [58] - would be built in the area on property purchased by the diocese at the corner of Dawson and Hilldale Road.[59] To this end, a steering committee led by Father Ermete Nazzani, c.s., pastor of St Anthony Parish, was formed and met regularly to plan fund-raising events and to discuss building plans and projected cost estimates for the new church. This process continued until Easter Sunday of 1989 when Father Nazzani announced that because of the shortage of priests within the Scalabrinian congregation further planning for the new church would have to be postponed indefinitely.[60] Understandably, this was a disappointment to the St Francis steering committee. Instead of disbanding they decided to remain dormant until Bishop O'Mara was able to provide a priest for the new parish.[61]

In the early morning of 6 March 1990, St Anthony Church on Banning Street was totally destroyed by fire.[62] As parishioners gathered to look at the ruins they reflected on the importance the church had in their lives. Italian immigrants arriving in Port Arthur since 1912 were drawn to St Anthony's because religious services were offered in their language and because the church soon became the focal point of their social lives. After the Second World War this tightly-knit Roman Catholic community looked outward and provided succour to refugee families. The fire was particularly tragic considering the extensive renovations made to the church during the 1970s. "The curious thing about St Anthony's" wrote one parishioner, "was that the more it changed, the more it stayed the same. The essence was always unchanging, that wonderful feeling of warmth, of community, of holiness."[63] Part of the

**St Anthony (Italian) Roman Catholic Church, 21 May 2002**
123 Hilldale Road, Thunder Bay, Ontario.
The church itself and the parish ("fellowship") hall to the right of the main entrance sit on a high elevation of land overlooking Thunder Bay Harbour. A two-level parking lot is available on the east side of the church. The new St Anthony Church was dedicated by the Most Rev. John A. O'Mara on 31 May 1992.

**St Anthony Church Interior, 21 May 2002.**
The impression one gets upon entering the new St Anthony church is one of brightness and delicacy. The white ceiling dominated by twelve ceiling leaves intended to distribute light and air and the light-coloured pews constructed of hardwood birch and maple contribute to this ambiance. These architectural features were meant to enhance the Christian celebration of the "Risen Christ". Father Ermete Nazzani's hope was that this church would be appropriate for "a community of souls". The overall design of the church interior supports the Vatican II concept of having the congregation as an integral part of liturgical celebrations. Architect Walter Kuch designed the pews and kneelers - a design which has since been used by other Roman Catholic churches in Canada.

**St Anthony Church Sanctuary, 21 May 2002**
The sanctuary is characterized by a simple elegance. The baptismal font (centre-left), the lectern, and altar are all made of solid granite hewn from the Canadian shield in northwestern Ontario. The marble floor tiles were imported from an Italian quarry and laid by St Anthony parishioners who volunteered their time and skills. The overall effect is one of natural beauty and permanence.

**St Anthony Church Tabernacle, 21 May 2002**
The hammered copper leaves behind the tabernacle were made by a St Anthony parishioner. The design in stainless steel was meant to echo the design of the twelve leaves positioned on the ceiling. The natural state of the granite tabernacle table is visible here.

renovations included upgrading the basement of the church into a multipurpose facility including a "home-away-from-home for senior citizens, a clothing and furniture depot for an unending stream of immigrants and refugees and a meeting place for all parishioners to enjoy fellowship and to plan fundraising for the latest needy cause." After the fire and particularly during Holy Week, St Andrew's Church 3 km away on Red River Road accommodated St Anthony's Italian and Portuguese Parish community pending a decision on the construction of a new church.

On 17 April 1990 Bishop O'Mara informed St Anthony's parishioners that their new church would be rebuilt on the corner of Hilldale and Dawson Roads.[64] The most compelling argument for this decision was the presence of over 1400 Roman Catholic families living in the Jumbo Gardens, Dawson Woods and County Park subdivisions west of the Thunder Bay Expressway. During the 1970s and 1980s young families had vacated the Banning, Secord, and Ontario Street area formerly served by St Anthony's Parish. The closure of St Joseph's Separate School and Cornwall Public school was visible proof of this. For those Roman Catholics still residing in that area two other Roman Catholic Churches - St Andrew's and Our Lady Queen of Poland - were close by. Given the shortage of priests in the Thunder Bay Diocese, two Italian parishes in the north ward of the city could not be justified. "While I realize this decision will not please everyone", concluded Bishop O'Mara, "I ask you to accept it in a spirit of faith and to cooperate with your pastor as he continues to shepherd your parish through this difficult situation. In this way the name and the wonderful tradition of St Anthony's Parish will be transferred to the new site and the parish will experience even greater vitality in the future."

Immediately following Bishop O'Mara's announcement a "Committee to save St Anthony's" was formed. Its members had no objection to building a new church on the Hilldale Road site but they wanted a modest church rebuilt on the original site to serve those (mainly senior citizens) who had attended daily Mass there for years.[65] As a symbol of their resolve they erected a wooden cross (and later an iron cross embedded in concrete) on the empty lot on the corner of Banning and Dufferin Streets where St Anthony's Church once stood. Moreover, they initiated legal proceedings to prevent Bishop O'Mara from using funds accruing from St Anthony's fire insurance policy in the construction of the new church. Notwithstanding this legal challenge and the resulting acrimony that developed between committee members and the diocese, construction began on the new church in 28 April1991 and

Bishop O'Mara presided at its official dedication and opening a year later. By 1992, 93 per cent of those who had attended the church on Banning Street were registered at the new St Anthony's parish.[66]

In the space of a decade the Diocese of Thunder Bay's two Italian national parishes were transformed. Both were relocated to new subdivisions of the City of Thunder Bay; the architecture of both reflected the ideals of Vatican II and both served a broader constituency of the Roman Catholic community within the north and south wards of the city. Both contributed generously to each other's building fund. It would be for future generations to decide whether the original Italian ethos of St Dominic and St Anthony parishes would endure the changes.

The architectural transformation of Notre Dame Du Portage parish church in Kenora was modest when compared to that of St Dominic and St Anthony in Thunder Bay. And yet, it took considerable thought and reflection on the part of their parish council to recommend in 1982 that a new facade be added that would dramatically alter the appearance of the church rebuilt in 1915 after fire had destroyed the original structure in 1914. The church was an architectural landmark in the town clearly visible from most points on Lake of the Woods. Most parishioners welcomed an expansion that would provide a narthex, a handicapped access ramp, washrooms on the main level of the church and much needed storage space.[67] Those with reservations questioned expenditures in excess of $100,000 on something other than helping the elderly and economically disadvantaged in the parish or in the community. When the project was tendered at the end of July 1982 construction costs exceeded what had been budgeted.[68] Even though many wanted this renovation to mark the centennial of the parish, it was temporarily postponed and re-tendered six months later when construction costs were within acceptable limits. Notre Dame Parish had little difficulty financing the project from funds deposited with the Chancery.[69] The dedication of the "vestibule" took place on Sunday, 30 October 1983. Notre Dame Du Portage Church took on a new look as it entered its second century of service to the Roman Catholics of Kenora.

Unlike Notre Dame in Kenora, Ignace's Immaculate Conception was a debtor parish. Almost two decades after its founding in 1960, it was not yet on solid foundations. During the 1970s the population of Ignace had doubled to about 4,000 due mainly to the mining operations of Falconbridge 48 km north of Ignace which attracted workers from a variety of cultural and linguistic backgrounds including English, French, Italian, Polish, Ukrainian,

Notre Dame Du Portage Roman Catholic Church, 23 May 2002
Kenora, Ontario.
The addition of the front vestibule with its repetitive arched window design is in harmony with the attractive rectory to the right of the church. The vestibule was dedicated on 30 May 1983.

Slovak, and some native Canadians.[70] The Italians who had been a part of the parish since its inception were leading the way in an attempt to complete the construction of the church which had not progressed much beyond its original crypt structure. With limited finances and the inability of the pastor and parishioners to form a parish council,[71] a major building project such as this seemed a remote possibility. "...It is a badly fragmented parish community that needs strong leadership from a wise and prudent priest who is experienced in the pastoral ministry," concluded Bishop O'Mara.

Such a priest was not available for transfer within the diocese. Consequently, Bishop O'Mara carefully guided the development of Immaculate Conception Parish from 1979 to 1984. Father Kenneth Pottie, former pastor of the parish, who had left in 1978 on a sabbatical year of renewal and study, was replaced by Father Jan Bednarz. Bishop O'Mara was delighted to receive another Polish priest in the diocese but in Ignace, Father Bednarz struggled "valiantly" to master the English language and to become acquainted with Canadian culture.[72] On several occasions in 1980 Bishop O'Mara visited Ignace to give the new pastor support and to show his concern for the people of the parish. In 1978, the Ignace Separate School Board was formed and the Immaculate Conception Roman Catholic Separate School promoted enrolment in its English and French instructional units.[73] During these visits, Bishop O'Mara concluded that a new church should be built on a new site where a church, rectory and school could be situated in close proximity to one other.[74] The diocese purchased a tract of land on Pine Street[75] and commissioned architects to design plans for a church. Father George Bourguignon, Pastor of Our Lady of Loretto Parish in Thunder Bay, was appointed Epsicopal Vicar to work with Father Bednarz and the Immaculate Conception building committee until construction was completed in October 1984. Donations and loans came from the Catholic Church Extention Society and other parishes in the diocese. For example, St Casimir Polish Parish in Thunder Bay gifted $25,000 and provided an additional $25,000 in the form of a loan.[76]

St John The Apostle Parish in Red Lake was equally dependent on the diocese for the creation of its new church. The parish reached a watershed in its history in 1977. The Missionaries of La Salette who had served the parish with dedication and distinction since 1953 were about to withdraw from the diocese because of a shortage of priests in their congregation thus leaving Red Lake without a religious community. To fill this void Bishop O'Mara appealed to various congregations of priests and women religious in the hope that one

**Immaculate Conception Parish Church, 20 May 2002**
Pine Street, Ignace, Ontario.
Bishop O'Mara's initial plan that a Roman Catholic School and a church rectory be built beside the new church did not materialize. The Immaculate Conception Parish received generous financial support from St Casimir Polish Parish in Thunder Bay. The new Ignace church was completed and opened in the fall of 1984.

**St Louis Parish Church, 23 May 2002**
Superior Street, Keewatin.

might "respond to the challenges of a frontier apostolate."[77] "...What we need", wrote Bishop O'Mara, "is a team who will inspire and organize and seek to evangelize the people of that area." The Sisters of St Joseph, Sault Ste. Marie, were the first to respond to his request by sending two sisters to the Red Lake region in 1978.[78] For three years they concentrated on home visitations, providing religious instruction to the approximately 100 students at St John Roman Catholic School, and organizing marriage and baptism preparation courses. In September 1981, they were replaced by a team from the Hamilton Diocese which included two diocesan priests, three Sisters of St Joseph and a lay couple. The Sisters of St Joseph assumed the responsibility as co-administrators of St John The Apostle Parish.[79]

It was under this pastoral team that the movement for a new church for St John Parish (the fourth in its history) began. Building and fund-raising committees were formed in 1982 and during Easter Holy Week of that year a series of open houses were held in the basement of the old church where the approximately 220 families in the Red Lake area were invited to offer suggestions, opinions and support for new church construction.[80] These meetings produced tangible results in that the parish organized fund-raising events such as a family fair, quilt raffle, and harvest ball.[81] The Red Lake Catholic Women's League and interestingly, the Hamilton Knights of Columbus and Holy Name Society, made significant contributions to the building fund. By January 1985 the parish was able to present Bishop O'Mara with a financial statement indicating an accumulation of $100,000 and plans for the new church.[82]

Most of the financing for the new St John The Apostle Church, however, came from outside Red Lake. By June 1985 loans from the Catholic Church Extension Society ($100,000) and the Diocese of Thunder Bay ($300,000) permitted construction to begin on the church itself together with extensive renovations to the rectory. Soon after its dedication on 5 January 1986 the reality of paying off the debt remained.[83] "We have social events to raise money and hopefully to build community", wrote Sister Jean Cunningham, the parish's administrator. "However, it will take a long time to pay for the church from the profit we make at social events." The years following revealed that the parish could manage its annual expenses but its indebtedness to the diocese and to the Catholic Church Extension Society continued well into the 1990s.

The Sisters of St Joseph ensured that St John The Apostle Parish played a pivotal role in the northern most reaches of the diocese. After 1986 it was without a parish priest. The pastor from Balmertown visited Red Lake each

**St John The Apostle Roman Catholic Church, 21 May 2002.**
Red Lake, Ontario.
Dedicated by the Most Rev. John A. O'Mara, 5 January 1986.
St John Church is built on the edge of a promontory of land overlooking Red Lake. On the lower level is the church hall and meeting rooms. The rectory to the left of the church, was built and enlarged during the 1960s.

**St John The Apostle Church Interior, 21 May 2002.**
The oak church pews came from the old St Dominic Church in Thunder Bay which was demolished in 1985.

**St John The Apostle Church Santuary, 21 May 2002**
On the wall behind the altar is a wooden sculpture by Miquel Joyal of Winnipeg. It depicts Christ on the cross with Mary and St John The Apostle.

Sunday to celebrate mass and to administer the sacraments as required. On a day-to-day basis, however, the Sisters of St Joseph of Hamilton tended to the spiritual needs of the parish. Bishop O'Mara applauded their work. "..I want to thank you...for the generosity that has been so evident in this Apostolate (Red Lake)" he wrote to Sister Rose Gabriel. "Church attendance is up; there are prayer groups and study groups; sacramental preparations programmes are in place and the Catholic Community is gradually coming to appreciate its Mission. In sum, there has begun a real transition."[84] In the parishes of Red Lake, Balmertown and Ear Falls, the Sisters offered the opportunity to study scripture; they had marriage preparation and R.C.I.A. courses and enriched the liturgy with music. When priests were not available, they conducted communion services and funerals. In short, they served wherever they recognized a need. From 1984 to 1990, their presence was made even stronger when members of their congregation agreed to become teacher-principals at St John's Separate School.[85] Not only did St John The Apostle Parish serve the spiritual needs of Roman Catholics in the Red Lake area but it was also the base from which the native apostolate was organized for Pikangikum and North Spirit Lake.

*Sharing the Challenges*

If the diocese was committed to supporting financially troubled parishes as well as the Native apostolate, then its financial base had to be broadened. In April 1989 Bishop O'Mara gave serious consideration to launching an annual diocesan fund-raising campaign similar to those so successfully organized by many Roman Catholic dioceses across North America..[86] Bishop Jennings launched the first such campaign on a limited basis during the 1960s as the "Bishop's Development Fund". Prior to engaging the services of a professional fund-raiser Bishop O'Mara presented the plan to the clergy, religious and pastoral workers of the diocese.[87] "The mission of the church is not to preserve the status quo," he wrote. "Instead, we must continually reach out through our programs and services...I believe we have an opportunity to position ourselves...for the challenges of the next decade." The challenges facing the diocese centred around the native apostolate, the education of future priests, the youth ministry, providing a chaplain for Lakehead University and a diocesan adult education coordinator. On behalf of the diocese, the Community Charitable Counselling Service of Canada planned a ten week campaign that was intended to generate gifts and pledges totalling $750,000. Each parish was assigned a specific goal which, if attained, would result in a twenty-five per cent return of that figure to the parish. Anything raised over their goal would be shared equally between the parish and the diocese. The first Sharing the Challenges Campaign was launched in September 1989.[88] Thirty-six (out of forty-one) parishes and seven missions participated. Pastors, parish teams, and several hundred canvassers throughout the diocese worked efficiently to surpass the stated goal.[89] In addition to the financial benefits accruing from the campaign, Bishop O'Mara summarized several intangible but no less important residual benefits for the diocese.

> ...I believe that our Catholic people understand in a new way, the Diocesan Church of Thunder Bay, and the services that are needed in order to build up and support the Church Community...Several of the volunteer canvassers have related incidents which occurred on the occasion of their visits, when they met shut-ins and lonely senior citizens who welcomed a chance to talk about their faith, their parish, and their families. Also, it has given the volunteers an experience of the diverse reception that can be given to those who have responsibility for leadership in the parish. Moreover, it has been an occasion to welcome back to the parish community, those who have strayed, or became lax in their religious practice.

As expected, the "Sharing the Challenges" campaign was not without its detractors. The "diverse reception" to which Bishop O'Mara referred was perhaps an oblique reference to those who refused to participate because the Catholic Education Campaign of the 1960s did not do what it was intended to do, namely, to construct a Catholic intercity high school.[90] Twenty years later, Bishop Jennings' diocesan fund-raising campaigns continued to be a liability for those involved in "Sharing the Challenges." In addition, the economic and personnel instability in several parishes prevented their participation in the campaign.[91] There was enough support for "Sharing the Challenges", however, to have it continue. Approximately one-third of Roman Catholics living within the diocese contributed to the campaign in 1989. Through the diocesan newspaper *The Northwestern Ontario Catholic* and circular letters to parish priests, Bishop O'Mara itemized the allocation of funds to the areas stated at the beginning of the campaign.

*"I was hungry, thirsty, lonely, and you helped me."*

The establishment of the Catholic Family Development Centre in 1979 was one diocesan initiative to benefit from the Sharing the Challenges campaign. Similar social agencies had been operating in Ottawa and Toronto since the mid-1970s. After discussions with pastoral councils in the diocese, the Priests' Senate and various Ontario bishops, Bishop O'Mara created the Catholic Family Development Centre as a social service agency to provide professional counselling and assistance to Christian families beset by worries and problems. The offices for the Centre, staffed by professional counsellors and social workers, were initially located in a home at 208 South Archibald Street directly across from St Patrick's Cathedral. Couples experiencing marital discord, single parents, young people estranged from their families, separated and divorced Catholics were referred to the Catholic Family Development Centre by parish priests, doctors, lawyers, school principals, and teachers. Although the agency was created by the Roman Catholic Diocese of Thunder Bay, it was estimated that after two years 50 per cent of its clientele was non-Catholic.[92] During its first year of operation the entire cost of providing this service to the Christian population of Thunder Bay and surrounding district was born by the diocese.[93] In subsequent years, diocesan funding was reduced to approximately 25 per cent of the centre's total budget as additional funding came from counselling fees, the United Way, and several Government of Ontario ministries.[94] A measure of the Catholic Family Development Centre's success was the increased demand for its services including the training of parish leaders for marriage preparation courses and requests for its staff to make presentations or conduct workshops for parishes, civic organizations and schools.[95] Offering a broader range of services permitted the Centre to move to a larger facility in the former St Anthony Parish rectory on Banning Street in 1990. It became well respected throughout northwestern Ontario for professional counselling services offered in a Christian context.

Parish support for the Catholic Family Development Centre through the "Sharing the Challenges" campaign was one example illustrating the expanded role of the parish in society. Father Pedro Arrupe, S.J., Superior-General of the Society of Jesus provided this description of what the parish might be in the post-Vatican II church:

> The parish is a most valuable apostolate in today's world and offers great possibilities.

But if the parish is to realize its potential, it should not merely be a place where sacraments are administered to a small number of practising Christians. Rather, it should be a centre where the Word of God is preached and inspires deep probing; where there is a sense of openness to the local social, economic and cultural problems. The parish should be a meeting place for everybody in the district. Its special concern should be the poor, the working people, the marginalized, the non-believers, and all who are at a distance from the church...

Although this vision of the modern parish was not universally accepted, the revised *Code of Canon Law* (1983) offered several "needs" for a pastor and parish council to consider in shaping the mission of its parish.[96] In addition to establishing a "sense of community", there was a need for growth, maturity, and the need for a parish to change and to accept the importance of change. Above all, there was a need for a parish to declare in some way its mission, its vision and its objectives.

To what extent then, did parishes within the Diocese of Thunder Bay measure up to Father Pedro Arrupe's vision or the guidelines set forth in Canon Law? During the 1980s and 1990s Canada became a haven for thousands of refugees escaping political and racial persecution in Vietnam, Eastern Europe, Central America and Africa. In the resettlement process they became a poor and marginalized group in Canadian society. The Thunder Bay Diocese was the first in Canada to sign a "Master Holder Agreement" with the Canadian Government whereby it agreed to guarantee refugee sponsorships entered into by individual parishes. Several parishes within the diocese demonstrated their charitableness by sponsoring a refugee or a refugee family. This meant providing the wherewithal for these people to settle comfortably in their adopted country. For example, refugees from Poland, Central America and Ethiopia were sponsored by St Casimir, St Anthony and Corpus Christi parishes in Thunder Bay.[97] Nortre Dame Du Portage in Kenora assumed similar responsibilities through its affiliation with the Sanctuary Movement which had begun in the United States.[98] It was an ecumenical movement where over 160 churches and synagogues offered sanctuary to a mere fraction of the estimated 200,000 refugees attempting to flee Guatemala and El Salvador in the mid-1980s. The movement's name was symbolic and appropriate for the times and the cause. Sanctuary refers to a church or other sacred place in which, by the law of the medieval church, a fugitive or debtor was immune from arrest. Interestingly, in the United States during the 1980s Central American refugees were considered "illegal aliens" and churches found harbouring these refugees were subject to criminal prosecution. In Canada, they were granted refugee status. Notre Dame Du Portage Parish in Kenora declared its solidarity with other Christian churches and synagogues by proclaiming itself a "sanctuary". Thousands of dollars were raised by the parish to sponsor and support thirty refugees from El Salvador from 1985 to 1991. Individual parishioners also provided shelter, hospitality and in some instances, employment. In the late 1980s, Thunder Bay became the North American terminus of an underground railway for Central American refugees. Each year thirty to forty would cross the Pigeon River border crossing into Canada and were assisted by The Ecumenical Sponsorship Group for Central American Refugees and the "Friends of Refugees".[99]

Bishop O'Mara's sympathy and support for this kind of "outreach" on the part of parishes was unequivocal.[100] "These people, our brothers and sisters in Christ, are in dire need of our support", he wrote, "and your response echoes the charity of the early Church Communities of whom it was said," 'See how these Christians love one another.'[101] In April 1977, Pope Paul VI appointed him to the Pontifical Council "COR UNUM "(one heart) for a period of five years.[102] The Council was, and still is, the instrument through which the Pope carries out special humanitarian initiatives wherever and whenever disasters occur.[103] Above all, it directs its charitable programmes toward developing countries. Through his participation in COR UNUM's deliberations Bishop O'Mara understood the plight of refugees around the world and the role a diocese could play in alleviating some of their suffering. In 1985 he toured El Salvador and agreed to share his experiences and observations with Notre Dame parishioners early in 1986.

A personal experience with refugees in Thunder Bay prompted Bishop O'Mara to encourage the formation of a Catholic agency in the diocese committed to the resettlement of refugees. In 1990, a refugee family that had crossed the Canada-United States border at Pigeon River appeared on the doorstep of his residence on Ridgeway Street seeking assistance.[104] That they would turn to the Roman Catholic Church as their first port of call in a foreign country emphasized the importance of the church in their lives and in their homeland. Bishop O'Mara's response was to refer these refugees to an individual representing the "Friends of Refugees"in Thunder Bay. Liz McWeeny and Bishop O'Mara discussed the formation of a Roman Catholic agency in the diocese that would specifically focus on the plight of refugees. Although some parishes willingly shouldered the responsibilities of refugee sponsorship, the administrative and moral support offered by the diocese perhaps would encourage others to become more involved.[105] Accordingly, under the leadership of its first executive director Liz McWeeny, the Diocesan Office of Refugee Services to New Life (D.O.O.R.S.) opened a centre in the former offices of the Catholic Family Development Centre at 208 S. Archibald Street in July 1991. Staffed by volunteers, it offered refugees clothing, furniture and short-term lodging. By the end of 1991 the executive director claimed that "newcomer refugees now know they have a place where they can come for shelter, for help, for fellowship and friendship. D.O.O.R.S. to New Life is becoming a valuable outreach to the refugee community."[106] The links parishes had with D.O.O.R.S. during the 1990s was uneven. It was mainly Thunder Bay parishes that worked through D.O.O.R.S. in sponsoring or assisting refugees.[107] St Dominic Parish for example, sponsored a refugee family through D.O.O.R.S. whenever the opportunity presented itself, financed their resettlement in Thunder Bay and through their parish bulletin appealed for furniture and clothing to assist them in the long-term. The Saint Vincent de Paul Society of St Agnes and Corpus Christi parishes donated generously in support of refugees but while the St Agnes group worked through the refugee committee the Corpus Christi organization operated independently. Similarly, food donations to refugees were made independently through St Anthony Parish. For the diocesan church, this lack of consistency was disappointing. Whenever a Catholic refugee family was settled in a home by D.O.O.R.S., their staff attempted to connect them with the closest parish. Frequently, this link was not nurtured and the refugee family moved to another Christian church where the reception was more positive and welcoming.

In addition to refugee sponsorship, parishes throughout the diocese sponsored a myriad of charitable projects to assist the poor in their communities. St Andrew's Parish in Thunder Bay for example, opened the Dew Drop Inn in their parish hall to meet the needs of the hungry and poor in the city.[108] Sister Roberta Derochier of the Sisters of St Joseph Congregation (Sault Ste. Marie), a social worker with St Andrew's Parish during the late 1970s, suggested to the St Vincent de Paul Society that a soup kitchen be opened for all people regardless of their religious beliefs. Since it opened its doors on 9 February 1981 it has provided meals each afternoon from 2:30 - 4:00 in the parish hall for the unemployed and homeless.[109] Groups from the Anglican, Lutheran, Presbyterian, and Christian Reform churches in the city regularly volunteered at the Dew Drop Inn as did service organizations such as the Port Arthur Rotary and Kiwanis clubs.[110] Similarly, Our Lady of Loretto Parish (Thunder Bay) became involved with the Current River Churches' Food Cupboard in 2000 to provide groceries for needy families every Tuesday morning from the basement of St Stephen's Anglican Church.[111] Examples such as these can be found in every parish of the diocese. That Christians in northwestern Ontario should cooperate on social justice issues revealed a dimension of ecumenism perhaps least expected in the decades following Vatican II.

How did the Diocese of Thunder Bay change during the Most Rev. John A. O'Mara's eighteen-year tenure as bishop and what on-going problems did it face as the new millennium approached? A perusal of the *Northwestern Ontario Catholic*, particularly over the years 1988–1992, reveals a liturgical renewal in the diocese as the laity assumed more responsibility for their parish communities and for Sunday celebrations of the liturgy.[112] This is not to suggest that there was a wholesale break with traditional Roman Catholic liturgy. Parishes continued to schedule Adoration and Benediction of the Blessed Sacrament as part of First Friday liturgical celebrations, to recite the Rosary before daily mass, to hold a parish mission every second year and to organize pilgrimages and processions on special feast days.[113] Adult communicants at Sunday masses remained high and there was an increase in those receiving the Eucharist at daily masses. Young adults, however, were not drawn to attend Sunday masses with the same frequency as their parents.[114] The laity expanded their roles from lectors, Eucharistic ministers, presiders at the altar, ministers of music and hospitality to ministers of prayer, teaching, and to visiting of the sick. Parishioners also took an active role, together with parish priests and deacons, in the preparation of parents of children to be baptized and of candidates for confirmation. Increasingly, they assisted pastors in offering marriage preparation courses and in preparing engaged couples "to understand the dignity and meaning of Christian marriage and their responsibilities as spouses and parents."[115]

Bishop O'Mara fulfilled the requirements as prescribed in Canon Law in enhancing the role of the laity in the governance of the diocese and individual parishes. By 1991, all parishes had parish councils; albeit, some were more active than others. Each parish council was represented on a Pastoral Council established in 1977. It met annually in plenary session and three times a year in each of the three regions of the diocese - Dryden (western), Nipigon (eastern) and Thunder Bay (central). Pastoral Councils became an important forum for the exchange of views and information between the bishop, clergy

**Catholic Pastoral Centre, Diocese of Thunder Bay, 13 August 2002**
1222 Reaume Steet, Thunder Bay, Ontario.

In 1991, the diocese rented space at the Sisters of St Joseph Avila Centre for the Chancery offices, Adult Faith Formation Office, and the Marriage Tribunal. When Avila Centre was sold to Lakehead University in 1993, a decision was made to construct a new pastoral centre on property purchased by the diocese in 1957 on which an intercity Catholic high school was to be built. The ground-breaking ceremony for the Catholic Pastoral Centre took place on 8 July 1993. All diocesan offices and services were moved to the completed building on 30 December 1993. The Catholic Pastoral Centre was blessed and dedicated by the Most Rev. John A. O'Mara on 6 April 1994.

and laity. It was on the recommendation of these councils that an Adult Faith Office was established (1990), a youth survey implemented (1989) and the "Sharing the Challenges" campaign inaugurated. (1989)

Geography was, and perhaps would always remain, an obstacle to the creation of a unified pastoral ministry. Great distances between parishes and missions led to a sense of isolation and parochialism among the clergy and laity whereby they identified with their parish as separate from the diocesan church. As noted above, Bishop O'Mara introduced practices and institutions to those already established by his predecessors to minimize the feeling of isolation Roman Catholics in northwestern Ontario had with their bishop.

One of the perennial problems facing many dioceses in North America was the shortage of priests. In the case of the Thunder Bay Diocese, the shortage was ever present. In 1992, fifty- three priests served in the diocese. Of this number, ten were retired from the parish ministry but were still called upon to substitute for priests temporarily absent from their parishes.[116] Twenty-four of these parishes were confided to diocesan priests while the remaining seventeen were served by religious orders and congregations. The role, responsibilities and expectations of the parish priest had grown significantly since Vatican II and extended well beyond the sacred liturgy. To compensate for the shortage of priests and to assist them in their various apostolates a permanent diaconate programme was inaugurated.

The position of the deacon within the Roman Catholic Church was somewhat chequered. In the early Church, the deacon assumed a role of service and was appointed a "minister of charity". Prior to the Middle Ages, married men were ordained deacons and during the celebration of the Mass they distributed the Eucharist and directed the prayers of the laity. Moreover, some became the bishop's principal administrative officer.[117] After the Council of Trent (1545-1563), however, ordinations came largely from the ranks of single men. Ordination as a deacon became a necessary stepping stone to the priesthood. This trend continued until the Second Vatican Council when Pope Paul VI encouraged bishops throughout the world to return to the practice of ordaining married men who wished to remain deacons for the rest of their lives in the service of the church.[118] In 1982, Bishop O'Mara assembled a team of clergy and laity to organize and implement a permanent diaconate training programme for the diocese.[119] The following September, the first 3fi year programme was launched with the first deacons being ordained in January and February of 1987.[120] A second programme followed from 1988 to 1991 resulting in the ordination of an additional seven permanent deacons. After ordination, deacons gave homilies at mass, performed baptisms, assisted at marriages in the name of the church and presided at wake and burial services. The deaconate apostolate focussed on the classic notion of service. For example, several deacons in Thunder Bay operated the Catholic Action/St Vincent de Paul Store which officially opened on 14 January 1997 at 129 Miles Street in Thunder Bay. The store offered clothing, furniture and other essentials to the poor and unemployed. Three of the permanent deacons that emerged from the initial programmes were Native Canadians. Their understanding of the unique spiritual needs of the Native Canadian community helped maintain that important link between them and the diocesan church. At a time when the Native population of northwestern Ontario was growing, the participation of deacons in this apostolate assumed greater importance.

If there is one area within the Roman Catholic Church which reveals the inequality between men and women it is the permanent diaconate. Admittedly, the shortage of priests within the diocese positioned women in prominent diocesan and parish administrative roles. Moreover, women who joined their husbands in the period of formation for the permanent diaconate were mandated to a Diocesan Ministry or Order of Service. And yet, it is this programme where the laity take notice of married men who received the sacrament of Holy Orders while women with degrees in theology and years of pastoral service are excluded simply because they are women.

The problem of inequality of women within the Roman Catholic Church pales in significance to the incidents of sexual abuse on the part of priests and religious. During Bishop O'Mara's period four priests and one religious brother were charged with sexual assault.[121] One was found not guilty. The Thunder Bay Diocese Quinquennial Report submitted to the Vatican in 1992 commented that "there is a sense of betrayal of a fundamental trust when a beloved and respected priest is found guilty, convicted of a crime and sent to prison. For some it is an obstacle in the way of continued practice of their faith; for others it is a deep sorrow." Each case tarnished the image of the Church.

The shortage of priests, the inequality of women within the Roman Catholic Church and the frequent charges of sexual abuse among the Catholic clergy were problems faced by all bishops in North America. On 2 February 1994 the Most Reverend John A. O'Mara was named third bishop of the St Catharines diocese. As he looked back on his eighteen years as Bishop of Thunder Bay, he could take some satisfaction in leading the diocese from a

**Pope John Paul II In Conversation with Bishop John O'Mara, Ad Limina Visit, 1983.**
According to Canon Law, Roman Catholic Bishops throughout the world visit the Pope in the year in which they submit their quinquennial report (every five years). The main purpose of this visit is to foster close contact between the pope and the bishops, to enable them to present their quinquennial report to the appropriate authorities, and to facilitate contacts between the bishops and various officials in the Roman Curia. This was Bishop O'Mara's first Ad Limina visit as Bishop of Thunder Bay.
(Courtesy *L'Osservatore Romano*)

state of adolescence to maturity. Once the Ontario Government announced its intention to extend full funding to Catholic high schools in 1984, he worked in concert with the Lakehead District Roman Catholic School Board in successfully implementing a dream which had eluded his predecessors, namely, the establishment of fully composite Catholic high schools in Thunder Bay. Moreover, participation in Development and Peace initiatives and the establishment of diocesan agencies such as the Catholic Family Development Centre and the Diocesan Office of Refugee Services to New Life (D.O.O.R.S.) afforded parishes the opportunity to look outward and to cooperate with other Christian denominations in assisting the poor, the working people and the marginalized in northwestern Ontario, Canada and the world. The regular publication of a diocesan newspaper *The Northwestern Ontario Catholic*, the organization and continuance of the "Sharing The Challenges Campaign" and the construction of a Catholic Pastoral Centre in Thunder Bay all contributed to a sense of unity and belonging among the parishes of the diocese. Above all, the steadfast support and encouragement Bishop O'Mara gave to parishes throughout the diocese in the construction of "second generation" churches placed its physical infrastructure on sound foundations for the new millennium.

## Notes

[1] *DTBA*, 4.01, +Angelo Palmas to Right Rev. F. Regis St James, 13 January and 3 February 1976. Normally, Diocesan Consultors elect from their group a Vicar Capitular to administer the diocese on the death of a bishop. Neither Bishop Jennings nor Bishop Gallagher appointed a separate group of Diocesan Consultors. Since Father Regis St James was the Dean of Port Arthur, the Apostolic Pro-Nuncio appointed him Vicar Capitular with the approval of the Priests' Senate. Monsignor George Bourguignon, telephone conversation, 13 May 2002.

[2] *DTBA*, 6.01, The Most Rev. Angelo Palmas to Right Rev. F.R. Saint James, 20 May 1976. See also The Most Rev. Angelo Palmas to Rev. Msgr. John A. O'Mara, 20 May 1974.

[3] *Ibid.*, 6.01/6, +O'Mara to +Angelo Palmas, 29 July 1976.

[4] *Ibid.*, Proclamation by Diocesan Consultors, 2 July 1976.

[5] *CJ*, 22 July 1976.

[6] *DTBA*, 2.013, Bishop John A. O'Mara Papers, birth certificate.

[7] The Most Rev. John A. O'Mara, telephone conversation with author, 10 May 2002 and 13 May 2002.

[8] For a retrospective of Bishop O'Mara's career see *The Vineyard: the Journal of the Diocese of St Catherines,* (June) 2001.

[9] John J. Stapleton, Ph.D., "Feasibility Study Re Expansion of Catholic Secondary Education in Thunder Bay, Ontario, Part II." (December 1981).

[10] *DTBA*, 10.02/14, +O'Mara to Thunder Bay Parishes, 1 May 1979; G. O'Brien to Lakehead District School Board Trustees, 21 July 1979.

[11] Stapelton Study, 1981.

[12] *Ibid.*, 10.02/14, *Profiles in Catholic Education*, September/October, 1982.

[13] Pedro Arrupe, s.j., "Our Secondary Schools: Today and Tomorrow", in *Our Way of Proceeding in the 1980s*, p. 42.

[14] "Declaration on Christian Education, 28 October 1965", in *The Basic Sixteen Documents, Vatican Council II: Constitutions, Decrees, Declarations* (New York: Costello Publishing Company, 1996), pp. 576-583.

[15] *Ibid.*, p. 577.

[16] *Ibid.*, p. 582.

[17] Guy O'Brien interview, 29 April 2002.

[18] *DTBA*, 10.02/17, +O'Mara to the Chairman and Members of the Lakehead District Roman Catholic School Board, 24 October 1983.

[19] *Ibid.*, Thunder Bay Catholic Education Adivsory Commission Minutes, 31 May 1984.

[20] *Ibid.*, Memorandum from G.S. O'Brien, Director of Education to Principals and Staffs, 27 October 1983.

[21] *Ibid.*, Minutes of the Thunder Bay Education Advisory Commission, 27 October 1983.

[22] See *Globe and Mail,* 13 June 1984, p. 1. To give this decision the force of law the Government of Ontario introduced and passed "Bill 30, An Act to Amend the Education Act, 1986"

[23] *DTBA*, 10.02/20, +O'Mara to the Honourable William Davis, 31 July 1984.
[24] *Ibid.*, Constitution, Board of Governors For the Private Catholic High Schools in the City of Thunder Bay, 11 October 1984.
[25] *Ibid.*, 4.04, Consultors' Minutes, 16 February 1989.
[26] *Ibid.*, Guy O'Brien interview, 29 April 2002.
[27] Mary Lillian Bergamo, "Perceptions of Catholic Administrators and Trustees Regarding Bill 30's Impact on the Mission of Separate Schools." Thunder Bay: Unpublished M.Ed Thesis, Lakehead University, 1989. pp. 20-25.
[28] *DTBA*, 8.07, Fr. John Davis, O.M.I. to +EQJ, 17 August 1965.
[29] *Ibid.*, Fr. J. Kerr, O.M.I. to +O'Mara, 2 June 1977.
[30] *Ibid.*, St Agnes Building Committee Minutes, 8 April 1979.
[31] *Ibid.*, Parish Council letter and brochure to St Agnes Parishioners, 12 May 1981.
[32] *Ibid.*, +O'Mara to the Members of St Agnes' Parish, Thunder Bay, 1 June 1982; Formal declaration by +O'Mara, 8 June 1982.
[33] See Roy and Diane Piovesana, *St Dominic Parish: A History, 1912-1987*, pp. 30-31.
[34] *DTBA*, 3.02/25, St Dominic Annual Parish Report, 16 January 1972.
[35] *Ibid.*, St Dominic Annual Parish Report, 1974. Cost of land was approximately $60,000.
[36] *Ibid.*, 8.12, +Gallagher to Rev. D. China, 19 July 1973.
[37] *Ibid.*, +Gallagher to Rev. D. China, 23 July 1973.
[38] *Ibid.*, 3.02/25, St Dominic Annual Parish Report, 31 December 1973. Building fund balance was $280,000.
[39] *Ibid.*, 6.01, +O'Mara to Most Rev. Angelo Palmas, Apostolic Pro-Nuncio to Canada, 25 March 1980.
[40] *Ibid.*, Rev. Francis G. Morrisey, O.M.I., "Statement regarding the canonical requirements relating to the re- establishment of Saint Anthony's Parish, Diocese of Thunder Bay", 8 October 1990, p. 6.
[41] *Ibid.*, 4.04, Diocesan Consultors Minutes, 20 October 1978.
[42] *Ibid.*, Diocesan Consultors Minutes, 18 January 1979.
[43] *Ibid.*, 6.01/8, +O'Mara to +Palmas, 25 March 1980.
[44] *Ibid.*, 4.04, Minutes of Consultors' Meeting, 29 May 1979.
[45] *Ibid.*, 8.12, +O'Mara to Louis Toneguzzi, George Facca, Dominic Boccalon, 14 Janury 1980.
[46] *Ibid.*, 8.12, Memorandum by +O'Mara on meeting with Rev. Daniel China, 30 May 1979.
[47] *Ibid.*, 6.01/8, +Angelo Palmas to +O'Mara, 14 March 1980.
[48] *Ibid.*, +Angelo Palmas to L.A. Toneguzzi, 22 May 1980.
[49] *Ibid.*, L.A. Toneguzzi to +Angelo Palmas, 21 May 1980.
[50] *Ibid.*, 8.12, +O'Mara to Parishioners of Northwood, 14 March 1980.
[51] *Ibid., 8.12,* Letter from St Dominic Church building committee and the building committee of Saints Joseph and Dominic Parish to +O'Mara, 15 September 1980.
[52] *Ibid.*, 8.12, DECREE CONCERNING St DOMINIC PARISH To the Priests, Religious and Laity of the Diocese of Thunder Bay, 12 November 1980. See also 4.04, Consultors Minutes, 1 October 1980; 8.12, +O'Mara to Rev. D. China, 14 November 1980; 3.02/25,

St Dominic Parish Report, 28 January 1982. Father China and the chair of St Dominic Parish Council, Louis Toneguzzi, surrendered to the Chancery $437,148.46 leaving the old St Dominic Church with $42,897.28. Father China remained at the old St Dominic Church and was appointed Vicar Cooperator to the Very Reverend Reginald Carroll, Rector of St Patrick's Cathedral.

[53] *Ibid.,* 5.07/18, Rev. A.J. Calandra, c.s. to +O'Mara, 27 April 1981; Calandra to +O'Mara, 28 April 1981.

[54] *Ibid.,* +O'Mara to Rev. A.J. Calandra, c.s. 4 May 1981.

[55] For a photo essay on the official opening of St Dominic Church see Roy and Diane Piovesana, *St Dominic Parish: A History, 1912-1987,* pp. 38-48.

[56] *DTBA,* 8.03, Rev. G. Bourguignon to +O'Mara, 10 January 1986.

[57] *Ibid.,* 5.07/18, +O'Mara to Very Rev. Peter J. Sordi, c.s. 24 March 1987. See also 5.10, +O'Mara to the Roman Catholic Community of Thunder Bay, 22 October 1987.

[58] *Ibid.,* 4.04, Consultors Minutes, 18 June 1987.

[59] *Ibid.,* +O'Mara to Rev. E. Nazzani, c.s. 25 March 1988. St Anthony and Corpus Christi Parishes shared the cost of this property by contributing $77,658.28 each.

[60] Thunder Bay *Chronicle-Journal (CJ),* 11 April 1989; *DTBA,* 5.07/18, +O'Mara to Rev. Dan Lapolla, c.s. 28 February 1989.

[61] *DTBA,* 5.10, John Potestio to +O'Mara, 12 April 1989; +O'Mara to Potestio, 17 April 1989.

[62] *CJ,* 6 and 7 March 1990.

[63] Rita Ubriaco, "Memories of St Anthony's Fire", in *Lakehead Living,* 21 March 1990, p. 3.

[64] *DTBA,* 8.10, +O'Mara to the Faithful of St Anthony's Parish, 17 April 1990.

[65] *CJ,* 7 May 1990.

[66] *DTBA,* 3.03, Quinquennial Report, 1988-1992, p. 18.

[67] *DTBA,* 8.46, Parish survey responses, 12 March 1982.

[68] *Ibid.,* Fr. Joseph Alarie, O.M.I. to +O'Mara, 11 May 1983.

[69] *Ibid.,* Fr. Albert Lafrenière, O.M.I. to +O'Mara, 20 October 1983; +O'Mara to Lafrenière, 24 October 1983.

[70] *Ibid.,* 8.29, +O'Mara to Very Rev. William F. Ryan, S.J., Provincial, 10 April 1979 (confidential)

[71] *Ibid.,* 8.29, +O'Mara to L. Zappitelli, 27 February 1979.

[72] *Ibid.,* 8.29, +O'Mara to Teresa Martin, 12 October 1979; 2.013, +O'Mara to Msgr. Francis J. Pluta, 17 January 1980.

[73] *Ibid.,* 8.29, Trustees, Ignace Separate School Board to +O'Mara, 19 March 1979.

[74] *Ibid.,* 4.04, Consultors' Minutes, 21 February 1980; 8.29, +O'Mara to Rev. Jan Bednarz, 21 February 1980.

[75] *Ibid.,* 8.29, +O'Mara to V. Maloney, 24 January 1983. A 266' x 168' lot was purchased for $24,000

[76] *Ibid.,* 8.29, +O'Mara to Rev. Marc Monforton, O.M.I., 28 December 1984. Total cost of Immaculate Conception Church was $525,694.87 of which $62,328.31 came from the sale of the old church and rectory.

[77] *Ibid.,* 5.23, +O'Mara to Rev. Colin MacKinnon, c.s.C, 8 March 1977.

[78] *Ibid.*, 2.013, +O'Mara to Sister M. Regina, Provincial Superior, 28 December 1978. Sisters Margaret Cushman and Mary Sheridan served in the Red Lake area for three years.
[79] *Ibid.*, 4.04, Consultors' Minutes, 1 October 1980. The team was comprised of two Diocesan priests, Father George Rich (1946-2001) and Father Earl Talbot; three Sisters of St Joseph of Hamilton - Sister Gemma (Barbara) Kernick, Sister Barbara Graf and Sister Rose Gabriel; and a married couple, Thea and Tony Kurtz.
[80] John Richthammer, "Red Lake Church" in *The Regional* (Red Lake), 28 March 1983.
[81] *DTBA*, 3.02/77, St John The Apostle Parish Report, 1982.
[82] *Ibid.*, 4.04, Consultors' Minutes, 24 January 1984.
[83] For construction and financial details relating to Red Lake Church see Ibid., 8.37, +O'Mara to Rev. John S. Knight, 6 September 1985; +O'Mara to Sister Rose Gabriel (Administrator), 6 September 1985; Tim Sullivan to +O'Mara, 17 September 1985.
[84] *Ibid.*, 5.15/16, +O'Mara to Sister Ann Marshall (Superior General), 31 October 1983.
[85] *Ibid.*, Sister M. Concetta to Sister Ann Marshall (Superior General), 10 May 1984; +O'Mara to Sister Ann Marshall, 28 May 1984.
[86] *Ibid.*, 12,25, +O'Mara to Members of the Council of Priests, 20 April 1989; +O'Mara to Vincent F. Saele, Community Charitable Counselling Service of Canada, 20 April 1989; Rev. Ken Beck to +O'Mara, 9 December 1988; +O'Mara to Beck, 14 December 1988.
[87] *Ibid.*, "Talk with clergy, religious and pastoral workers", 25 May 1989.
[88] The Diocese signed a Professional Service Agreement with the Community Charitable Counselling Service of Canada on 22 August 1989. The length of the agreement was for twelve weeks. The professional fee was $42,000 and the operation budget was $12,000.
[89] *Ibid.*, +O'Mara to pastors and parishes in the Diocese, 18 January 1990. Total pledges amounted to $876,918 from 5,867 individual donors. By January 1990 $627,128 had been received.
[90] *Ibid.*, 12.25, Dr. Peter DeGiacomo to Mr. Glen Brassard, 2 November 1989 (copy); +O'Mara to Dr. Peter DeGiacomo, 16 November 1989.
[91] *Ibid.*, Rev. Allan Savage to +O'Mara, 9 September 1989.
[92] Thunder Bay *Chronicle-Journal,* 31 January 1981.
[93] *DTBA*, 4.04, Consultors' Minutes, 29 May 1979.
[94] During the late 1990s, the "Sharing the Challenges Campaign" provided $85,000 - $88,000 annually to the Catholic Family Development Centre. The Ministry of Community and Social Services as well as the Ministry of Correctional Services funded the Centre.
[95] *Ibid.*, 3.03, Quinquennial Report 1988 to 1992, pp. 7-8.
[96] Coriden, ed., *The Code of Canon Law*, p. 432.
[97] *Ibid.*, 8.03, Rev. P. M. Stilla to Manager, Employment and Immigration Canada, 7 November 1985.
[98] *Ibid.*, 8.32, Notre Dame Du Portage Parish Council Minutes, 8 January 1986. See also *NWOC*, November 1996.
[99] Liz McWeeny, telephone conversation with author, 4 June 2002.
[100] *Ibid.*, +O'Mara to Liz McWeeny, 12 December 1991.
[101] *Ibid.*, 8.10, +O'Mara to Rev. Carlo Titotto, c.s. 31 January 1985.
[102] *Ibid.*, 6.01/7, +Angelo Palmas to +O'Mara, 1 March and 6 April 1977 (confidential).

[103] Apostolic Constitution *Pastor bonus*, art. 145.

[104] Liz McWeeny, telephone conversation, 4 June 2002.

[105] *DTBA,* 12.18, Liz McWeeny to Sr. Liana Glynn, O.P., Chancellor, 10 April 1991.

[106] *Ibid.,* 12.18, D.O.O.R.S. to New Life Report, December 1992. In 1992, twenty-eight families were resettled through the diocesan Office of Refugee Settlement.

[107] *Ibid.,* 12.18, D.O.O.R.S. Report, 16 April 1993.

[108] *Ibid.,* 5.08, Fr. George Leach, s.j. to +O'Mara, 30 October 1983.

[109] *CJ,* 12 February 2002.

[110] Rev. Scott Gale and Terry Favreau, telephone conversation with author, 6 June 2002.

[111] *DTBA.,* 8.04, "Social Justice Initiatives at Our Lady of Loretto Parish, Thunder Bay, 2001.

[112] *Ibid.,* 3.03, Quinquennial Report, 1988-1992, p. 20.

[113] *NWOC,* September 2000, p.1.

[114] *Ibid.,* p. 22.

[115] *Ibid.,* p. 23.

[116] *Ibid.,* p. 28.

[117] F.L. Cross, ed., *The Oxford Dictionary of the Christian Church*, p. 455.

[118] *DTBA*, 12.03, Rev. P. M. Stilla to L. Johnson, 16 March 1984. See also Rev. Pasquale M. Stilla, "The Permanent Deacon In Vatican Council II and the Post Canciliar Church" (Roma: The Pontifical University of St Thomas Acquinas, 1983).

[119] The team included Rev. Pat Stilla, J.C.L., Armand and Mary Danis and Gene and Cookie Bannon.

[120] The first deacons to be ordained in the diocese by Bishop O'Mara were Rev. Mr. Hugh Evans of Kenora in January of 1987 and Rev. Mr. Armand Danis in February. An additional eight deacons were ordained from the first programme in 1987.

[121] *DTBA*, 3.03, Quinquennial Report, 1988-1992, p. 12.

**Pope John Paul II with Ontario Roman Catholic Bishops, Ad Limina Visit, 1988.**
(L.–R: Fr. Angus MacDougall, Bishop Brendan O'Brien, Bishop Michael Rusnak, –, Archbishop Francis Spence, Archbishop Marcel Gervais, Bishop Thomas Fulton, Bishop John A. O'Mara, His Holiness Pope John Paul II, Bishop Eugene LaRocque, – , Bishop Frederick Henry, Bishop Anthony Tonnos, Bishop Jacques Landriault, Bishop Matthew Ustrzycki, Bishop Jean-Louis Plouffe, Msgr. Robert Borne.
(Courtesy *L'Osservatore Romano*)

# TOWARDS JUBILEE YEAR 2000

## III

CHAPTER SIX

# BISHOP FREDERICK BERNARD HENRY

The Most Reverend Frederick Bernard Henry became the fourth Bishop of Thunder Bay at a time when governments in Canada were preoccupied with cutting deficits, balancing budgets, and lowering taxes. To many, these draconian measures were long overdue and considered fiscally responsible. To religious leaders like Bishop Henry, however, they exacerbated an already deplorable state of unemployment, homelessness, child poverty, and labour unrest in Canadian cities. During his brief sojourn at the helm of the Thunder Bay Diocese, he spoke out often and eloquently in defence of the disadvantaged and marginalized. "I never perceived myself as an agent for social justice", wrote Bishop Henry in the Thunder Bay *Chronicle-Journal*. "But the poor and unfortunate have no voice. So I think of what Jesus would do for them and he would speak up. I have a voice - so I do."[1]

Frederick Bernard Henry was born on 11 April 1943 in London, Ontario, the eldest of four sons born to Leo and Noreen Henry. In Southwestern Ontario, his elementary and secondary years of catholic education were unbroken as he attended St Joseph, St Peter, and Holy Rosary elementary schools. He was a graduate of London's Catholic Central High School and the Sacred Heart Junior Seminary in Delaware, Ontario. In 1961, he entered St Peter Seminary in London and seven years later (25 May 1968) was ordained

The Most Reverend Frederick Bernard Henry, D.D.
Fourth Bishop of Thunder Bay, 11 May 1995–19 March 1998
(John Nistico photo, Thunder Bay)

to the priesthood by Bishop G. Emmett Carter for the Roman Catholic Diocese of London.

Father Frederick Henry's one year as associate pastor of Christ the King Parish in Windsor was followed by further studies in philosophy and theology. In 1970 he entered the University of Notre Dame (Notre Dame, Indiana) and graduated three years later with a Master of Arts degree in philosophy. He continued his post-graduate studies at the Gregorian University in Rome where he earned a Licentiate in theology.

He now seemed destined to assume an academic post at a Catholic Canadian theological college. From 1974 to 1981 he was on the faculty of St Peter Seminary in London followed by four years as its Rector. Perhaps his most important contribution to this institution was the supervision of an expansion of its library facilities and the initiation of an accreditation process which ultimately led to the seminary's membership in the Association of Theological Schools in Canada. While Rector of St Peter's, he was made an "Honourary Prelate" on 18 April 1985 with the title Monsignor. After a decade in academia, Monsignor Henry was ordained a bishop on 24 June 1986 in Saint Peter's Cathedral Basilica. He became Auxiliary Bishop to the Most Reverend John Sherlock, Bishop of London and took up residence in Windsor, Ontario.

Bishop Henry was drawn out of the Southwestern Ontario that he loved so much when His Holiness Pope John Paul II named him Bishop of Thunder Bay on 24 March 1995. He took possession of the diocese on Thursday, 11 May 1995 during the installation ceremonies in St Patrick's Cathedral led by His Excellency Aloysius Cardinal Ambrozic, Archbishop of Toronto. For the next two-and-a-half years the Roman Catholics in the Thunder Bay Diocese came to know Bishop Henry as a man of decisive action and as a champion of social justice. His letters to the editor and feature articles appeared with remarkable frequency in the Thunder Bay *Chronicle-Journal*. He argued against the establishment of a charity casino in the city,[2] deplored the impact deficit reductions had on child poverty and single mothers in Ontario[3], supported teachers' right to protest over the Ontario Government's Bill 160 which removed legitimate working conditions from negotiations and supported the right of nurses not to assist doctors who performed abortions.[4] On the latter topic he wrote:

> Given that abortion is elective surgery, and not life threatening (unless you happen to be the child in the womb), it's sadly ironic that in our times when we tend to exalt free-

dom of choice – a woman can choose to have an abortion, a doctor can choose to perform or not perform an abortion, but a nurse and the unborn child have absolutely no choice in the matter…"

Bishop Henry's letters appeared so frequently in the *Chronicle-Journal* that he was periodically given space as a guest columnist. At times, he was criticized for political bias unbecoming a Minister of Religion and for stepping on the toes of local politicians. "The process I have followed", replied Bishop Henry, "is a rather classical one: careful analysis, distancing oneself from collusion with any political party, challenging injustice, and participation in the design of realistic alternatives."[5]

Bishop Henry soon discovered that the Diocese of Thunder Bay faced problems that cried out for his ability to design realistic alternatives. The shortage of priests in the diocese, the responsibility for the well-being of retired priests, and the lingering problem of what was to become of the Banning and Dufferin Streets property on which stood the former St Anthony Church were issues that demanded his attention. In a clever diplomatic manoeuvre the diocese sold the property to the not-for-profit Habitat For Humanity organization. The proceeds from the sale were directed to reducing the mortgage on the new St Anthony Church on Hilldale Road.[6] He also sold a cottage belonging to the diocese on Loon Lake and placed the monies accruing from the transaction into the priests' pension fund.[7] It was Bishop Henry's wish that retired diocesan priests should live in a modest but comfortable manner.

Bishop Henry's motto: "Dobo Vobis Pastores" (I will give you pastors) understandably raised great expectations among the laity and the clergy as to his strategies for bringing more priests to serve in the diocese. He found this problem as difficult to solve as his predecessors. "It's God's Church, it's not my Church" he concluded. "And God is going to give me enough priests to do my job."[8] As a short-term solution to the priests' shortage he introduced the concept of "clustering" parishes to be served by one priest. Moreover, he initiated a third training programme for the permanent deaconate.

As the following images suggest, Bishop Henry made a lasting contribution to the Thunder Bay Diocese by having a new coat of arms designed, by initiating the construction of a mausoleum at St Andrew's Cemetery, and by canonically erecting an additional native parish in the diocese.

**Diocese of Thunder Bay Coat of Arms**

The heraldic symbols and colours of the new coat of arms were chosen to reflect our faith and the character and culture of our diocese.

The shield-shaped field or ground is divided into five areas. The top left area is a Celtic cross, representing St Patrick, the secondary patron saint of our diocese. The top right area shows lilies and a crown, representing Our Lady of Charity, our principal patron saint. In the bottom left is a fort, representing how the diocese was initially settled by the fur traders. Three eagle feathers, representing our native community, occupy the bottom right. At the centre base are the Sleeping Giant and Lake Superior which are well-known geographic features of Thunder Bay. The partition lines form another cross which connect all the symbols into a unified family: the Diocese of Thunder Bay. The mitre is the ornamental head dress which represents the office or dignity of the bishop. The colours represent the continents and countries of the world where the people of the diocese originated: yellow for Asia, black for Africa, blue for Europe, green for Australia and red for the Americas.

**Our Lady of Charity Mausoleum in St Andrew's Cemetery, 13 August 2002.**
On 6 October 1995 Bishop Henry announced that a new community mausoleum would be built at St Andrew's Cemetery providing 418 crypts for casket burials and 360 niches for cremains. "A Catholic cemetery is an extension of the parish church", he remarked, "and a visible sign of our unbroken relationship with the community of saints…It exists to serve the people of our faith community." Construction on the $2.3 million mausoleum began in April 1997 and it was officially opened and blessed as "Our Lady of Charity Mausoleum" by Apostolic Administrator, Msgr. Roger Bazin on 7 October 1998.

**Kitchitwa Kateri Anamewgamik Roman Catholic Parish Church, 23 July 2002**
451 Syndicate Avenue, Thunder Bay.
The Kateri Church Centre was dedicated and blessed by Bishop Henry on 7 January 1996 under the patronage of Kateri Tekawitha, a seventeenth century Mohawk woman who converted to Christianity and devoted her life to the service of God. It became the most recent native Roman Catholic parish in the diocese with approximately 150 members. In addition to serving St Anne (Fort William First Nation) and Our Lady of the Snows (Armstrong) parishes, the Jesuits made a commitment to serve the Kateri Centre as well.

## NOTES

[1] *CJ*, 15 March 1996.
[2] *Ibid.*, 20 August 1996.
[3] *Ibid.*, 10 August 1995; 27 October 1995.
[4] *Ibid.*, 15 July 1997
[5] *Ibid.*, 24 August 1994.
[6] *Catholic Register*, 12-19 August 1995; *CJ*, 19 July 1995.
[7] *CJ*, 15 July 1995.
[8] *CJ*, 18 November 1995.

CHAPTER SEVEN

# BISHOP FREDERICK J. COLLI

As the Roman Catholic Church was about to enter the new millennium, the Most Reverend Frederick Joseph Colli became the fifth bishop of the Thunder Bay Diocese. "Jubilee Year 2000" was more than simply another "Holy Year" or a "year of remission". His Holiness Pope John Paul II saw it as a new beginning for all Christians. Bishop Colli explained it this way in his installation address delivered in St Patrick Cathedral on 25 March 1999:

> The greatest challenge of our journey will lead us into the new millennium - in the new "era of faith". As our Holy Father has noted, it will be a time of struggle and testing as we promote the "culture of life" against the assaults of the culture of death in our world. It will challenge us to bear witness to Christ and the life He has shared with us, from our Baptism. It will be a challenge, and at the same time an opportunity to show to the world our faith and our trust in the Lord, and our cooperative spirit toward one another. It will be a challenge, but also a wonderful experience. I look forward to sharing that journey with you as a faith family here in our diocese.

Bishop Colli began sharing this journey by energetically and enthusiastically participating in the special events and liturgical celebrations of parishes and missions which extended across the vast expanse of northwestern Ontario.

Frederick Joseph Colli was born in St Catharines, Ontario on 17 June 1949.

After completing his catholic elementary and secondary education there, he entered St Augustine's Seminary, Toronto in 1968 and seven years later was ordained to the priesthood by the Most Reverend Thomas J. McCarthy, Bishop of St Catharines, on 21 June 1975. Apart from a two-year interlude of post graduate study in Rome at the Pontifical Gregorian University where he earned a Masters Degree in Canon Law, Father Fred Colli served the St Catharines Diocese at the pastoral and administrative levels for almost two decades. He served first as associate pastor of St Theresa (Port Colborne) and St Kevin (Welland) parishes and then as pastor of St Julia Parish, St Catharines from 1985 to 1995. During this period, he was also Chancellor of the St Catharines Diocese and Associate Judicial Vicar of the Catholic Marriage Tribunal.

On 22 February 1995, the Feast of St Peter, in Ottawa's Notre Dame Cathedral, Father Frederick Colli was ordained a bishop by Archbishop Marcel Gervais of Ottawa. He became Auxiliary Bishop of Ottawa with specific responsibilities for the English sector of the Archdiocese.

Four years to the day of his episcopal ordination, the Most Reverend Frederick J. Colli was named Bishop of Thunder Bay by His Holiness Pope John Paul II. Bishop Colli took possession of his diocese on 25 March 1999.

Pope John Paul II with Bishop Frederick J. Colli, Ad Limina Visit, 1999.
Bishop Colli points out location of the Thunder Bay Diocese
(Courtesy *L'Osservatore Romano*)

**Bishop Frederick J. Colli's Coat of Arms**

The crest is divided into two sections by a chevron. The upper half contains a "peace dove" which is a symbol from the crest of the Diocese of St Catharines, Bishop Colli's place of birth. The dove also represents Bishop Colli's first name which is "Frederick" and means "peaceful ruler." The Lily represents the Blessed Virgin Mary who was a faithful servant of God, and whose words are in the motto of Bishop Colli's crest, "Holy is God's Name," from Mary's great prayer, the Magnificat. The lower part of the crest contains a red cross, showing that a bishop is a servant of Jesus and the three hills at the bottom of the crest, represent the bishop's surname, "Colli", which means "hills".

**St Casimir Parish celebration of the Feast of Corpus Christi, Thunder Bay, 25 June 2000.**
Bishop Colli participated in many parish liturgical celebrations during Jubilee Year 2000. Here, flanked by the Knights of Columbus and members of St Casimir Polish Parish, he carries the Blessed Sacrament through the streets of Thunder Bay's East End during the parish's celebration of the Feast of Corpus Christi.

**St Casimir (Polish) Parish Corpus Christi Procession, Thunder Bay, 25 June 2000**
The young ladies of St Casimir Parish scatter rose petals along the procession route.

# World Youth Day 2002

World Youth Day 2002 was held in Toronto from 23 – 28 July. Pope John Paul II chose the theme: "You are the salt of the earth...You are the light of the world." (Mt. 5:13-14) for this special bi-annual world event. The Thunder Bay Diocese received the WYD Cross in Kenora on Monday, 14 January. To mark this special event in the diocese services were held in Kenora, Fort Frances, and Dryden. The next evening the cross was welcomed in Thunder Bay with visitations to Old Fort William, St Patrick Cathedral, and St Agnes and St Elizabeth parishes. On 16–17 January the WYD Cross remained in Thunder Bay with visitations to St Patrick's High School, Lakehead University, St Ignatius High School, Correctional Centre (Hwy 61), Confederation College, Shelter House, and St Anthony Parish. On Friday, 18 January, the WYD Cross was transported along the north shore of Lake Superior to the Annunciation of the Blessed Virgin Mary Parish in Nipigon and to Holy Angels Parish, Schreiber. From there, the cross was taken to the Moosonee Diocese. The photographs that follow illustrate some of the activities surrounding the reception of the WYD Cross and the "Days In the Diocese" of Thunder Bay - 18-20 July 2002.

Raising the World Youth Day Cross at Old Fort William, Thunder Bay, 15 January 2002 (DTBA)

Pilgrims sign World Youth Day Board at Old Fort William, Thunder Bay, 19 July 2002

**Bishop Colli arrives at the wharf of Old Fort William, Thunder Bay, 19 July 2002**
A special historical and cultural programme was provided at Old Fort William for World Youth Day pilgrims en route to Toronto. Here Bishop Colli participates in a re-enactment of voyageurs approaching Fort William in the early nineteenth century perhaps in the company of a Jesuit priest.

**School groups assemble for the "Days In the Diocese" Outdoor Mass, Marina Park, Thunder Bay, 20 July 2002.**
Each elementary and secondary Catholic School in the diocese sent teacher and student representatives to the outdoor Mass. Shown here are John Prezio, Karen Watt, and students from Our Lady of Charity School.

If there was any event in the history of the diocese which reflected its unity, diversity, and geographic extent it was the presence of parish and mission representatives at the "Days in the Diocese" outdoor World Youth Day Mass held at Marina Park, Thunder Bay on 20 July 2002. Shown here are the various delegations preparing to take their place on the field where the Mass was to be celebrated.

**World Youth Day Mass, Marina Park, Thunder Bay, 20 July 2002**
Bishop Fred Colli concelebrates World Youth Day Mass with priests from across the Thunder Bay Diocese.

**Bishop Frederick J. Colli Ordains Thomas Mullamangalam to the priesthood
17 August 2002**

Father Thomas Mullamangalam kneels before Bishop Fred Colli in St Patrick Cathedral after his ordination to the priesthood. In this photograph, Father Mullamangalam accepts his chalice and paten. Assisting are deacons Rev. Mr. John McKeown, Rev. Mr. Charles Johnston and seminarian Terry Sawchuk. Father Mullamangalam was appointed to serve Notre Dame and St Louis Parishes in Kenora with Father Alan Campeau. His ordination marks the first in the new millennium for the Diocese of Thunder Bay. It was fitting that an ordination to the priesthood for the Thunder Bay Diocese took place during its fifieth anniversary year.

# NECROLOGY, 1952 – 2002

Compiled by Sr. Teresa Sabatini, c.s.j. with Anita Schick

| Name | Birth | Ordination | Death |
| --- | --- | --- | --- |
| Aubin, Paul o.m.i. | 1911 | 1937 | 25 January 1978 |
| Audette, Denys o.m.i. | 10 February 1907 | 24 June 1934 | 20 October 1976 |
| Azzolini, J. i.m.c. | | | 27 July 1976 |
| | | | |
| Baillargeon, Eugene, o.m.i. | 1878 | 1911 | 24 September 1959 |
| Bathurst, Charles, s.j. | 2 August 1903 | 25 July 1936 | 23 March 1987 |
| Bazinet, Gordon, s.j. | 23 October 1926 | 9 June 1963 | 4 August 1998 |
| Beaudin, Alfred, o.m.i. | 1882 | 1909 | 9 May 1965 |
| Beaulieu, J. Fidelis, o.m.i. | 1899 | 1929 | 5 April 1962 |
| Beaulieu, Romeo, o.m.i. | 11 August 1908 | 24 June 1935 | 8 May 1983 |
| Belanger, Maurice, o.m.i. | 1896 | 1932 | 12 October 1969 |
| Benoit, Euchariste, o.m.i. | 10 September 1910 | 12 June 1938 | 16 May 1994 |
| Bernard, Ralph, o.m.i. | 20 October 1925 | 15 April 1956 | 23 September 1991 |
| Bortignon, Joachim | 16 April 1902 | 23 February 1929 | 13 December 1977 |
| Brachet, Joseph, o.m.i. | 30 November 1886 | 28 July 1918 | 27 August 1982 |
| Brennan, Donald, o.m.i. | 1924 | 1950 | 9 September 1990 |
| Bruyere, Paul, (Deacon) | 30 April 1902 | 14 September 1974 | 21 December 1976 |
| Bunyan, Emmett | 23 September 1894 | 6 June 1920 | 21 December 1959 |
| | | | |
| Cahill, Lawrence | 1925 | 5 June 1948 | 27 April 1990 |
| Carrano, Anthony, c.s. | 1921 | 1954 | 5 July 1993 |
| Carriere, Regalis, o.m.i. | 9 July 1907 | 10 September 1944 | 16 November 1969 |
| Carroll, Reginald | 30 June 1918 | 10 April 1943 | 11 February 1995 |
| Chatelain, Placidus, o.m.i. | 1900 | 1941 | 15 January 1971 |
| Chavely, Joseph | 23 November 1952 | 23 March 1989 | 1 May 1995 |
| China, Daniel | 15 November 1911 | 2 June 1940 | 3 December 1990 |
| Colliard, Alfred, s.j. | 21 February 1918 | 20 June 1954 | 22 March 1988 |
| Comeau, Charles, o.m.i. | 1899 | 1924 | 13 October 1980 |
| Cowan, James | 14 September 1909 | 27 March 1937 | 30 September 1966 |
| Crawford, Joseph, C.Ss.R. | 13 March 1938 | 21 June 1964 | 29 January 1992 |

| Name | Birth | Ordination | Death |
|---|---|---|---|
| Desautels, Isaie, o.m.i. | 19 March 1903 | 20 March 1927 | 29 April 1982 |
| Desrochers, Henri, o.m.i. | 1909 | 1933 | 29 June 1965 |
| DeVarennes, Vincent, o.m.i. | 2 September 1909 | 2 June 1928 | 24 November 1991 |
| Devine, Francis, s.j. | 18 September 1907 | 18 August 1940 | 8 April 1995 |
| Doherty, Marcus, s.j. | 31 December 1898 | 22 June 1930 | 2 July 1970 |
| Dorge, Emilien, o.m.i. | 8 September 1916 | 29 June 1941 | 25 April 1998 |
| Dugal, Marcel | 29 October 1908 | 30 June 1935 | 12 February 1965 |
| Duplain, Emmanuel, o.m.i. | 1892 | 1920 | 8 November 1972 |
| | | | |
| Epoch, George s.j. | 18 April 1920 | 22 June 1952 | 1 October 1983 |
| Estok, Michael s.j. | 17 October 1906 | 27 June 1949 | 2 February 1989 |
| | | | |
| Feeley, Ross s.j. | 18 July 1929 | 17 June 1962 | 4 October 1992 |
| Ferus, Joseph m.s. | 9 August 1911 | 25 June 1939 | 12 June 1973 |
| Fiori, Frank (Deacon) | | | 16 August 1999 |
| Florentin, Andre o.m.i. | 22 October 1913 | 29 June 1941 | 5 November 1983 |
| | | | |
| Gallagher, Gerald s.j. | 24 June 1916 | 25 June 1950 | 12 December 1975 |
| Gallagher, Nornam (Bishop) | 24 May 1917 | 24 March 1941 | 28 December 1975 |
| Gatien, Leonard | 15 October 1920 | 3 June 1955 | 18 March 1991 |
| Gauvin, Stanislaus | | 1932 | 18 May 1985 |
| Giroux, Louis-Philippe o.m.i. | 1903 | 1932 | 6 May 1984 |
| Gragnani, Giulio c.s. | 1911 | 1934 | 7 February 1979 |
| Greengrass, Alexander | 2 January 1918 | 31 May 1947 | 25 July 1986 |
| Gurka, Joseph m.s. | 7 October 1914 | 7 June 1941 | 16 October 1988 |
| | | | |
| Harrow, Joseph (Deacon) | | | 25 April 1997 |
| Hawkins, Michael s.j. | 24 July 1901 | 15 August 1937 | 28 February 1965 |
| Hebert, Eugene | 29 July 1901 | 11 June 1927 | 22 February 1971 |
| Hennessey, John s.j. | 23 May 1902 | 31 July 1936 | 11 August 1982 |
| Hogan, Albert | 7 April 1891 | 26 May 1923 | 24 April 1966 |
| Hyrchenuk, Stephen s.j. | 6 March 1918 | 27 June 1949 | 20 November 1993 |
| | | | |
| Janicki, John m.s. | 26 April 1926 | 25 May 1963 | 24 July 1991 |
| Jaworski, Peter m.s. | 15 May 1900 | 18 July 1926 | 6 November 1959 |
| Jennings, Edward Q. (Bishop) | 4 October 1896 | 27 December 1925 | 22 October 1980 |
| Jordan, Joseph s.j. | 4 February 1901 | 16 August 1936 | 5 July 1991 |
| Jubinville, Denys o.m.i. | 1901 | 1925 | 2 December 1968 |
| | | | |
| Karpinski, Leonard m.s. | 6 November 1928 | 28 October 1956 | 10 October 1971 |
| Kennedy, Raphael s.j. | 25 October 1889 | 15 August 1926 | 17 December 1961 |
| Killorin, Donald s.j. | 14 August 1910 | 17 June 1942 | 13 March 1992 |

# NECROLOGY

| Name | Birth | Ordination | Death |
|---|---|---|---|
| Lafreniere, Leo o.m.i. | 1910 | 1937 | 23 December 1974 |
| Laliberte, Leo | 17 March 1905 | 14 June 1930 | 8 May 1972 |
| Lambert, Jean o.m.i | 16 March 1912 | 29 June 1939 | 23 May 1986 |
| Lemire, Francois o.m.i. | 1910 | 1937 | 15 January 1982 |
| Lemire, Jean o.m.i. | 1906 | 1931 | 4 March 1984 |
| Lewandouski, John m.s. | 10 November 1930 | 8 December 1954 | 19 May 1989 |
| Lizee, Aime o.m.i. | 17 December 1905 | 28 June 1931 | 12 January 1981 |
| | | | |
| MacGilvray, Roderick s.j. | 1 November 1899 | 12 August 1934 | 29 October 1964 |
| Malloy, Wilfred o.m.i. | 1911 | 1939 | 15 November 1969 |
| Masse, Joseph o.m.i. | 1905 | 1930 | 6 December 1975 |
| Mateuszek, Ladislas m.s. | 30 November 1899 | 24 June 1928 | 10 February 1975 |
| Maurice Edouard o.m.i. | 30 December 1916 | 28 September 1941 | 29 August 1972 |
| McCarthy, John s.j. | 2 July 1906 | 14 August 1938 | 23 August 1981 |
| McKey, John s.j. | 8 August 1911 | 17 June 1942 | 1 January 2000 |
| McKinnon, William (Deacon) | | | 8 February 2000 |
| McGarry, James s.j. | 7 November 1899 | 13 August 1933 | 12 April 1987 |
| McGrath, James o.m.i. | 31 August 1909 | 29 June 1934 | 7 January 1986 |
| McGuire, Patrick | 1893 | 29 June 1923 | 11 September 1974 |
| McHardy, Patrick s.j. | 28 September 1907 | 18 August 1940 | 4 May 1965 |
| McHugh, John s.j. | 28 August 1916 | 16 June 1948 | 18 November 1993 |
| McHugh, Joseph | | 15 June 1935 | 7 October 1958 |
| Messier, Louis | 22 February 1884 | 25 July 1910 | 14 October 1957 |
| Meyer, Francis | 15 May 1925 | 19 May 1951 | 13 September 1988 |
| Michael, Joseph o.m.i. | 1906 | 1934 | 18 January 1975 |
| Monaghan, Joseph s.j. | 26 December 1884 | 27 June 1924 | 29 February 1980 |
| Montag, John | 18 October 1915 | 8 April 1939 | 28 June 1978 |
| Morin, Julien o.m.i. | 26 June 1914 | 25 June 1944 | 24 November 1993 |
| Morris, Garrett | | 5 June 1938 | 26 February 1969 |
| Muldoon, James | 7 July 1916 | 30 May 1942 | 2 February 1997 |
| Murphy, Vincent s.j. | 21 June 1903 | 13 August 1939 | 19 October 1984 |
| Murray, Joseph s.j. | 2 October 1926 | 21 June 1959 | 13 January 1977 |
| Murtagh, Michael | 9 December 1918 | 10 June 1945 | 28 July 1994 |
| | | | |
| Nolan, Francis o.m.i. | 1913 | 29 June 1942 | 23 November 1976 |
| | | | |
| O'Donnell, Hugh s.j. | 21 May 1919 | 20 June 1954 | 16 March 1976 |
| | | | |
| Paradis, Alphonse o.m.i. | 1897 | 1923 | 16 August 1969 |
| Pinette, Gerard o.m.i. | 10 January 1910 | 29 June 1937 | 18 July 1986 |
| Przysienzniak, Stanley m.s. | 8 February 1922 | 30 May 1959 | 5 February 1968 |

| Name | Birth | Ordination | Death |
|---|---|---|---|
| Reguly, Joseph | 18 May 1918 | 10 April 1943 | 18 October 1988 |
| Rio, Marcel  o.m.i. | 4 May 1899 | 11 May 1925 | 28 April 1992 |
| Robertson, Robbie  o.m.i. | | | 25 September 1998 |
| Roenicke, John | 16 March 1918 | 10 April 1943 | 21 March 1969 |
| Rolland, Alexander  s.j. | 3 March 1904 | 12 August 1934 | 23 May 1987 |
| Ruest, Adeodat  o.m.i. | 4 March 1914 | 29 June 1941 | 2 May 1986 |
| Rushman, Clifford  s.j. | 8 February 1909 | 1 July 1945 | 28 July 1990 |
| | | | |
| St. Jacques, Michael  o.m.i. | 1911 | 1938 | 3 August 1962 |
| St. James, Regis | 29 March 1911 | 20 February 1938 | 29 June 1976 |
| Savoie, Elie  o.m.i. | 1898 | 1924 | 5 April 1962 |
| Schretlen, Aloysius  s.j. | 7 June 1921 | 1 June 1952 | 25 February 1996 |
| Shea, Dennis  o.m.i. | 1912 | 13 June 1948 | 24 April 1974 |
| Spada, Mario  c.s. | 28 August 1924 | 13 March 1948 | 10 February 1977 |
| Stankiewicz, Joseph | 21 March 1910 | 20 February 1938 | 20 April 2002 |
| | | | |
| Tetrault, Paul Emile  o.m.i. | 1 December 1907 | 29 June 1937 | 17 May 1973 |
| Trembley, Ernest Norman | 21 February 1922 | 8 May 1960 | 20 April 1996 |
| Turner, Anthony | 16 August 1925 | 8 December 1978 | 20 April 1996 |
| | | | |
| Venti, Rosario | 24 December 1905 | 8 February 1931 | 10 February 1986 |
| | | | |
| Wittig, Lawrence | 4 July 1909 | 15 June 1935 | 9 May 1977 |
| | | | |
| Zanoni, Gregory  c.s. | 29 June 1908 | 21 March 1931 | 28 September 1995 |
| Ziliotto, Rino  c.s. | 31 August 1919 | 25 June 1944 | 30 March 2002 |
| Zimmerman, John  m.s. | 3 January 1890 | 26 June 1917 | 30 January 1978 |

# CHRONOLOGY

### 1891

4 October – The Most Rev. Alexandre-Antonin Taché (1823-1894) Archbishop of St Boniface, blesses the bell for the newly constructed Notre Dame du Portage Parish Church, Rat Portage (Kenora).

10 October – James Murphy, chairman of committee to build a new church in Fort William, submits a tender notice in the *Fort William Journal* calling for expressions of interest from local contractors to begin laying foundations for a new church at the corner of Archibald and Donald Streets.

### 1892

21 August – First mass is celebrated in St. Patrick's Church, Fort William, by Father Remi Chartier, Superior of Jesuits in Thunder Bay District and pastor of St Andrew's Parish, 1890-1894.

### 1893

8 May – Father Joseph Hébert, S.J., 59, Superior at the Fort William Mission (1880-1890) dies at Fort William Mission and is buried in the Mission Bay cemetery.

2 September – The Most Rev. Richard A. O'Connor, Bishop of Peterborough, on a pastoral visit to Fort William announces that the new church in Fort William would be under the patronage of St Patrick, that an incumbent priest would henceforth remain with the congregation and that a stained glass portrait of St Patrick would be placed over the main altar.

9 September – The Most Rev. Richard A. O'Connor makes the first pastoral visit of any Bishop to Schreiber in the western portion of his diocese.

21 September – Mission at Fort Frances is

founded by Father Adelard Langevin, o.m.i.

### 1894

19 March – Rev. Adélard Langevin, o.m.i. (1855-1915) is consecrated Archbishop of the Archdiocese of Saint- Boniface by Bishop Édouard-Charles Fabre of Montréal.

### 1895

11 January – Under the direction and leadership of Father Edward Devine, SJ, chaplain to the workers and their families on the Lake Superior division of the C.P.R., (1893-1896) a modest Roman Catholic chapel is built in the hamlet of Murillo, approximately 30 km west of the town of Fort William.

10 April – Fire destroys orphanage and Immaculate Conception Church at the Fort William Mission.

1 June – Father Jean-Baptiste Baudin, o.m.i. ends a thirteen year tenure (1882-1895) as pastor of Notre Dame Parish, Kenora.

28 July – First mass is celebrated in the Fort Frances "Chapel House" by Father Dorais, o.m.i.

8 September – Father J. B. Baudin, o.m.i. becomes first resident priest at "Our Lady of Perpetual Help" mission in Fort Frances.

### 1896

18 November – Construction of the first Roman Catholic Church in Schreiber is completed under the supervision of Father Louis Lafortune,s.j. who becomes its first resident priest in 1912.

### 1897

4 November – Sisters of Charity (Grey Nuns) assume responsibility as teachers in the Rat Portage (Kenora) Boarding School (three miles south of Notre Dame du Portage church) with Rev. Charles-Arthur Cahil, o.m.i. as principal.

### 1898

8 October – Father Roger Arpin, s.j. (1841-1908), pastor of St Patrick's Parish, Fort William purchases land south of Neebing Avenue to serve as a Roman Catholic cemetery.

### 1900

5 March – A Temperance Society is formed in St Andrew's Parish, Port Arthur.

20 March – Slovak members of St Patrick Parish, Fort William arrange to bring in a Slovak priest from Pennsylvania, USA to give a six day mission in their language.

26 December - A group of Roman Catholic families meet in St Patrick's church hall at 12:00 noon to establish the Roman Catholic Separate School Board of Fort William and to elect eight trustees.

### 1902

7 January – St Stanislaus School on Myles Street opens as the first Roman Catholic elementary school in Fort William.

### 1903

12 July – The Roman Catholics of Norman, Ontario purchase a former Methodist church in their town for $700 and have it

dedicated as their own by the Archbishop of St Boniface, the Most Rev. Adélard Langevin, o.m.i., under the patronage of "Our Lady of the Sacred Heart."

## 1904

24 May – Because of the influx of thousands of immigrants into northern and northwestern Ontario, the region lying north of Lake Nipissing and the French River is detached from the Peterborough Diocese by Pope Pius X to form the new Diocese of Sault Ste Marie with its Episcopal Seat in the town of Sault Ste. Marie, Ontario. Henceforth, all parishes and missions from North Bay to Fort William fall under the aegis of the new diocese.

20 September – David Joseph Scollard is selected and appointed the first bishop of the newly formed Diocese of Sault Ste. Marie by Pope Pius X.

## 1905

8 December – Sisters of St Joseph convent at 213 Myles Street Fort William is officially opened and blessed by Bishop David J. Scollard of Sault Ste Marie.

## 1906

22 March – Ecole Ste-Marguerite Residential School for Indian children opens on the Couchiching Reserve.

## 1907

1 May – Father François Maynard, s.j. begins his apostolate among the Slovaks of Fort William's East End.

28 July – Bishop David J. Scollard blesses the cornerstone and foundation of St Peter's [Slovak] Roman Catholic Church at 615 Connolly Street in Fort William's East End.

2 November – St Peter's [Slovak] Roman Catholic Church is totally destroyed by fire.

## 1908

21 May – With the financial support of the Diocese of Sault Ste. Marie, construction begins on the new St Joseph's Boarding School (formerly located on the Fort William Mission) at the corner of Arthur and Franklin Streets, Fort William, Ontario.

## 1909

8 November – Architectural plans for a new church by Montreal architect G.E. Tanguay submitted by St Andrew's Parish building committee, Port Arthur, for Bishop Scollard's approval are rejected as being beyond the financial means of the parish. Construction is postponed indefinitely.

25 June – The first Corpus Christi procession in Thunder Bay is organized by Father François Maynard, s.j. and the parishioners of St Peter's parish in Fort William's East End.

## 1910

1 September – St Agnes mission at the corner of Frederica and Brown Streets, Fort William, is canonically proclaimed a parish with Father Louis Ragaru S.J. as pastor (1910-1913).

6 September – St Martin's Roman Catholic School, Brown Street, Fort William, opens.

9 December – In his report to Fort William City Council, Assessment Commissioner John Wells establishes the Roman Catholic population of the city at 6,421 - being 32.3% of a total population of 19,858.

## 1911

24 March – Notre Dame Du Chemin Parish, Pinewood Ontario is canonically erected by Bishop Emile Yelle of Saint-Boniface.

8 October – St Peter's (Slovak) Roman Catholic Church is formally dedicated by Bishop Scollard.

## 1912

2 January – A group representing Fort William's Italian community meet in the basement of St Peter's (Slovak) Church to form an organizational committee to direct the fundraising and construction of their own church in the city's East End.

21 July – Notre Dame du Portage parish, Kenora, celebrates the first ordination to the priesthood of one of its own parishioners - Joseph Alfred Baribeau - by Archbishop Adélard Langevin of St Boniface.

29 November – The Roman Catholic Parish of Our Lady of Perpetual Help, Fort Frances is canonically erected by the Most Rev. Louis Philip Adélard Langevin, o.m.i., Archbishop of Saint-Boniface.

24 December – St Anthony's Italian Roman Catholic Church at the corner of Dufferin and Banning Streets, Port Arthur, officially opens with a midnight mass celebrated by Rev. Francis Crociata.

## 1913

9 January–St Joseph's Italian Roman Catholic Church is officially opened and dedicated by the Rev. Francis Crociata.

## 1914

27 July– Most Rev. D.J. Scollard officiates at the cornerstone laying ceremony for St Agnes Roman Catholic Church. Westfort William. Estimated cost of construction is $50,000.

22 December–Fire and water damage destroy St Anthony's Roman Catholic Church,Port Arthur, Ontario.

24 December–Notre Dame Church, Kenora, Ontario is destroyed by fire. The loss to the parish is estimated at $35,000.

## 1915

17 January–New St Agnes Church in Westfort William is dedicated by Bishop Scollard.

17 May–Rev. Domenico Tomaselli arrives in Thunder Bay to become pastor of St Anthony and St Joseph Italian parishes in Port Arthur and Fort William.

19 December–The first mass is celebrated in the new and enlarged reconstruction of Notre Dame du Portage church, Kenora.

## 1917

28 June – Bishop David Scollard and Father Louis Lafortune, s.j. visit Dorion, a hamlet 20 km east of Port Arthur, Ontario and meet with the 12 Catholic families to plan the completion of their new chapel.

## CHRONOLOGY

### 1920

15 November – World War I memorial in Port Arthur is unveiled on the front lawn at St Andrew's Roman Catholic Church.

### 1921

17 June – St Agnes' Ladies Aid and Dramatic Club unite in promoting a circus and garden party fund raiser on the church lawn.

### 1922

1 October – Our Lady of the Holy Rosary Church (St Casimir, Thunder Bay) is dedicated with Father Francis B. Tomanek officiating.

### 1925

3 May – The new St Andrew's Church, Port Arthur, is dedicated by Bishop Scollard. Cost is $100,000, leaving the parish to carry a $75,000 debt.

### 1928

21 November – St Patrick Arpin Memorial High School (Fort William) is built at a cost of $100,000 and officially opened.

### 1931

23 January – Rev. Sr. Monica, founder of St Joseph's Hopsital (Port Arthur) dies at age 80.

8 June – Fr. Joseph C. Salini, born in Fort William and ordained in the Pro-Cathedral of North Bay, celebrates his first Mass at St Agnes Church. Fr. Salini is the first Canadian-born Italian to be ordained in Canada.

### 1932

12 January – Father Peter J. Monahan, Pastor of St Patrick's parish, Fort William makes an appeal to his congregation for funds to purchase food and clothing for the needy of the parish and other parishes in Thunder Bay. Three thousand dollars is raised for this purpose.

### 1935

19 March –The Most Rev. Ralph H. Dignan is consecrated as Bishop of Sault Ste. Marie at St Peter's Cathedral, London, Ontario, by the Most Rev. Andrea Casulo, Apostolic Delegate to Canada.

### 1936

3 April – Bishop Dignan canonically changes the name of St Joseph's Italian Roman Catholic Church, Fort William to St Dominic and Our Lady of the Holy Rosary Polish Roman Catholic Church, Fort William to St Casimir.

28 May – Bishop Dignan canonically erects the Parish of St Augustine of Baird, comprising the Missions of Harstone and Hymers with the Rev. Joseph Carmel McHugh as its first resident parish priest, succeeding Rev. V.J. McGivney.

19 June – Bishop Dignan canonically erects the Parish of the Annunciation B.V.M. of Nipigon with the Rev. John M. Leacy as its first parish priest.

### 1937

1 July – The Diocese of Sault Ste. Marie purchases the Croation Hall, Current River, Port Arthur for $650 to be used as a chapel

to be known as Our Lady of Loretto. Rev. Alexander J. MacDonald, S.J is in charge.

13 August – Mgr. V. Mazzoni, Chargé d'Affaires, Ottawa, notifies Bishop Dignan that the Holy See has canonically ratified the establishment of the Sisters of St Joseph of the Diocese of Sault Ste. Marie.

## 1938

6 March – Bishop Dignan canonically establishes the Deanery of Thunder Bay and appoints Rev. Patrick J. McGuire of St Patrick parish as its dean.

## 1939

8 December – St Joseph Manor, Port Arthur, Ontario (formerly the Wiley residence, Red River Road) the new home for the aged, receives its first resident. Mother M. Clara is its first Superior.

## 1940

21 April – Monsignor Domenico A. Tomaselli, pastor of St Anthony's R.C. Church for 25 years, dies at age 64 in St Joseph's Hospital, Port Arthur after a lengthy illness.

## 1941

3 June – La Verendrye Hospital, Fort Frances, Ontario, owned and operated by the Sisters of Charity (Srs. Grises de Montréal) is officially opened.

24 October – Rev. Joseph S. Stankiewicz, formerly assistant pastor at St Patrick's Parish, becomes pastor of St Casimir (Polish) Parish, Fort William, Ontario.

## 1942

21 June – The Indian Missions of Lake Nipigon are detached from those of Long Lac and constituted as a separate unit with Father Alexander Rolland, s.j. in charge and headquartered at MacDiarmid.

## 1943

10 April – Reginald Carroll, Edward Kennedy, Joseph Reguly and John Roenicke, all of Fort William, ON., are ordained to the Holy Priesthood in the Pro-Cathedral of the Assumption, North Bay, by Bishop R.H. Dignan.

2 August – Holy Angels Catholic Separate School, staffed by the Sisters of St Joseph (Sisters St Bride, St Jude, Inez Marie and Carmela), is opened in Schreiber, Ontario.

28 October – Sisters of St Joseph sell the historic Whalen Residence, Algoma Street, Port Arthur, to the Dominion Government for $12,000. The property is to be used for a Naval Barracks.

## 1947

9 April – St Martin of Tours Parish, Terrace Bay, Ontario is canonically erected with Rev. E.M. Skillen as its first pastor.

18 April – The Holy Saviour Parish, Marathon, Ontario is canonically erected with Rev. Regis St James as its first pastor.

## 1949

20 March – The new Church of the Annunciation, Nipigon, Ontario is officially opened with Rev. J.J. Muldoon as pastor. It replaces a smaller frame church which had become inadequate for the congregation.

# CHRONOLOGY

## 1952

27 January – Corpus Christi Parish Church and Rectory on Red River Road, Port Arthur are officially opened and dedicated. Fathers Regis St James, Pastor; Charles Bathurst, S.J., of St Andrew's; and Rosario Venti, of St Anthony's assist Bishop Ralph Dignan of Sault Ste. Marie at the ceremony.

29 April – The Roman Catholic Diocese of Fort William is created comprising that part of the Diocese of Sault Ste. Marie west of 86 longitude and all territory in Ontario that once came under the aegis of the Archdiocese of St Boniface.

21 May – The appointment of The Most Rev. E.Q. Jennings as the first Bishop of Fort William is given official notice in *L'Osservatore Romano*.

26 August – Roman Catholics from northwestern Ontario gather in St Patrick's Cathedral to celebrate the installation and enthronement of Bishop Jennings by The Most Rev. Ildebrando Antioniutti, Apostolic Delegate to Canada.

## 1953

22 February – Official name of the Roman Catholic Church on the Fort William Mission is changed from The Church of the Transfiguration to St Anne.

19 May – One hundred and thirty-two members of the Catholic Women's League of Canada in the Diocese of Fort William gather in the city to organize a Diocesan Council of the League.

20 May – Bishop E.Q. Jennings officially installs the first Diocese of Fort William Council of the Catholic Women's League.

18 July – Separate parishes are erected in Nipigon (Annunciation of the Blessed Virgin Mary) and Red Rock (St Hilary) by Bishop E.Q. Jennings

7 December – Under the guidance and leadership of Father Lawrence Wittig (1909-1977) the parishioners of St Patrick Parish, Atikokan complete construction of a new church in the Dunbar Heights area of the town.

## 1954

6 March – Very Reverend Corrado Martellozzo, C.S., Provincial Superior of the Missionaries of St Charles (Scalabrinians) offers the services of his priests to Bishop Jennings and the Diocese of Fort William.

15 August – Roman Catholics of Current River gather for the official opening of Our Lady of Loretto Parish Church at 290 Grenville Avenue, Port Arthur, Ontario.

## 1957

20 June – As part of their seventy-fifth anniversary celebrations the parishioners and pastor of Notre Dame du Portage, Kenora witness the ordination of Father Leroux by Bishop Jennings as the first priest to be ordained for their parish.

29 July – Bishop Jennings blesses the newly constructed church in Sioux Narrows.

28 August – The first diocesan fund-raising campaign – "The Bishop's Development Fund"– is launched with a goal of $875,000.

## 1958

5 March – The Scalabrini Order (Missionaries of St Charles) begin their pastoral work in the Thunder Bay Diocese with the direction of St Patrick Parish, Atikokan.

7 October – The Roman Catholic Diocese of Fort William purchases twenty-eight acres of land west of Balmoral Street and south of the Lakehead College of Arts, Science and Technology campus from the City of Port Arthur on which to build an intercity catholic high school.

## 1959

7 June – Father Peter Jaworski, M.S., a former Provincial with the La Salette Fathers and the first pastor of Our Lady Queen of Poland Parish, Port Arthur dies and is succeeded by Father Joseph Ferus, M.S.

## 1960

15 February – Bishop Jennings engages the services of Mickelson, Fraser and Haywood Architects to prepare conceptual drawings for the proposed intercity Catholic high school.

8 August – Bishop Jennings makes an unprecedented commitment that the Bishop of Thunder Bay would in perpetuity confide Our Lady Queen of Poland Parish "to priests of Polish ethnic origin and language."

12 August – Construction begins on new St Mary's Parish Centre and Rectory, Fort Frances.

## 1961

16 January – St Margaret "Chapel-of-Ease" in the Brent Park subdivision of Port Arthur is elevated to the status of a parish with Father J.E. Roenicke as its first full-time pastor.

15 November – Bishop E.Q. Jennings blesses and officially opens St Joseph Roman Catholic School in Dryden, Ontario.

## 1962

11 July – Missionary Father Euchariste Benoit, o.m.i. observes on his first visit to North Spirit Lake (170 km north of Red Lake) that all but one family in the community are Roman Catholic.

5 August – Newly renovated church in Armstrong is blessed by Bishop Jennings.

## 1963

13 August – Father Benoit builds a temporary church at North Spirit Lake, the most northerly mission in the Diocese, made out of lumber hewn from the logs of the region. After a year of construction this modest church is finally usable by the Oblates and the natives of the area.

15 September – Corner stone for the new St Patrick Cathedral, Fort William, Ontario is blessed by Bishop Jennings.

## 1964

6 September – Corner stone is laid for Our Lady Queen of Poland Church, Port Arthur, Ontario.

## 1965

28 March – The new St Patrick Cathedral, Fort William, Ontario is dedicated.

13 June – Holy Family Parish Rectory and Outdoor Shrine at 2055 Rosslyn Road Fort William (Neebing),Ontario is blessed by Bishop Jennings.

22 August – Our Lady Queen of Poland Church, 93 N. Algoma Street, Port Arthur, Ontario is dedicated in time to commemorate the first millennium of the Polish nation (966-1966)

## 1966

23 October – A testimonial dinner is held in honour of Father Joseph Stankiewicz to celebrate his 25th anniversary as Pastor of St Casimir(Polish) Roman Catholic Parish, Fort William, Ont.

24 September – New Holy Angels' Parish Centre and Rectory in Schreiber is officially opened.

21 November – Father Bernard Campbell celebrates the first mass in the newly constructed Immaculate Conception crypt church in Ignace, Ontario.

## 1967

3 February – First mass is celebrated by Father E.J. Duplain in Our Lady of Fatima Church, Vermillion Bay, Ontario.

28 February – An advisory board is formed to govern the private sector (grades 11 and 12) of St Patrick's Arpin Memorial High School, Fort William, Ontario.

25 June – Bishop E.Q. Jennings blesses and unveils a Trans Canada Highway plaque at Nipigon, Ontario commemorating the first Holy Mass celebrated in northwestern Ontario by Father Claude Jean Allouez, S.J. near Virgin Falls on the Nipigon River (1667).

4 November – St Margaret Parish rectory at 88 Clayte Street, Port Arthur, Ontario is blessed by Bishop E.Q. Jennings.

## 1968

11 May – Sisters of St Joseph Avila Centre, south of Lakehead University campus, is dedicated and officially opened.

16 July – The inaugural meeting of the Diocesan Senate of Priests is held in Fort William, Ont.

26 October – The Missionaries of St Charles (Scalabrinians) assume direction of St Anthony's (Italian) Parish (Port Arthur) with Father Umberto Rizzi, c.s. as Pastor and Father Lino Santi, c.s. as Assistant Pastor.

## 1969

6 July – St Anne's Church on the Fort William Mission is officially opened and dedicated.

20 July – Our Lady of the Lake Mission Church on Eva Lake (Mission of St Patrick Patrick Parish, Atikokan) is blessed by Bishop Jennings.

21 August – The Most Rev. E.Q. Jennings submits his resignation as Bishop of Fort William to the Holy Father, Pope Paul VI.

21 September – Sacred Heart Parish in Sioux Lookout celebrates the opening of their new church.

21 November – Cornerstone of Holy Family Church, Fort William (Neebing) is layed.

### 1970

15 April – The Most Reverend Norman Joseph Gallagher, 53, Auxiliary Bishop of Montréal, is named Bishop of Thunder Bay.

17 April – As Apostolic Administrator, The Most Rev. E.Q. Jennings officially changes the name of the Diocese from Fort William to Thunder Bay ("Dioecesis Sinus Tonitralis")

26 May – The Most Reverend Norman J. Gallagher is installed as the Second Bishop of Thunder Bay in St Patrick's Cathedral.

### 1971

21 February – On the recommendation of the Senate of Priests, Bishop Gallagher announces the first major transfer of priests throughout the diocese.

12 June – Some parishes in the diocese begin the practice of celebrating the Sunday liturgy on Saturday evenings.

3 September – St Patrick Church in Emo is totally destroyed by fire.

10 December – Bishop Gallagher elevates two Indian Missions – St Francis Xavier in Heron Bay and St Anne on Mission Road in Thunder Bay – to full parish status.

14 December – After much reflection, Bishop Gallagher decides to end diocesan financial support of St Patrick Arpin Memorial High School.

### 1972

22 February – Twenty years after its founding, the number of Catholics in the Diocese of Thunder Bay rises from 32,000 to 54,000 - an increase of 68.8%.

12 December – A six per cent assessment is levied on all parishes in the diocese to assist in paying off the Cathedral debt.

### 1974

10 September –Paul Bruyère, from Fort Frances, is the first native Indian in the diocese to be ordained to the Permanent Deaconate.

27 May – Bishop Gallagher recognizes the establishment of the Thunder Bay Catholic Croatian Congregation under the leadership of Rev. Julius Balog. Services are temporarily held at St Andrew's Church.

### 1975

28 December – Bishop Norman Gallagher dies at age 58 in Saint Joseph's General Hospital, Thunder Bay.

### 1976

24 May–Pope Paul VI appoints Msgr. John A. O'Mara, 52, Pastor of St Lawrence Parish, Scarborough, Ontario, Bishop of Thunder Bay.

29 June–Msgr. John A. O'Mara is consecrated a Bishop by The Most Rev. Philip Pocock, Archbishop of Toronto, in St Michael's Cathedral, Toronto.

21 July–The Most Rev. John A. O'Mara is installed as the third Bishop of Thunder Bay at St Patrick's Cathedral.

27 December–Bishop O'Mara establishes a body of Diocesan Consultors to advise him on

matters relating to the Thunder Bay Diocese.

### 1977

20 January–Bishop O'Mara establishes a Pastoral Council for the Diocese of Thunder Bay Diocese.

6 April–Pope Paul VI appoints Bishop John O'Mara to the Pontifical Council "Cor Unum" for a period of five years.
12 June–The Catholic Women's League of Sacred Heart Parish, Sioux Lookout, celebrate their twenty-fifth anniversary.

19 August–Because of personnel shortages the Missionaries of La Salette withdraw from the Red Lake area.

### 1978

28 April–The first Diocesan Charismatic Conference, organized by the Oblate Fathers at St Agnes Parish (Thunder Bay), is held at St Patrick High School.

### 1979

18 January–Bishop O'Mara canonically erects St Theresa Parish in Ear Falls.

29 May–Bishop O'Mara canonically erects the Croatian Catholic Parish in Thunder Bay under the patronage of The Assumption of Mary with Father Iligia Puljic, O.F.M. as its first pastor.

### 1980

12 November – St Dominic Parish at 700 McLaughlin Street, Thunder Bay is suppressed and a new parish under the patronage of St Dominic is erected as the national Italian parish for Thunder Bay South and the territorial parish for the Northwood subdivision.

### 1981

8 January – An elementary separate school with twenty students is opened in the basement of Holy Saviour Church, Marathon.

4 May – Scalabrinian Congregation accepts Bishop O'Mara's invitation to assume responsbility for the pastoral care of St Dominic Parish with Father Umberto Rizzi, c.s. as pastor.

1 October – Sisters of St Joseph (Hamilton) assume responsibility for the administration of St John the Apostle Parish, Red Lake.

### 1982

6 June – New St Agnes Church in Thunder Bay is dedicated by Bishop O'Mara.

### 1983

7 May – New St Dominic Church is officially opened and dedicated.

1 September – Training programme for Permanent Diaconate begins in diocese.

20 October – Inaugural meeting of The Thunder Bay Education Advisory Commission is held to explore feasibility of extending Catholic secondary education in Thunder Bay beyond grade ten.

30 October – Renovations to the entrance of Notre Dame du Portage Church in Kenora are completed.

### 1984

12 June – Hon. William Davis, Premier of Ontario, announces that his government would grant Roman Catholic Schools equality of status and financing with the province's public education system commencing in September 1985.

3 October – New Immaculate Conception Church, Ignace is dedicated.

### 1986

1 February – New St John The Apostle Church in Red Lake is dedicated.

### 1989

12 September – "Sharing the Challenges" campaign is launced in Thunder Bay Diocese.

### 1990

6 March – Fire destroyes St Anthony's Church in Thunder Bay.

### 1991

17 December – Decision is made to build Diocesan Catholic Pastoral Centre south of Avila Centre in Thunder Bay.

### 1992

31 May – New St Anthony Church at corner of Dawson and Hilldale Roads is officially opened and dedicated.

1 November – Two Franciscan priests - Rev. Fidelis Wyrabkiewicz, O.F.M. Conv. and Rev. Andrew Werner, O.F.M. Conv. - come to the Thunder Bay Diocese to serve the Polish parishes of St Casimir and Our Lady Queen of Poland.

### 1993

18 April – Sisters of St Joseph welcome the community to the twenty-fifth anniversary and closing of Avila Centre, Thunder Bay.

30 August – Sod-turning ceremony is held in Kenora for the new St Thomas Acquinas Catholic High School

### 1994

2 February – The Most Rev. John A. O'Mara is named third bishop of the St Catharines Diocese by Pope John Paul II after spending eighteen years as Bishop of Thunder Bay.

6 April – Catholic Pastoral Centre in Thunder Bay is blessed and dedicated by Bishop John A. O'Mara.

13 April – Episcopal See of Thunder Bay is vacant as The Most Reverend John A. O'Mara is installed as the third Bishop of St Catharines. Father Edward Kennedy is named Apostolic Administrator of diocese.

### 1995

24 March – The Most Reverend Frederick Bernard Henry, Auxiliary Bishop of the London Diocese is named fourth Bishop of Thunder Bay by Pope John Paul II.

11 May – The Most Rev. Frederick B. Henry is installed as Bishop of Thunder Bay by His Excellency Aloysius Cardinal Ambrozic, Archbishop of Toronto.

18 July – Diocese of Thunder Bay sells property on corner of Banning and Dufferin Streets, former site of St Anthony's Church, to Habitat For Humanity.

## 1996

7 January – Kateri Church Centre, 451 Syndicate Avenue, is dedicated by Bishop Henry as the third Native parish in Thunder Bay.

4 June – Bishop Frederick Henry officially dedicates a monument to the unborn erected by the local Knights of Columbus in St Andrew's Cemetery, Thunder Bay.

## 1997

14 January – Catholic Action/St Vincent de Paul store officially opens at its new location on 129 Miles Street, Thunder Bay.

## 1998

7 October – Our Lady of Charity Mausoleum in St Andrew's Cemetery is officially opened and blessed by Apostolic Administrator, Msgr. Roger Bazin.

## 1999

22 February – The Most Reverend Frederick Joseph Colli, Auxiliary Bishop of the Archdiocese of Ottawa, is named fifth Bishop of Thunder Bay by Pope John Paul II.

25 March – The Most Reverend Frederick J. Colli is installed as Bishop of Thunder Bay in St Patrick's Cathedral by His Excellency Aloysius Cardinal Ambrozic, Archbishop of Toronto.

30 May – An Ecumenical Faith Gathering is held in the Fort William Gardens, Thunder Bay, as a prelude to the celebration of the Jubilee Year 2000.

## 2000

22 February – Fourth Degree Knights of Columbus celebrate their 100th anniversary with a mass at St Patrick Cathedral.

30 June – Our Lady of the Way Parish, Pinewood celebrates the 100th anniversary of their church.

## 2002

14 January – World Youth Day Cross arrives in Kenora and the Thunder Bay Diocese.

15 January – World Youth Day Cross is raised at Old Fort William, Thunder Bay.

18 January – World Youth Day Cross is brought to the Annunciation of the Blessed Virgin Mary Parish (Nipigon) and to Holy Angels Parish (Schreiber) before leaving for the Moosonee Diocese.

18 – 20 July – WYD "Days In the Diocese" of Thunder bay welcome pilgrims en route to Toronto for World Youth Day 2002 (23 – 28 July) with Pope John Paul II.

17 August – Bishop Frederick J. Colli ordains Deacon Thomas Mullamangalam to the priesthood in St Patrick Cathedral. This is the first ordination in the diocese for the new millennium.

# INDEX

Adult Faith Office 257
Ad Limina Visits, 259, 266, 279.
Amadio, Father Luigi. 123
Ambrozic, Aloysius Cardinal 271
Annunciation of the Blessed Virgin Mary
Parish 148, (photo) 150
Arpin, Father Ludger, s.j. 28-32
Arrupe, Father Pedro, s.j. 220
    on Christian secondary education 220
    post-Vatican II parish 251
Association of St Francis 133
Avila Centre 222
Bathurst, Father Charles, s.j. 289
Baggio, Most Rev. Sebastiano 186
Batterton, Father William T., 27
Baudoux, Archbishop Maurice 187
Baxter, Father Richard, s.j. 24, 35, 57
Bednarz, Father Jan 243
Bélanger, Father Rudolphe 130
Bellavance, Father Joseph 128
Benoit, Father Eucharistе, o.m.i. 289
Bishop's Development Fund 153-155
Bournemouth 184
Bortignon, Father Joachim 112, 117
Bourguignon, Msgr. George 207, 211-213, 217

Budka, Bishop Nykyta 96-97
Bunyan, Father Emmett 112
Brachet, Father Joseph, o.m.i. 190
Bruyère, Paul 203-205
Campbell, Father Bernard 131-132
Campeau, Father Alan 288
Capresi, Father Ferdinando 86
Carey, Father Roy 112
Carrano, Father Anthony, c.s. 116
Carter, Bishop Alexander 186
Carter, Bishop Emmett 186
Carroll, Msgr. Reginald 112, 146, 195
Cathedral debt, 196-197
Cathedraticum 194-195
Catholic Canada, 1893 (map) 4
Catholic Church Extension Society 132, 243, 245
Catholic Family Development Centre 251
Catholic Pastoral Centre 256
Catholic Women's League 152-153, 177
Chartier, Father Remi, s.j. 28
China, Father Daniel 112, 229, 230-231
Choné, Father Pierre, s.j. 6
Colli, Bishop Frederick J. 277
    and the new millennium 277

birth 277
Coat of Arms 280
episcopal ordination 278
graduate studies 278
ordination 278
ordination of Thomas Mullamangalam 287
pastor 278
St Augustine's Seminary 278
with Pope John Paul II 279
World Youth Day 284
Consolata Missionaries 123
Corpus Christi Parish 143-144
Cowan, Father James 112
Crawford, Fr. Joseph, C.Ss.R. 289
Croation Catholic Church 202
Crociata, Father Francis 76-78
Current River Churches' Food Cupboard 255
D.O.O.R.S. 254-255
Dallaire, Father Arthur, o.m.i. 113
Daughters of the Immaculate Heart of Mary 17
Davis, Father John 127
Davis, Premier William 222
Days in the Diocese 285
DeLaronde, Henry 12
Declaration on Christian Education 220
Del Mestri, Archbishop Guido 208
Desrochier, Sr. Roberta, c.s.j. 254
Descoteaux, Father H.M., s.j. 25
Devine, Father Edward J. 44
Dew Drop Inn 254-255
DiGiacinto, Father Ralph 231-232
Diocesan Consultors, 261
Diocesan Senate of Priests 169
Diocese of Fort William 109
  bilingual diocese 110
  change of name 170
  *Dioecesis Arcis Gulielmi* 170
  geographic extent 106
  Heraldic Crest 111
  reasons for creation 109
Dowling, Bishop Thomas 24

Dugal, Father Marcel 112, 129-130
Dugas, Father Louis Napoleon, s.j. 13
Favotto, Father Joseph 117
Ferus, Father Joseph, m.s. 142
Flahiff, Cardinal George 187
First Church United 224
Fort Frances Mission 51
Fort William Mission 6
  cemetery 7, 22
  Church of the Immaculate Conception 16
  farm 7
  Fort William 17, 21
  fire 7, 17
  Grand Trunk Pacific Railway 20
  importance to Thunder Bay Diocese 23
  Jesuit missionary activity 6
  Jesuit scholars 8
  Kaministiquia River 6
  move to Mission Bay 22
  Pennassi, Chief J. B. 20
  photo (1898) 7
  registers 13
  Sisters of St Joseph 17
  Squaw Bay (Mission Bay) 21
  St Joseph's Orphanage 17
  Wikwemikong 8
Fort William's East End 66-68
Franciscan Fathers o.f.m. (conv.) 95
Frémiot, Father Nicolas s.j. 6
Frytek, Father Ladislas, o.f.m. 134-135, 175
Gallagher, Father Edward 112
Gallagher, Bishop Norman J. 181-214, 229-230
  administrative changes 195
  ecumenism 191
  post-Vatican II Roman Catholic Church 188
  World War II 184
  appointed Bishop of Thunder Bay 187
  auxiliary bishop (military vicariate) 185
  Auxiliary to the Archbishop of Montréal 186
  birth 183

cathedral debt 196
chaplain, Royal Canadian Air Force 184
comparisons with Bishop Jennings 183
daily Mass in No. 39 Wing 184
death 209
education 183
failing health 207
legacy to Thunder Bay Diocese 209
new parishes 197
ordination 184
portrait 182
priestly personal integrity 197
priests' transfers 195
record as military chaplain 185
symbol of diocesan unity 189
Gauvin, Father Stanislaus 115
Jérôme, Brother Louis s.j. 7
Gorek, Father Anthony 91
Gragnani, Father Julio, c.s. 116
Gravelbourg Diocese 185-186
Greengrass, Father Alexander 112
Grenier, Father Joseph, s.j. 36
Gull Lake Parish 184
Hebert, Father Eugene 112
Hébert, Father Joseph, s.j. (photo) 9
Henry, Bishop Frederick B. 269-276
    against charity casino 271
    and abortion 271
    and priest shortage 272
    and social justice 269
    and St Anthony property 272
    birth 269
    education 269
    episcopal ordination 271
    graduate studies 271
    Kateri Church Centre 275
    Mausoleum at St Andrew's Cemetery 272
    new coat-of-arms 272
    ordination 271
    portrait 270
    retired priests 272
    St Peter Seminary, London 271
Hogan, Msgr. A. J. 27, 112, 126

Holy Angels Parish 151
Holy Family Parish 198
Holy Rosary (Polish) Parish 88-93
    church ownership 90
    conflict with pastors 90
    legal dispute 91
    new church 93
Holy Saviour Parish 150
Immaculate Conception Parish (Ignace) 130-132, 241-244
inequality of women 258
Intercity Catholic High School 153, 154
    and Arpin Memorial 154, 155
    and Oblates 157
    changed relationship to St Patrick Parish 163
    curriculum 157
    fund-raising for 159
    property acquisition 158
    reasons for failure 160
    St Patrick High School Board 163
    eaching staff for 156
Jamot, Bishop John Francois 5
Jaworski, Father Peter, m.s. 140, 176
Jennings, Bishop E.Q. 105-180
    attendance at Vatican II 168
    Coat-of-Arms 166
    death 170
    Edmonton Diocese 106
    education 105
    installation ceremony 108
    Kamloops Diocese 106
    named Bishop of Fort William 106
    ordination 106
    portrait 107
    record 169
    retirement 170
    World War I 106
Johnston, Rev. Mr. Charles 288
Karpinsky, Father Leonard, m.s., 137
Kehoe Renewal Centre 197
Kowalski, Father F., o.m.i. 88
Kula, Father Francis, m.s. 137
Lacombe, Father Albert, o.m.i. 45

Lafortune, Father Louis, s.j. 44
Lakehead District Roman Catholic School Board 221
Laliberte, Father Leo 112
Lamarche, Father Prosper, s.j. 21-22, 24, 34
Langevin, archbishop Adélard 44-48, 51, 54, 65, 66.
Lakeview High School 222
Leacy, Father John M. 150
Leger, Paul-Emile Cardinal 186
Lizee, Fr. Aime o.m.i. 291
Loretto Sisters 122
MacNeil, Father Edward 127
Mally, Father Wilfred 127
Matthews, Owen 134
Maurice, Father E., o.m.i. 113
Maurice, Father William, s.j. 202
Maynard, Father Francois, s.j. 69-73
McCarthy, Father T. J., s.j. 112
McCullough, Father N.F. 25
McDougall, Father Donald 129
McGuigan, James Charles Cardinal 217-218
McKeown, Rev. Mr. John 288
McHugh, Father Joseph 112
McHugh, Father John 152
McWeeny, Elizabeth 254
Meyer, Father Francis J. 112
Mission Boarding school/orphanage 20
Missionaries of Our Lady of La Salette 135
Missionaries of St Charles (Scalabrinians) 116
    and St Anthony's Parish 117, 120
    Baird 117
    in Atikokan 116
    origins 116
Monahan, Father Patrick J. 35
Montag, Father John 112
Moreau, Father Armand 112
Morris, Father Garret 112
Moss, Father William, o.m.i. 48, 50
Muldoon, Father James J. 112, 152
Mullamangalam, Father Thomas 288
Murray, Father Arthur Joseph 86-87

Murray, Father Joseph s.j. 291
Nazzani, Father Ermete, c.s. 235
Nestor Falls Chapel 200
Northwestern Ontario Catholic 255
Notre Dame Du Portage Parish 45-48, 241, 288
    "vestibule" dedication 241
    church photo 242
    new facade 241
    Sanctuary Movement 252-253
    "Lake of the Woods Missions" 48
    early growth 45
    Ecole Mount Carmel 47
    fire destroys church 46
    log chapel 45
    parish status 45
    reconstruction after fire 46
    social make-up 46
    Ukrainian parishioners 47
O'Connor, Bishop R.A. 11-14
O'Dwyer, Father Cornelius 121, 127
O'Mara, Bishop John A. 215-266
    and "COR UNUM" 253
    and Archdiocese of Toronto 217
    attendance at Second Vatican Council 218
    birth 217
    Catholic Secondary Education 217-218
    episcopal ordination 215
    legacy to Thunder Bay Diocese 260
    Monsignor 217
    ordination 217
    pastoral work 217
    portrait 216
    Rector of St Augustine's Seminary 218
    with Pope John Paul II 259
Ontario Secondary School Teachers' Federation 222
Our Lady of Fatima Roman Catholic Church 200
Our Lady of Good Counsel Parish 55
Our Lady of Loretto Parish 144, 145
Our Lady of Lourdes Parish 52
Our Lady of the Lake chapel 116

Our Lady of the Way Parish 54
Our Lady Queen of Poland Parish, Thunder Bay 140-142
Parish Councils 195, 255-256
Palmas, Most Father Angelo 215
paroikia 3
Pastoral Council 255
Permanent diaconate programme 257-258, 265
Peterborough Diocese 5
Planet, Father E. 121
Pocock, Archbishop Philip F. 187, 217
Poitras, Father F. 122
Polish National Church 91
Pottie, Father Kenneth 243
Primeau, Father Albini, s.j. 68
Reguly, Father Joseph, 73-74, 112
Red Lake District Ministerial Association 192
Rodger, Father William 191, 210
Roenicke, Father J. E. 112, 146
Rolland, Father Alexander, s.j. 152
Roy, Archbishop Maurice 185
Ruest, Father Charles, o.m.i. 190
Sacred Heart Parish, Gull Bay 202
Sacred Heart Parish, Sioux Lookout 120-125
Sault Ste Marie Diocese 5
School Sisters of Notre Dame 122
Second Vatican Council, 1962–1965 167
    see also Vatican II
    Bishop Jennings' attendance 168
    study sessions for Canadian bishops 168
sexual abuse cases 258
Sharing the Challenges 249
    detractors 250
    first campaign 250
Shea, Father Denis, o.m.i. 126
Specht, Father Joseph, s.j. 11-13
Shumay, Father B 112
St Agnes Parish 24-28, 126-127, 224-229
    church bell 24
    Church of the Nativity and St Agnes 24
    debt 27
    demolition of the old church 224
    fund-raising for new church 224
    Italians 27
    mission church 24
    need for new church 224
    new church dedication 229
    new church photo 225
    new church, (1914) 25
    photo, 1926 26
    photo, interior 1936 26
    and Ragaru, Father A. A., s.j. 25
St Andrew Parish 35-45
    Bishop Scollard 36
    Port Arthur's Catholic population 36
    Dew Drop Inn (photo) 43
    first church 35
    need for new church 36
    new church building committee 37
    new church construction 40
    photo 42
    similarities with St Patrick (Fort William) 35
    vision of new church 39
St Anne Parish 202
St Anthony (Italian) Parish 78, 235
    dedication of church 78
    financial assistance 81
    fire (1914) 81
    "Committee to save St Anthony's" 240
    church fire 235
    decision to build new church 240
    importance of church 235
    photo 236
St Augustine Parish 118
St Benedict Roman Catholic Church 199
St Casimir (Polish) Roman Catholic Parish 94-95
    see also Holy Rosary Parish
St Dominic (Italian) Parish 229-232
    See also St Joseph Italian Church
St Elizabeth Parish 144, 146
St Francis Xavier Parish (Balmertown) 138
St Francis Xavier Parish (Heron Bay) 202
St Hilary Parish 149, 152

St Isidore Roman Catholic Church 201
St James, Father Regis 112, 144, 178, 215, 261
St John The Apostle Parish (Red Lake) 133-141, 243-249
St Joseph Boarding School 19
   move to Fort William 23
St Joseph Italian Roman Catholic Parish 80-87
St Joseph Parish (Northwood) 231
St Joseph Parish (Dryden) 127-129
St Louis Parish 244, 288
St Margaret Parish 145-146, 176
St Martin of Tours Parish 151-152
St Mary Parish (Fort Frances) 51
St Patrick Arpin Memorial High School 205
St Patrick Cathedral Church Construction 161
St Patrick Intermediate School 221
St Patrick Parish, Atikokan 113-117
St Patrick Parish (Emo) 55
St Patrick Parish (Thunder Bay) 28-35
St Patrick Secondary School 221
St Peter Parish (Fort William) 68
   and Jednota 68
   church bell 70
   church construction 70
   church interior 74
   church photo 71
   early spiritual growth 70
   first Corpus Christi outdoor procession 70
   new church dedication 72
   property purchase 68
   Stations of the Cross 72, 75
St Peter Roman Catholic Separate School 71
St Rose of Lima Church, Silver Islet 24
St Stanislaus Roman Catholic School 31
St Sylvester Church 14
   Lake Helen Reserve 15
   photo 15
St Theresa Parish (Kakabeka Falls) 119
St Theresa Roman Catholic Church (Ear Falls) 139
Stankiewicz, Father Joseph 92-94, 112
Taché, Archbishop Alexander 45
Tanguay, G.E. 38-39
The Northwestern Ontario Catholic 250
The Saint Vincent de Paul Society 254
Thunder Bay Catholic Education Advisory Commission 219
Tomanek, Father Francis B. 88
Tomaselli, Father Domenico 83-84
Ukrainian Catholic Church of the Transfiguration 97
Ukrainian Catholics 93
Urzedowski, Father Chester, m.s. 192
Vatican II 189
   annual parish report changes 189
   Decree on Ecumenism 191
   ecumenism 191
   new liturgy 190
   parish councils 194-195
   sanctuary, physical changes to 190
Whelan, James 37-38
Wittig, Father Lawrence 112, 116
Wojnowski, Father John 92
World Youth Day 2002, Thunder Bay 282-287
Ziliotto, Fr. Rino c.s. 292
Zimmerman, Father John, m.s. 135-141, 192